BORDE

Solving Social Problems

Series Editor:
Bonnie Berry, Director of the Social Problems Research Group, USA

Solving Social Problems provides a forum for the description and measurement of social problems, with a keen focus on the concrete remedies proposed for their solution. The series takes an international perspective, exploring social problems in various parts of the world, with the central concern being always their possible remedy. As such, work is welcomed on subjects as diverse as environmental damage, terrorism, economic disparities and economic devastation, poverty, inequalities, domestic assaults and sexual abuse, health care, natural disasters, labour inequality, animal abuse, crime, and mental illness and its treatment. In addition to recommending solutions to social problems, the books in this series are theoretically sophisticated, exploring previous discussions of the issues in question, examining other attempts to resolve them, and adopting and discussing methodologies that are commonly used to measure social problems. Proposed solutions may be framed as changes in policy, practice, or more broadly, social change and social movement. Solutions may be reflective of ideology, but are always pragmatic and detailed, explaining the means by which the suggested solutions might be achieved.

Borderline Slavery
Mexico, United States, and the Human Trade

Edited by

SUSAN TIANO
University of New Mexico, USA

MOIRA MURPHY-AGUILAR
University of Texas at El Paso, USA

With Brianne Bigej

Routledge
Taylor & Francis Group

LONDON AND NEW YORK

First published 2012 by Ashgate Publishing

Published 2016 by Routledge
2 Park Square, Milton Park, Abingdon, Oxfordshire OX14 4RN
711 Third Avenue, New York, NY 10017, USA

First issued in paperback 2016

Routledge is an imprint of the Taylor & Francis Group, an informa business

British Library Cataloguing in Publication Data
Borderline slavery : Mexico, United States, and the human trade. – (Solving social problems)
    1. Human trafficking – Mexican–American Border Region. 2. Human trafficking – Mexican–American Border Region – Prevention.
    I. Series II. Tiano, Susan. III. Murphy-Aguilar, Moira.
    364.1'5'09721–dc23

Library of Congress Cataloging-in-Publication Data
Borderline slavery : Mexico, United States, and the human trade / [edited] by Susan Tiano and Moira Murphy-Aguilar.
        p. cm. – (Solving social problems)
    Includes bibliographical references and index.
    ISBN 978–1–4094–3968–4 (hbk. : alk. paper)
    1. Human trafficking – Mexican–American Border Region. 2. Human smuggling – Mexican–American Border Region. 3. Illegal aliens – Mexican–American Border Region. 4. Foreign workers – Mexican–American Border Region. 5. Slave labor – Mexican–American Border Region.
    I. Tiano, Susan. II. Murphy-Aguilar, Moira. III. Murphy, Moira.
    HQ281.B67 2012
    306.3'6209721–dc23   2012012823

ISBN 13: 978-1-138-27906-3 (pbk)
ISBN 13: 978-1-4094-3968-4 (hbk)

Contents

vi *Borderline Slavery*

List of Figures

List of Contributors

Brenner Allen is a legal analyst with the American Bar Association Rule of Law Initiative (ABA ROLI). She is responsible for developing and implementing legal research projects to complement ABA ROLI's global programming, including the Human Trafficking Assessment Tool (HTAT), to facilitate the collection of detailed, comprehensive data on human trafficking in any given country. Her primary focuses are human rights and access to justice, as well as legal profession reform.

Brianne Bigej is pursuing her Juris Doctorate degree as well as her Masters in Latin American Studies at the University of New Mexico. She has worked on issues of human trafficking on the U.S.–Mexico border, human rights, gender and development, and labor in the Americas. Upon graduation in July 2012, she plans to continue work on labor issues, employment law, and workers' rights through her legal practice.

Sandro Calvani was the Chairman for 2009–2010 of the Global Agenda Council on illicit trade of the World Economic Forum, Davos and Dubai. In 2007 UN Secretary-General Ban Ki-moon appointed him as Director of the United Nations Interregional Crime and Justice Research Institute (UNICRI), where he served until 2010. Prior to this post he served as the Director of the United Nations Office on Drugs and Crime (UNODC) Office in Colombia (2004–2007). To date, Dr. Calvani has worked in 135 countries and has authored 19 books and more than 600 articles on sustainable development, humanitarian aid, public health, and the convergence of emerging threats to human security.

Jenny Clark is an instructor of Political Science at South Texas College and is Chair of both the Women's Studies Committee and the Distinguished Speaker Series. Clark serves on a state-wide Anti-Trafficking Coalition and on various state-wide anti-trafficking task force working groups. In 2009, Clark received the South Texas Civil Rights Project's Emma Tenayuca award for her work in bringing to light the forms of trafficking and coercion that affect women.

Gustavo de Unánue Aguirre is a Mexican diplomat currently working in the Department of Political Affairs of the Organization of American States (OAS) in Washington D.C. Prior to his current post, he was the Mexico Consul in Albuquerque, New Mexico. His areas of expertise and interest are foreign affairs, human rights, and conflict resolution.

Kathryn Farr is a Professor Emeritus in the Department of Sociology at Portland State University. Her research interests encompass global human trafficking, violence against women and children in war-torn areas, and the sexual exploitation of refugee and internally displaced women and children. Her 2004 book, *Sex Trafficking: The Global Market in Women and Children,* was one of the foremost academic publications on sex trafficking and continues to be incorporated in a variety of courses in sociology, social problems, culture and sexuality, history, and women's studies.

Carolyn Gonzales is a Senior Communication Representative in University Communication and Marketing at the University of New Mexico. She is a co-founder of the Cross-Border Issues Group, a collaboration between UNM and Mexican faculty and students who travel to immigration hot spots to produce journalistic and academic reports. Ms. Gonzales is currently a cultural studies graduate student in the UNM Department of Foreign Languages and Literatures.

David B. Ham is the President of the Board of Governors, National Border Patrol Museum. He served for over 31 years in the United States Border Patrol, spending more than a decade as part of the El Paso Anti-Smuggling Unit (ASU) where he supervised criminal investigations against large-scale smuggling organizations in the El Paso sector. He rose to Assistant Chief Patrol Agent, El Paso Sector, before his retirement in 2003.

Stephanie Hepburn is an independent journalist. She is the author of several books related to women and children, including *Women's Roles and Statuses the World Over* and *Hidden in Plain Sight: Human Trafficking the World Over* (with R.J. Simon), which examines the current situation of human trafficking within 24 nations.

Olivia Jung has worked as a speech writer and executive assistant at the United Nations Interregional Crime and Justice Research Institute (UNICRI). Her focus on human rights developed during her studies at the College of William and Mary, while she was actively involved in Amnesty International, and it further expanded into international humanitarian law with her MA in Peacekeeping Management from the University of Turin. She is also a published translator and illustrator.

Virginia McCrimmon was the Point of Contact for the Anti-Human Trafficking Program of the Salvation Army in El Paso, Texas, which has been recognized by the U.S. State Department as a "must visit location" for international visitors interested in combating human trafficking because of its exemplary anti-human trafficking task force. She focused on providing vital services to trafficking victims and served as a liaison among several agencies. She has hosted three annual anti-human trafficking conferences with nationally recognized speakers, and has provided assistance to the State Attorney General of New Mexico in the formulation of task forces to implement recently passed anti-human trafficking laws in the state.

Moira Murphy-Aguilar works at the Center for Inter-American and Border Studies at the University of Texas at El Paso and teaches in the Latin American and Border Studies Program. Previously she was a Professor of Administration and Social Studies at Monterrey Tech in Mexico. Her areas of specialization include border studies, gender studies, development in Latin America and internationalization of education. Her publications include the books: *Ciudad Juárez: Entre la Frontera y el Mundo* and *Educación e Investigación: Retos y Oportunidades.*

Lise Olsen is an investigative reporter at *The Houston Chronicle* and has served as a board member of the non-profit Investigative Reporters & Editors. Olsen extensively interviewed trafficking victims, law enforcement officials, attorneys and others as part of a *Chronicle* series on human trafficking in Texas cantinas. She has twice been named Texas newspaper reporter of the year by the AP Managing Editors. She has changed laws and public policy through her stories and frequently presents her work at major reporting conferences in both the US and in Latin America.

Tony Payan is an Associate Professor of Political Science at the University of Texas at El Paso. He is co-editor of two books: *Gobernabilidad en la Región Paso del Norte: Reflexiones desde Distintas Perspectivas* (with S. Tabuenca) and *Human Rights along the U.S.–Mexico Border* (with K. Staudt and T. Kruszewski); and the author of two other books: *Cops, Soldiers and Diplomats: Explaining Agency Behavior in the War on Drugs* and *The Three U.S.–Mexico Border Wars: Drugs, Immigration and Homeland Security.* His research areas are the U.S.– Mexico border and governmental structures and human rights within the region. He has written columns for the *New York Times* and *Newsweek.*

Roberto Rodríguez Hernández was born in Cuernavaca, Morelos, on March 23, 1954. He graduated from the Universidad Autónoma de Morelos School of Law and began his career in the Mexican Foreign Service in 1977. In 1989 he studied for his Master's Degree in Criminal Science at the University of Valle De Bravo. In 1991 he was promoted to the rank of Minister in the Mexican Foreign Service, and in November 2002 he was given the title of Ambassador. He has been Consul General in San Juan, Puerto Rico (Oct. 2004–Oct. 2007); Nogales, Arizona (1995–2001); Budapest, Hungary (1987–1988); San Francisco, California (1985–1987); Laredo, Texas (1982–1985); and Havana, Cuba (1980–1982). His ambassadorial duties have included efforts to combat human trafficking regionally and globally.

Richard Schaefer is an Associate Professor in the Department of Communication and Journalism at the University of New Mexico. His teaching specialties are broadcast journalism, media writing and immigration issues. He is a co-founder of the UNM Cross-Border Issues Group.

Susan Tiano is the Director of the Latin American and Iberian Institute and a Professor in the Department of Sociology at the University of New Mexico. Her areas of specialization include women and labor within Latin America and along the U.S.–Mexico border, the *maquiladora* industry, and the effects of economic crises on women and households. She has written numerous book chapters, journal articles and books, including *Women on the United States–Mexico Border: Responses to Change (with Vicki Ruiz) and Patriarchy on the Line: Gender, Labor, and Ideology in the Mexican Maquila Industry.*

Acknowledgements

(This narrative begins from the perspective of senior editor, Susan Tiano, who for stylistic reasons finds it easier to frame it from her own point of view. It switches from "I" to "we" at the historical juncture when Moira Murphy-Aguilar joins the project.)

This volume is the result of synchronicities and lucky accidents whose orchestration can only be appreciated in retrospect. The institutional context for the project is the Latin American and Iberian Institute at the University of New Mexico, which drew together the cast of characters and provided the infrastructure to implement what would otherwise have been a laudable but unrealistic objective. As a long-time scholar of gender and labor in northern Mexico, I was becoming increasingly alarmed about sex and labor trafficking in the U.S.–Mexico borderlands but could find little scholarship on the topic. I got my chance to do something about this when my recruitment as LAII Director gave me the contacts and wherewithal to organize a bi-national conference on human trafficking in the Americas, which laid the foundation for this volume.

Since the mid-2000s, when I began using Kathryn Farr's seminal book (*Sex Trafficking: The Global Market in Women and Children*, 2004) as a case study in my graduate seminar on gender and international development, a small but devoted cadre of current and former students had been coalescing around the problem of human trafficking. Including both social scientists and attorneys-in-training, all shared my vision of linking academic and activist approaches to combating the human trade in New Mexico and elsewhere in the borderlands. Billy Ulibarri (who was earning his Ph.D. in sociology) helped me stay abreast of the rapidly emerging academic literature, while Carolina Ramos (who was simultaneously pursuing her degrees in law and Latin American Studies) shared her insights for harmonizing the contrasting legislation of Mexico and the United States into a collaborative effort to halt human trafficking across their shared border. Strengthening our links to the non-profit sector was Megan Jordi, a dual-degree law and LAS student specializing in immigration law, who worked closely with Catholic Charities to serve immigrant communities in New Mexico; and two UNM LAS alumni, Claudia Medina and Sandra Ortsman, who were leading *Enlace Comunitario*, an Albuquerque-based non-profit organization devoted to assisting immigrant women involved in violent and abusive relationships.

Carolina, Megan, Claudia, and Sandra were all involved in our state's first anti-trafficking task force, which had consolidated around recent New Mexico legislation designed to thwart the human trade, and was being led by Assistant Attorney General Maria Sanchez-Gagne. Maria was spearheading a multi-state effort to train criminal justice agents to recognize and assist international and domestic trafficking victims, and was using her considerable energy, contacts and resources to make New Mexico a regional leader in anti-trafficking programs and policy-making. With the addition of Brianne Bigej, a dual-degree student in law and LAS with a specialization in human rights, the stage was set for developing an outreach agenda that would link academic and advocacy-focused approaches to understanding and combating human trafficking in the borderlands.

Key to setting the process in motion was Pedro David, former chair of the UNM Sociology Department and current World Court judge (for the International Criminal Tribunal for the former Yugoslavia). Pedro serves on the board of directors of the United Nations Interregional Crime and Justice Research Institute (UNICRI)—the branch of the UN that is most responsible for researching and informing international policy on human trafficking. Excited by the prospects of promoting collaboration between the LAII and UNICRI, Pedro suggested that I invite Sandro Calvani, then-Executive Director of UNICRI and an expert on organized crime and the illicit global trade, to visit UNM on one of his many trips to the Americas. Sandro accepted my invitation, and this astoundingly busy man spent two days with us in Albuquerque, meeting with students and faculty, energizing our community, and helping us to consolidate our outreach agenda. We decided that the LAII and UNICRI would collaborate on a joint conference on human trafficking.

To ensure that our efforts were truly bi-national, we partnered with the Mexican Consulate in Albuquerque. Then-Consul Gustavo de Unánue Aguirre, who had been working with his government to combat trafficking within the Mexican interior and its borderlands, co-sponsored the conference and collaborated on its organization and content. Both the Consul and the Consulate's educational coordinator, Emy Kamata, were centrally involved in planning for the conference and ensuring participation from representatives of the Mexican government. "Modern-Day Slavery in the Americas" would, to our knowledge, be the first bi-national conference on the human trade in Mexico and the U.S.–Mexico borderlands to be organized jointly by the Mexican Consulate and a U.S. university.

From its inception, the conference was designed to integrate academics, policy-making, and advocacy in order to broaden its appeal and utility. We wanted it to be a truly bi-national endeavor, with presenters and audience members from both Mexico and the United States. Its unique contribution would reflect its focus on the U.S.–Mexico borderlands, though global dynamics would need to be addressed to create a fuller picture of the conditions promoting the human trade. Our aim was to focus on both sex and labor trafficking, and to show their links to other phenomena such as immigration and organized crime. Our objectives went beyond sharing knowledge of human trafficking and enslavement in the borderlands. We wanted the conference to feature an "applied" component that would encourage more enlightened policy formation and more effective service delivery to victims of the trade, and we wanted to forge networks and alliances that would last beyond the parameters of the conference. And we wanted the conference to lay the groundwork for a book on the U.S.-Mexico borderlands to advance the scholarly literature, most of which focused on Europe and Asia.

In addition to the essential contributions of the graduate student team (Billy Ulibarri, Brianne Bigej, Carolina Ramos, and Megan Jordi), I convened a planning group of UNM faculty with expertise in immigration (Manuel García y Griego and Dely Alcantara), Maria Sanchez-Gagne from the State Attorney General's Office, and Emy Kamata from the Mexican Consulate, whose ideas helped shape the list of invited presenters and the strategy for organizing the sessions and inviting the participants. Three media savvy people, Tony Tiano, Chris Schueler and Phil Cisneros, offered invaluable suggestions for garnering local media attention for the event.

We decided that Sandro Calvani would give the keynote address for the opening dinner, and New Mexico Attorney General Gary King graciously agreed to deliver a luncheon address centering on New Mexico's attempts to combat human trafficking in our state. Invited presenters would include U.S. and Mexican government officials, leaders of anti-trafficking organizations in Mexico and the United States, journalists, and academics, all of whom would share their distinctive perspectives and experiences on the problem of human trafficking. Invited presenters included Kathryn Farr, Jayne Huckerby, Tony Payan, Heidi Rummel, Gretchen Kuhner, Gustavo de Unánue Aguirre, Paula Goode and Maria Sanchez-Gagne.

Careful planning may set the stage for a successful conference, but plans must be effectively implemented for an event to reach its full potential. From the outset we were blessed to have the committed and efficient assistance of the LAII staff. Directing all of the local arrangements was Amanda Wolfe, who generously assumed this challenging task on top of her other duties as academic advisor for the LAII's Latin American Studies Program. With Amanda's remarkable foresight and organizational abilities, the conference proceeded without a hitch. Other LAII staff members, particularly Vickie Madrid Nelson and Frances Rico, deserve a tremendous amount of credit for their contributions to making the conference a success, as do Brianne Bigej, Megan Jordi, and Billy Ulibarri. A grant from the Gorham Foundation provided financial support for the event, and the University of New Mexico offered various kinds of assistance for the conference and our follow-up activities.

A particularly useful source of advice was my cousin Kat Tiano, who encouraged me to think outside the box of the typical academic conference. She suggested that we devote the second day of the conference to generating a set of applied strategies for combating human trafficking by means of an audience-centered exercise that would allow them to use the information they had gleaned from hearing the presenters' talks—in light of their own expertise as activists, service providers, journalists, or researchers—to identify the barriers to combating human trafficking, and to formulate strategies for surmounting these obstacles. I would facilitate a discussion designed to "surface" the obstacles; then we would take a short break in which we would thematically sort the items; and when we reconvened we would organize participants into small groups, each assigned to a particular theme or set of barriers. Their job would be to suggest solutions for dealing with their assigned set of barriers, which would be compiled by the group's "recorder" and presented to the larger audience for discussion and analysis. (I am grateful to Patricia Covarrubias, Susan Loubet, Dely Alcantara, Suzanne Schadl, Brianne Bigej and Chris Schueler for leading the groups.) The goal was to transform the resulting strategies into a written report that would be distributed to audience participants at a later date, and would be available for dissemination to other interested parties. This turned out to be an extremely useful exercise, leading to a report (which Kat prepared with the assistance of Billy Ulibarri and myself) intended for distribution to the audience members after the conference.

After the event had taken place, we aimed to keep the conference-generated enthusiasm alive by helping attendees network and exchange relevant information. Those who agreed to share their emails were added to a list-serve of conference participants, who would receive information about anti-trafficking initiatives in the region. While budget cuts to the LAII over the next several years precluded our ability to maintain the information-exchange, we were able to secure the necessary funding for follow-up conferences and activities to maintain energy and commitment in the regional network. The most successful post-conference initiative, as it turned out, has been the production of the present volume, *Borderline Slavery: Mexico, the United States, and the Human Trade.*

As any editor knows, transitioning from a series of oral presentations to an edited collection worthy of publication is a complex process. I knew from the outset that success in this endeavor would require a talented and academically respected co-editor with deep roots in the U.S.–Mexican borderlands and academic affiliations with universities on both the Mexico and U.S. sides of the border. Fortunately for me—and for this volume—my friend, former student, and current research collaborator, Moira Murphy-Aguilar, fit the bill exactly. Moira had earned her Ph.D. in Latin American Studies at UNM under my mentorship, and had produced a brilliant, Fulbright-funded dissertation on the impacts of the North American Free Trade Agreement (NAFTA) on transportation networks in the borderlands. Her decision to pursue her Ph.D. at UNM had been a fortuitous turn of events. We were both alumni of Brown University—she as an undergraduate and myself as a Ph.D. recipient—with equally strong commitments to Latin American research and scholarship, but we knew nothing about each other until she registered for my gender-and-development seminar. After that, our shared interests in gender and labor in the U.S.–Mexico borderlands and our mutual respect for each other and our abilities forged an enduring bond that continued to evolve after she earned her doctorate and pursued her academic career. Her exceptional scholarly skills, her academic affiliations with universities in both Cd. Juarez and El Paso, her network of contacts throughout the borderlands, and her pronounced commitment to combating human trafficking, made her the ideal partner to produce the volume. With her collaboration, the effort shifted from a solitary scholarly endeavor to a full-fledged partnership, as is reflected in the shift in this narrative from the first-person singular "I" to the plural "we."

Another vital member of the production team is Brianne Bigej. Brianne transitioned seamlessly from assisting Amanda Wolfe to organize the conference, to working closely with us to produce *Borderline Slavery*, a title she suggested herself. While the two co-editors were juggling the demands of their jobs as professors and administrators at UNM and the University of Texas, El Paso, it fell to Brianne to help us maintain momentum on the project. The conference presenters had been carefully selected to represent the full spectrum of specialists (academics, journalists, service providers and government and NGO leaders) so when any of the original presenters opted not to participate, their "slots" had to be filled by writers with comparable expertise. Brianne's diplomacy in encouraging busy people to make good on their commitments to produce papers for the volume was a godsend to the project. Her extensive knowledge of the applied and scholarly literature on human trafficking, her understanding of the legal aspects underpinning global and regional approaches to solving the problem, her intelligence, leadership, and interpersonal skills, and her unusual organizational abilities combined to make her an invaluable part of the production team.

Equally essential to the project were the multifaceted contributions of LAS Master's student Kristen Mattila, whose LAII-funded graduate assistantship supported her participation on the project. Known affectionately as "Wonder Woman" for her talent, flexibility, and enthusiasm, Kristen juggled a multitude of tasks involved with this complex enterprise. Without her vast range of expertise we would never have been able to meet our project deadlines.

The final, indispensable component of the web of connections that have made this book a reality is Bonnie Berry, the editor of the Solving Social Problems series with Ashgate Publishing in which this book will appear. Bonnie and Susan have been friends for many years, brought together by their beloved mutual friend and sociology colleague, Keiko Nakao. Just as we were beginning to explore our options for publishing the volume, Bonnie happened to notify us that she was soliciting contributions for her series. Assuming that human trafficking in the U.S.–Mexican borderlands was a fairly regional topic that might not be the best fit for a United Kingdom-based publisher, Susan mentioned the volume-in-progress to Bonnie, and was delighted by her expression of interest. Bonnie's gentle persistence in nudging us to produce and submit the prospectus, her help with negotiating the contract, and her consistent support and feedback throughout the production process have been essential to bringing this project to fruition. We are equally indebted to Neil Jordan, Senior Commissioning Editor, and all the staff at Ashgate for their expertise and patience.

This narrative, while accurate in its attributions and sincere in its gratitude, is inadequate to account for all of the fortuitous events, connections, and contributions that have made this volume a reality. And it fails to do justice to the underlying reality of human trafficking globally and regionally which *Borderline Slavery* attempts to illuminate and assuage, as well as the countless numbers of victims whose lives are diverted, distorted, and truncated by this horrendous practice. If the information in this volume can help combat the human trade and assist those it victimizes, this will be our greatest source of satisfaction and gratitude.

List of Abbreviations

ABA ROLI	American Bar Association Rule of Law Initiative
AFESIP	Acting for Women in Distressing Situations (Agir pour les Femmes en Situation Précaire)
AFL-CIO	American Federation of Labor-Congress of Industrial Organizations
ASU	Anti-Smuggling Unit
ATF	Bureau of Alcohol, Tobacco, Firearms and Explosives
CAFV	Center against Family Violence
CARICOM	Caribbean Community
CBIG	Cross –Border Issues Group
CBP	Bureau of Customs and Border Protection
CEDAW	Convention on Elimination of All Forms of Discrimination against Women
CEIDAS	*Centro de Estudios e Investigación en Desarrollo y Asistencia Social* (The Center for Study and Research on Development and Social Assistance)
Cd.	*Ciudad* (City)
CIS	Commonwealth of Independent States
DEA	Drug Enforcement Administration
DHS	Department of Homeland Security
DMRS	Diocesan Migrant and Refugee Service
DOJ	Department of Justice
DOL	Department of Labor
DOS	Department of State
ECPAT	End Child Prostitution, Child Pornography and Trafficking of Children for Sexual Purposes
ETA	Employment and Training Administration
EZLN	*Ejercito Zapatista de Liberación Nacional (*Zapatista National Liberation Army)
FBI	Federal Bureau of Investigation
FEVIMTRA	*Fiscaliza Especial para los Delitos de Violencia contra las Mujeres y Trata de Personas* (Special Prosecutor for Crimes of Violence against Women and Human Trafficking)
FLSA	Fair Labor Standards Act
GDI	Gender Related Development Index
GDP	Gross Domestic Product
GEM	Gender Empowerment Measurement
HTAT	Human Trafficking Assessment Tool

IBRD	International Bank of Reconstruction and Development
ICE	Immigration and Customs Enforcement
IDP	Internally Displaced Person
ILO	International Labor Organization
IMF	International Monetary Fund
INEGI	*Instituto Nacional de Estadística y Geografía* (National Institute of Statistics, Geography and Information)
INM	*Instituto Nacional de Migración* (National Institute of Migration)
INS	Immigration and Naturalization Services
IOM	International Organization for Migration
IT	Information Technology
ITP	Industrial Training Program
LAS	Latin American Studies
LPSHT	Law for Preventing and Sanctioning Human Trafficking
MHMR	Mental Health and Mental Retardation
MOU	Memorandum of Understanding
MSA	Metropolitan Statistical Area
NAFTA	North American Free Trade Agreement
NETS	Network for Emergency Trafficking Services
NGOs	Non-governmental organizations
NIM	Mexico's National Institute of Migration
NIS	Newly Independent States
NOSC	New Orleans Survivor Council
NOWCRJ	New Orleans Workers' Center for Racial Justice
OAG	Office of Attorney General
OAS	Organization of American States
OECD	Organization for Economic Co-operation and Development
POC	Point of Contact
RUF	Revolutionary United Front
SSA	Supervisory Special Agent
TIP	Technical Internship Program
TOC	Transnational organized crime
TVPA	Victims of Trafficking and Violence Protection Act of 2000
UACJ	*Universidad Autónoma de Ciudad Juárez*
UDHR	Universal Declaration of Human Rights
UN	United Nations
UNDP	United Nations Development Program
UNESCO	United Nations Educational, Scientific and Cultural Organization
UNICEF	The United Nations Children's Fund
UNICRI	United Nations Interregional Crime and Justice Research Institute
UNIFEM	United Nations Development Fund for Women

UNM	University of New Mexico
UNODC	United Nations Office on Drugs and Crime
UNTOC	United Nations Convention against Transnational Organized Crime
UPI	Universal Placement International
URM	Unaccompanied Refugee Minor
USAID	United States Agency for International Development
USCIS	U.S. Citizenship and Immigration Services
UTEP	University of Texas at El Paso
VSC	Victim Services Coordinator
WHD	Wage and Hour Division (of the U.S Department of Labor)

PART I
The Global Context: Setting the Stage for Sex and Labor Trafficking

Chapter 1

Introduction

Susan Tiano

Concern is building across North America about the growing violence along Mexico's northern border. Thousands have died in the bloody conflict between the criminal networks and Mexican law enforcement that has ensued in the wake of President Calderón's get-tough policies. Recognition is just beginning to dawn that border violence and the illicit trade that fuels it is not just about drugs and guns—it is also about human trafficking. Growing numbers of people are being transported against their will across the increasingly militarized but persistently permeable border between Mexico and the United States to labor in households, fields, factories, and brothels. Some travel to the borderlands from home communities in Mexico; some arrive after traversing Mexico from its southern border with Guatemala; others are shipped from Europe or Asia to northern Mexican border cities serving as entry points into the lucrative U.S. market for sex workers and other kinds of coerced labor.

Many traffickers obtain their victims legally via a labor contracting system established through guest-worker provisions within U.S. immigration law. Many victims begin their journeys voluntarily, paying smugglers huge sums to transport them to the beckoning U.S. labor market—only to become enslaved, exploited, and exchanged, often repeatedly, with the profits from their sale increasing with each transaction. Many are trafficked by the same networks that move drugs and other contraband, after being kidnapped from or sold by migrant smugglers (called "coyotes" or "*polleros*" in the borderlands) who have betrayed their clients' trust. Many end up dead, used as pawns to manipulate rival trafficking rings, or killed for failing to conform to their traffickers' dictates.

The steady stream of news about the border violence mostly focuses on drug trafficking and gun running, the better known forms of the illicit border trade. But accounts are beginning to emerge of humans who are being bought, sold, and transported through Mexico and across the borderlands. The world was shocked to discover the murders of 72 Ecuadorian, Guatemalan, and Honduran immigrants in San Fernando, Tamaulipas, a short distance from the border with McAllen, Texas, in August 2010. They were victims of Los Zetas, a criminal cartel known for dominating the illicit smuggling channel running up the Mexican gulf coast from Quintana Roo to Tamaulipas and into South Texas. The few survivors were unclear whether the group had been kidnapped by the violent cartel, or were instead delivered into its hands by unscrupulous migrant smugglers. But even if some media accounts have been reluctant to label the tragedy as a straightforward

case of human trafficking (*The Economist* 2010), security experts have recognized
the signs (Burton 2010).

Since then, a growing range of similar incidents has come to light. Tamaulipas
is increasingly being seen as a "black hole" for migrant deaths in the borderlands
(Pastrana 2010). In April 2011, the corpses of 183 murdered men and women,
most of them migrants from Central or South America, were discovered in some
40 mass graves in San Fernando—the same town where the 72 migrants had been
murdered eight months earlier. Their deaths were similarly attributed to Los Zetas,
though the rival cartel, El Golfo, may also have been involved (Sicar 2011). In
July 2011, National Public Radio investigator Jason Beaubien reported that some
150 Central and South American migrants had been captured, tortured, and held
hostage for days waiting for their families back home to pay exorbitant ransoms;
those whose families were unable to wire the funds were shot at blank range in
front of the others (Beaubien 2011). While Tamaulipas is especially notorious for
migrant victimization, Sonora, Chihuahua, and Baja California are also witnessing
a growing plague of cartel-induced torture, extortion, and murder of migrants.
Regardless of how the migrants had begun their journeys, they had ended them as
victims of human trafficking.

Mexico's role in the human trafficking chains that increasingly blanket the
globe is not simply as a transit site for victims from Central America or elsewhere
in the Global South attempting to enter the United States, either as their final stop
or before being trafficked somewhere else. It is a destination country for many
trafficked victims who remain in Mexico's mines, sweatshops and brothels—or
in upper-class households whose longstanding cultural traditions of domestic
servitude can obscure evidence of human trafficking occurring in their midst.
More often, Mexico serves as a source country whose citizens are absorbed in
substantial numbers into the trafficking chains that transit the globe. In Cd. Juárez,
Chihuahua, a steady stream of teen-age women have gone missing—389 cases
were reported in 2010, up from 326 in 2008 and 259 in 2009, according to an
October 17, 2011, issue of the *El Paso Times* (Cárdenas 2011). Juárez is not alone;
women and children are going missing all along the borderlands and in many other
parts of Mexico. But whether it is losing its own young citizens or is becoming a
murder site for uncooperative passengers en route to the United States, Mexico's
trauma is not always portrayed as human trafficking.

Until human trafficking is seen for what it is—the involuntary transport of
men, women and children within and across national borders for purposes of
exploitation, extortion, or other kinds of victimization—its looming presence in
U.S.–Mexican borderlands will not be recognized to its full extent. Nor will we
make much progress in tracing the intricate links between human trafficking,
migrant smuggling, and the illicit trade in drugs, guns, and other contraband that
can compound the dangers for trafficked victims. As long as drug trafficking takes
center stage in media reports and political discussions of border violence; human
trafficking is seen as something confined to women and youth forced into the
sex industry; and the increasing migrant death toll in the borderlands is blamed

on the migrants themselves and their "reckless" decision to allow themselves to be smuggled through a region dominated by drug cartels, human trafficking is unlikely to be recognized for the widespread and systematic danger it poses to growing numbers of men, women, and children in and beyond the borderlands.

This volume was written to dispel these and other misleading stereotypes and to shed light on the reality of the human trade. Faced with the irrefutable evidence that human trafficking is a reality in 21st century United States and its borderlands, many within the academic, law enforcement, and victims' services communities are calling for concerted political action to apprehend the perpetrators, rescue and rehabilitate the victims, and eliminate the practice altogether. A key component of this effort is to educate the public about the existence, nature, and scope of human trafficking so that they might become allies in the effort to end the practice. Human trafficking is occurring world-wide, with victims being trafficked to and from all of the world's regions; but the conditions on the U.S.–Mexico border add a unique regional cast to this global phenomenon, and they need to be understood before effective strategies can be developed for halting its progress in the borderlands.

As long-time residents and scholars of the borderlands, we have produced *Borderline Slavery* with this end in mind. The chapters in this volume situate human trafficking within the global context that is encouraging its proliferation, and show how its manifestation in the U.S.–Mexican borderlands is assuming its own distinctive shape reflecting regional conditions. Mexico's unique status as a key "portal" to the world's richest economy for goods and people from Latin America and other parts of the world poses unique challenges for law enforcement efforts to thwart the lucrative trade in humans and other contraband commodities. Yet we are only beginning to understand how trends in Mexico are influencing and in turn being shaped by, the human trade. Our aim is to trace the contours of human trafficking in the U.S.–Mexico borderlands toward the end of illuminating the kinds of social changes, policy shifts, law enforcement strategies and victims' services and advocacy that will be needed to confront the problem in the years ahead.

Clarifying Our Focus on Human Trafficking

During the past decade, human trafficking has morphed from an obscure or unknown practice into a salient social issue, as journalists have begun reporting on it and academics have attempted to study it empirically and explain it theoretically. Our growing awareness reflects not only the dramatic increase in the illicit human trade in the globalization era, but also the perceptual shift among politicians, law enforcement officials, and the public at large, as they abandon preconceived stereotypes that disguise or conceal it—such as the myth that slavery in the United States ended with the Civil War—and begin to see it for what it is: a widespread scourge that is destroying lives, wrecking communities, and endangering national security.

Human trafficking dwarfs most kinds of crime in creating public disdain and igniting punitive impulses. Who could fail to be horrified by the buying and selling of human beings in order to enslave them for power and profit? The fact that most recognized victims are women and children and that many are trafficked outside of their home countries to places where they are helpless in the face of foreign languages, cultures and legal systems, compounds public sympathy for the victims and disgust for their traffickers. One would think that a practice so alien to American values would mobilize a massive public outcry and a determined demand for law enforcement to devote the necessary resources to halt the practice—even though this might require taxpayers to dip into their pockets to foot the bill. Yet, as often as not, the U.S. media, politicians, and the public at large engage in "selective perception": they just don't see it for what it is because it is so antithetical to their cultural ideals of human freedom and equality.

So they confuse it with other phenomena: enslaved migrant laborers are simply undocumented workers who are in the country illegally; sex trafficking victims are merely prostitutes plying an illegal trade. With such conceptual sleights of hand, trafficking disappears behind other kinds of crimes, themselves neither effectively monitored nor consistently prosecuted, rather than showing itself for the real and growing social problem that it is. Misinformation and stereotypes feed this selective perception and the resulting masking of the problem behind other, lesser offenses: when traffickers can disguise themselves as "pimps" or "coyotes" rather than revealing themselves as traders in human beings, the human trade can continue to operate invisibly under the radar of law enforcement and public opinion. And when apprehended human traffickers receive the relatively light sentences meted out to petty pimps and smugglers, the threat of criminal prosecution offers little deterrence against the practice.

A key contribution to the cultural myopia that keeps us from facing the facts about human trafficking in North America is its confusion with one of the key "hot button" issues of the 21st century—immigration and the complicated economic, political, and social issues that accompany this intensely debated phenomenon. The discussion is so raucous and politically charged that questions such as whether border crossers entered into their travel arrangements voluntarily or under coercion, become irrelevant. And it is easy for human trafficking to disappear behind the smuggling of undocumented workers because the latter is much more pervasive and politically salient.

The two are indeed closely linked. Undocumented immigration can fuel human trafficking in times like the present, when stepped-up border patrol attempts to apprehend undocumented crossers promote migrants' reliance on coyotes—and in so doing, increase their vulnerability to trafficking networks such as Los Zetas or El Golfo, to which the human smugglers are increasingly connected. As Sandro Calvani and Olivia Jung convincingly argue in Chapter 3, when lawful immigration becomes ever-more restrictive relative to the number of cases seeking admission into the United States or elsewhere, this promotes both migrant smuggling and human trafficking. Yet while the intimate links between the two practices need to be understood to derive a more complete picture of the factors that promote human trafficking, conflating them does little to illuminate the complex forces promoting the human trade and the necessary strategies for confronting it.

This conceptual confusion between the two allows human trafficking to flourish under the radar of news reporters and law enforcement officials alike. When migrants' bodies are exhumed from mass graves in Tamaulipas or found decaying in the Arizona desert, attributing their deaths to their unfortunate choice to place themselves in the inept hands of coyotes who carelessly put them at risk of cartel violence, belies the reality of how human trafficking rings operate in the borderlands. Traffickers often pose as mom-and-pop smuggling operations just long enough to entrap their victims, or they purchase their human cargo from unscrupulous coyotes at some point along the transit route. Migrants held hostage in order to extort their families for huge sums of money may have been "kidnapped" by criminal elements—but they are just as likely to have been victimized by their own traffickers-posing-as-smugglers.

Cartels like Los Zetas and El Golfo traffic in humans as well as drugs, weapons, and other kinds of contraband, and often force trafficked victims to act as "mules" to transport the illicit goods. Those who are murdered are often killed to punish them for their refusal, or to set an example to make others in their group more compliant. When investigators dismiss their cases as smuggling gone awry rather than the purposive and systematic strategies of human trafficking cartels, they unwittingly—or perhaps deliberately, if they are in cahoots with the traffickers, as some law enforcement authorities appear to be—perpetuate the conditions that allow human trafficking to flourish undetected. When this happens, the supply of unwitting migrants who are fodder for the trafficking cartels is undiminished because knowledge of the cartels' ways of operating fails to percolate back through migrant networks to the victims' home communities to deter others from taking the same risks. In this way, human trafficking in the borderlands continues unabated, hidden in the shadows of misinformation, selective perception, and stereotype.

Human trafficking needs to be acknowledged as a unique phenomenon that is shaped by different socioeconomic forces and responds to different kinds of preventive strategies, than the smuggling of undocumented migrants. The two practices may share certain similarities in that both are ultimately rooted in the desire for a better way of life and the willingness to travel to a new context in the hopes of achieving it. But the process and end points are drastically different: the smuggled migrant, once delivered to his or her destination, is free to experience the opportunities and pitfalls of the new context, while the trafficked victim is enslaved, abused, and exploited by the traffickers.

Trafficking cases are more apt to be acknowledged as such when they involve living victims who understand and are able to relate their victimization histories to investigators. They are also more likely to be detected when they involve women and children, whose presumed defenselessness makes them more apt than men to be seen as having been entrapped and transported involuntarily. The typical image of adult men is that they are autonomous agents in charge of their own destinies;

when migrant men are found *en masse* at a U.S. worksite or appearing as though they might be in transit to one, they are more likely to be seen as undocumented workers (or "illegal aliens") who are willingly taking (scarce) U.S. jobs to which they are not entitled, than as coerced or enslaved victims of human trafficking.

Human trafficking is more apt to be seen for what it is when its victims are found in the sex industry than in other economic sectors. The U.S. public is so accustomed to enjoying a steady stream of migrant labor to staff their fields, farms, and households that they have no need to assume that the machinations of human traffickers would be required to ensure a sufficient supply of suitable migrant labor power. By contrast, the moral and material conditions surrounding sex work are so abhorrent to the average U.S. citizen that finding enough prostitutes to meet the demand might easily be assumed to require manipulation, coercion, or enslavement. Thus, when Soledad Griensen Porras was accused of forcing into prostitution 13 women and girls who were staying at a domestic violence shelter she was operating in Cd. Juárez, the October 2011 *El Paso Times* article did not equivocate in describing it as a straightforward case of alleged human trafficking (Martínez-Cabrero 2011).

Although it is gratifying to realize that human trafficking is finally being revealed for the horrendous problem it is, its frequent framing as something confined to the sex industry leaves many of its victims unnoticed and unprotected. In the chapters that follow, you will learn how human trafficking and migrant smuggling parallel and reinforce each other in the borderlands as they channel victims into various economic roles and sectors—some illicit and some legitimate. And you will come to see that failure to understand their contrasts and continuities, whether on the part of scholars, researchers, policy makers, law enforcers, or the public at large, works to the advantage of traffickers while undermining victims' welfare.

Human Trafficking in the Borderlands: A Regional Twist on a Global Problem

While confusion about the nature and magnitude of human trafficking certainly perpetuates the problem, it can hardly be considered to be a primary cause. Both globally and regionally, human trafficking reflects a broad range of causal conditions that are allowing it to flourish in the 21st century. Changes related to globalization are causing trafficking networks to proliferate by shifting the conditions and incentive structures of the human trade. Globalization is also expanding the pool of potential victims by increasing people's propensity both to want and need to migrate in search of a better way of life, and to be forced into the hands of smugglers and traffickers in order to do so. International borders magnify the complex consequences of globalization as it promotes immigration, commodity trade, and other international exchanges, at the same time that it challenges the ability of law enforcement and border control agents to regulate these exchanges.

Such dynamics take a particular form on the U.S.–Mexico border, where trade in humans, alongside and in interaction with other kinds of illicit trade, is on the rise.

The Global Context

In Chapter 2, Susan Tiano frames the historical and theoretical context for understanding human trafficking in terms of World System Theory approaches that view the practice as an integral component of the emerging world economy in the 16th and 17th centuries. While slavery and the human trade had existed throughout human history, with the advent of modernization, market capitalism, and the rise of the world economy they became more global—and more deeply entrenched. Trading in humans was both a key element of the economic exchange network on which trading companies depended for their profits, and a source of labor for mines, plantations, and other enterprises whose profits were augmented by employing vulnerable, low-cost labor. During the next several centuries, attempts to control the human trade had some effect in the West—for example, in eliminating overt race-based slavery in 19th century United States. But the practice continued in weak states with nonexistent or unenforceable laws and in cultural contexts where it shaded into, and could thus hide behind, normatively acceptable practices such as indentured servitude, military conscription, child apprenticeship and arranged marriage.

By the late 20th and early 21st centuries, just as globalization was diffusing Enlightenment values of individual freedom and human dignity worldwide, the illicit global trade in human beings was booming due to an unanticipated convergence of trends that have increased the economic incentives to human trafficking while substantially decreasing the risks of apprehension and punishment. As Sandro Calvani and Olivia Jung maintain in Chapter 3, the unsubstantiated popular fear of immigration, and the often misguided policy attempts to restrict what has conventionally been an accepted global practice, is leading increasing numbers of international migrants into the hands of human traffickers. Their numbers have been augmented by the profusion of wars and civil conflicts that have marked the 20th and 21st centuries, uprooting communities and initiating streams of political refugees and asylum seekers—a dynamic poignantly described by Kathryn Farr in Chapter 4. Women and children are disproportionately apt to pay the costs of the political and economic dislocations in their countries, and to be victims of the poverty and violence that can also make them vulnerable to human trafficking (Jenny Clark, Chapter 7).

Global problems require international solutions, which began to emerge in the late 20th century though the efforts of the United Nations and various global NGOs. As Roberto Rodríguez Hernández (Chapter 6) relates in his discussion of Mexico's implementation of the United Nations' Blue Heart campaign, such international campaigns support and legitimize national efforts to mobilize resources to combat human trafficking. When they are based on sophisticated methodological tools for assessing societal impacts, as Brenner Allen (Chapter 8) describes in her discussion of the American Bar Association's Rule of Law Initiative in Mexico, international campaigns can be monitored in the national context and adjusted to reflect local conditions more closely.

Globalization and Borders

The human trade flourishes in international border regions that can magnify the contradictions of globalization. By definition, borders connect adjoining nations with distinctive economies, polities, cultures, and population dynamics. Contrasts between the two nations in product supplies, market demand, and job opportunities encourage trade, immigration, capital investment, and other kinds of cross-border flows. The cross-border movements of goods, people, and capital in response to divergent market dynamics has been heightened under globalization, as governments around the world have attempted to promote economic growth by removing barriers to free trade and capital investment.

Difficult to monitor under the best of circumstances, these increasing cross-border flows are flourishing in the nebulous "grey zones" created by inconsistencies in regulatory regimes between adjoining nations. As Tony Payan describes in Chapter 9, the growing volume of licit trade in goods and services, and the rising number of migrants moving across national borders, have made it easier to conceal illicit commodity trade and human trafficking. Yet one of the contradictions of globalization is that at the same time that the accelerated rate of cross-border trade activity heightens the need for resources to enforce national regulatory policies, globalization ideologies and policies favor reduced government regulation and limited state spending in order to lower taxes and diminish national debt, all of which decrease the resources available for border law enforcement. And relaxing regulations such as those that have protected U.S. workers since the 1930s can be a boon to human traffickers, as Stephanie Hepburn describes in Chapter 12.

To compound the challenge of regulating cross-border flows, borders often link two "frontier" regions that are geographically, culturally, and politically distant from their national capitals. This distance can hamper efforts to monitor activity and enforce national laws and regulations in border zones. This is particularly likely if many frontier residents lack commitment to or harbor an active distain for national norms and values and thus have little internal motivation to comply voluntarily with federal regulatory or legal policies. In the absence of both "external" and "internal" social controls, crime can flourish, law enforcement can be hobbled, and official corruption can run rampant.

Another paradox of globalization, which favors "free trade" unhampered by state regulation, is that it creates a world economy that is increasingly transnational, while public administration and other governmental functions continue to be nationally bounded. Even though the accelerated flows of goods and people across borders increase the need for governmental regulation, states' ability to do so is often hampered by discrepant laws and regulatory regimes between adjoining countries. In such a situation, as Gustavo de Unánue Aguirre maintains in Chapter

5, bi-national collaboration becomes all the more essential for harmonizing divergent regulatory regimes; but it can be hampered by cultural, linguistic, and ideological differences between the two contexts.

The U.S.–Mexico Border

These dynamics take a particular shape on the U.S.–Mexico border, where the world's richest economy abuts a nation that is facing growing economic, political and law-enforcement challenges. This conjuncture promotes human trafficking in various ways. The seemingly insatiable U.S. demand for sex workers, cheap labor, low-cost domestic help, and other services that are not effectively supplied by U.S. citizens—which diminishes only slightly in recessionary times like the present—creates a ready market for trafficked victims and huge profits for their traffickers. In many Latin American labor markets the supply of workers exceeds their available employment opportunities, forcing many people to move elsewhere in search of a better way of life for themselves and their children. The marked discrepancy between employment opportunities, wage levels, and working conditions between the United States and much of the rest of the world stimulates immigration. Yet the limited options for legal entry into the United States funnel much of it into undocumented channels. The more rigidly enforced the border, the more likely are would-be migrants to be forced to depend on coyotes to get them into the country. The line between immigrant smuggling and human trafficking is a fine one because once migrants put themselves in the smugglers' hands, they are vulnerable to being deceived, coerced, and enslaved by the smugglers themselves or by traffickers to whom the smugglers may be linked.

Part of the problem for those who want to restrict cross-border flows is that communities on both sides of the border share a history, culture, and kinship network that predates the current placement of the border. Their shared ties encourage the trans-border circulation of goods and peoples through well-established networks that defy regulatory attempts. In fact, as Richard J. Schaefer and Carolyn Gonzales document in Chapter 11, many border residents feel as much affinity with the transnational frontier culture of the border region as they do with their national centers, which they often perceive as uninformed and uncaring about their unique problems as border residents.

The paradoxical U.S. political agenda in which economic migrants are both needed and feared further complicates things. It leads to inconsistent law enforcement, legal loopholes, and a porous border where immigration control and law enforcement agents are so busy apprehending smugglers and unauthorized migrants that they have little left over for combating human trafficking operations, as Tony Payan explains in Chapter 9. The U.S. government's preoccupation with the "war on drugs" leads it to privilege enforcement of drug laws to the neglect of human trafficking—and to be so preoccupied with the former that agents may not notice the latter when it occurs. The long-standing history of illicit trade across the U.S.–Mexico border has created well-entrenched criminal networks that can easily expand their scope of activity to include human trafficking. Mexico's recent efforts under President Calderón to combat drug smuggling and the violent backlash from organized crime have created tremendous turmoil in much of the country. This is particularly the case along the northern border, where crime, illicit trade, and official corruption are rampant and seemingly beyond government control. The vast cultural, legal, and linguistic differences between the United States and Mexico compound the difficulties of bi-national cooperation among law enforcement agencies attempting to combat human trafficking.

Eradicating human trafficking across the U.S.–Mexico border requires a multipronged approach emphasizing bi-national cooperation and coordination as well as accurate information and understanding of its global and regional causes on the part of politicians, law enforcement agents, and the public at large, in both Mexico and the United States. Awareness of the ways human trafficking is linked to, and different from, immigrant smuggling is essential for effectively detecting and prosecuting it. The sensationalism of sex trafficking must not occlude the frequency and severity of labor trafficking. As David B. Ham demonstrates in Chapter 10, law enforcement officials must coordinate their efforts with other agencies (immigration enforcement, public health, education, victims' rights, the mass media, and so on) to create a holistic approach that maximizes resources and emphasizes prevention as much as prosecution. Bi-national cooperation is essential to harmonize the contrasting law enforcement approaches to combating human trafficking in Mexico and the United States.

The emphasis on prosecuting offenders needs to be balanced against the need for protecting vulnerable victims. Although both the United States and Mexico have implemented tough federal anti-trafficking laws and many borderlands states have done the same, apprehensions and victim rescues have not kept pace with the volume of labor and sex trafficking occurring within and across their borders. Victims are often reluctant to report their experiences to law enforcement when they risk deportation; and as Lise Olsen reports in Chapter 13, the awarding of T-visas (visas offered to trafficking victims willing to testify against their traffickers) is not occurring in sufficient numbers to be much of a motivation. Yet as cases described by Gustavo de Unánue Aguirre, Roberto Rodríguez Hernández, and David B. Ham all demonstrate, growing awareness on the part of law enforcement officials is enabling them to detect and rescue some victims in the borderlands. As Virginia McCrimmon outlines in Chapter 14, providing the necessary services to rescued victims requires a coordinated response among social service agencies, victims' advocates, and medical and mental health professionals to assist victims' recovery from the traumas of their captivity and enslavement.

Human trafficking is a reality in the borderlands, but with knowledge, awareness, and commitment we can apprehend its perpetrators, protect its victims, and, in the long run, bring an end to the conditions that enable it to flourish. The contributors to this volume have offered their insights and recommendations in the hopes that someday all the world's citizens will be free from the scourge of the human trade.

Bibliography

Beaubien, J. 2011. Drug Cartels Prey on Migrants Crossing Mexico. *NPR, All Things Considered* [Online, July 7]. Available at: http://www.npr.org/2011/07/07/137626383/drug-cartels-prey-on-migrants-crossing-mexico [accessed: November 23, 2011].

Burton, F. 2010. Dispatch: Massacre in Mexico and Human Trafficking Video [Online, August 26]. Available at: http://www.youtube.com/watch?v=WOWwJnmP1mU [accessed: November 23, 2011].

Cárdenas, L. 2011. Juarez: Daughters may be missing, but still cherished. *El Paso Times*, October 17.

Martínez-Cabrera, A. 2011. Human Trafficking investigated at Juarez shelter for battered women. *El Paso Times* [Online, October 20]. Available at: http://www.elpasotimes.com/ci_19143438 [accessed: November 23, 2011].

Pastrana, D. 2010. Tamaulipas, Mexico's Black Hole. *IPS* [Online, September 2]. Available at: http://www.ipsnews.net/news.asp?idnews=52705 [accessed: November 23, 2011].

Sicar, M. 2011. Searching Among the Dead. *Human Journalism* [Online, May 30]. Available at: http://www.english.periodismohumano.com/tag/tamaulipas/ [accessed: November 23, 2011].

The Economist. 2010. No Safe Passage: Add Drugs and Gangs to the Long List of Dangers Facing Migrants. *The Economist* [Online, September 9]. Available at: http://www.economist.com/node/16994348 [accessed: November 23, 2011].

Chapter 2

Human Trafficking: A Perfect Storm of Contributing Factors

Susan Tiano

People have captured, traded and enslaved one another throughout human history, though their practices have shifted over time with changing political and economic conditions. Warfare, economic profiteering, and family formation have all served as motives for enslavement, though it may not have been widely recognized as such at the time. Social norms are fluid: what is seen as acceptable practice in one era may be considered a horrendous offense in another, and normative ideals can be dramatically different from actual practice. At the 16th century inception of what some (Chirot 1977, Wallerstein 1974) have called the "modern world system," slavery was a key source of labor and profits though it was often rationalized away or hidden from the public eye.

The paradox of slavery heightened in the 17th and 18th centuries, as the same Liberal Enlightenment values of human freedom and liberty that galvanized abolitionist sentiment also stimulated the entrepreneurial behaviors that fueled the market economy which made the human trade so profitable. The motors of European development were the same colonial expansion and international trade patterns that coerced and enslaved many people throughout the globe (McMichael 2008, Frank 1972). Slavery was but one of the practices to highlight the contradictions between the real and ideal in the treatment of human beings: various patterns of un-free labor such as the Latin American *encomienda* system and the European practice of indentured servitude also facilitated migration flows and accommodated labor shortages in the boom years of European commercial expansion.

Although slavery had been formally abolished in much of the world by the end of the 19th century, by that point the conditions of forced labor, sexual servitude and un-free human transport had been deeply ingrained, used by businesses and governments alike to meet their needs for workers and soldiers. Outlawing the human trade did not eliminate slavery—it simply drove it underground. There the global trade in humans has boomed[1] due to the same economic laws of supply and

---

1   The U.S. State Department estimates that on a global scale, every year 2–4 million people are trafficked (Siskin and Wyler 2010).The International Labor Organization reports that at least 2.4 million victims are trafficked each year (UN.GIFT). Renowned abolitionist and writer, Kevin Bales, estimates that currently 27 million of the world's inhabitants are enslaved (Bales, Trodd, and Williamson 2009).

demand as the more legitimate kinds of global commerce, though it has presented even greater opportunities for profits by avoiding tariffs, taxes, and other costs of doing lawful business. The contemporary human trade received a huge impetus from globalization, with its accelerating flow of ideas, products, and people within an ever-expanding world economy. Modern-day slavery is rooted in the past but is being shaped in unique ways by a novel conflux of circumstances that are enabling it to flourish in contemporary times.

In its 21st century incarnation, the human trade responds to a complex set of factors that shape the supply and demand for trafficked persons, while at the same time promoting the institutional context that enables it to flourish. To illustrate the factors that have contributed to the human trade, both historically and currently, it is useful to consider Figure 2.1, which situates human trafficking in the bull's-eye of a series of concentric circles. These are meant to symbolize the various interconnected "environments" that interact to give rise to any and all social practices, whether conventional or deviant.

Like any social practice, human trafficking takes place within social networks and organizations that promote it or allow it to occur. These in turn exist within societal and political contexts that support them or at least fail to prevent them from existing. These social and political processes and structures are embedded in economic contexts that mobilize resources to facilitate or impede their operation, and sustain a population with its own characteristic demographic processes, including births, deaths, and migrations. And all of these processes are physically situated in space and sustained by a physical environment that provides both opportunities and constraints for the populations that dwell there and utilize available environmental resources. In each of these spheres, various conditions have arisen over time to promote, allow, or fail to prevent human enslavement and trafficking.

Physical Environment

Throughout much of human existence, the cultures people have created to enable them to adapt to their natural environments have generally allowed them to subsist without destabilizing their surroundings—though archeological evidence abounds of over-farming and other kinds of resource depletion that brought the end to particular societies. This environmental equilibrium shifted with modernization and the advent of capitalism,[2] when the natural environment came

---

2   While the term "modernization" may carry negative connotations in today's post-colonial world, it is still the most commonly used label for the complex of technological, cultural, social, and political changes that propelled European development—even though the term rarely connotes the colonial incursions that financed the growth of Europe and its Western colonies. The economic motor of European modernization was capitalism, which was nurtured by the then-revolutionary belief systems of Protestantism and the Liberal Enlightenment.

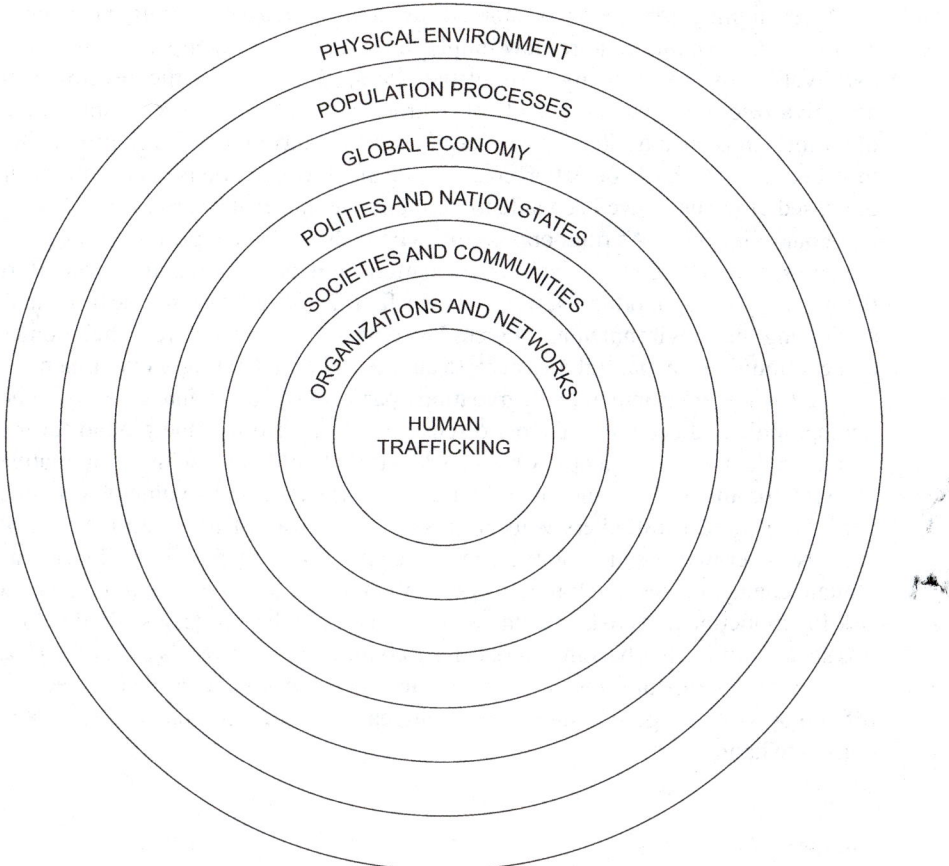

Figure 2.1   Context for Human Trafficking

Source: Susan Tiano 2011

to be seen as a set of resources to meet market demand, generate profits, and offer economic incentives for new products and technologies. With urbanization and industrialization, a "human-built" environment that depended on culture as much as nature and required a constant infusion of resources to sustain itself and its population, was juxtaposed to the natural world. When the two are in balance they can promote sustainable socioeconomic development, but imbalances can cause resource depletion, destruction of wildlife habitat, and other forms of environmental degradation. Today such dislocations are occurring on a global scale. Contemporary climate change is causing adverse weather events that threaten crops, make lands uninhabitable, and expose growing numbers of people to natural disasters that rob them of life and property.

As sustaining life becomes more difficult in increasingly marginal natural environments, people require new employment options to compensate for their lost livelihoods. Yet in many parts of the Global South, economic development has privatized land ownership and concentrated agricultural resources into large, often foreign-owned agribusiness enterprises. Many have mechanized production in order to scale back on labor costs by hiring fewer workers, and with their increased efficiency have been able to out-compete the smaller producers, driving them out of business. As rural opportunities have dwindled people have flooded to the cities, and often beyond them to destinations outside their country, in an effort to find a way to support themselves and their families. These "economic migrants" are joining the "environmental refugees" who have been evicted from their homes and communities by natural disasters, to augment the global migratory stream.

Increasing environmental degradation, particularly as it interacts with the demographic and economic factors discussed below, fertilizes the ground for the human trade. Desperate people who have lost their livelihoods, with no alternative in sight for themselves and their households, are especially vulnerable to the appeals of human traffickers who promise a better way of life. And the lack of security in crowded cities or the refugee camps that are poised to flourish as climate change makes many regions uninhabitable could put growing numbers at risk for abduction and enslavement. With the demographic shifts described below, this state of affairs has become increasingly common as the world's population has grown while the natural resources available to sustain it have eroded or become off limits to many people due to their increasing concentration in private and corporate hands.

Population Processes

As the modern world has evolved, its technological and social advances have increased the planet's capacity to support an ever-larger global population. As recently as 400 years ago, only about a half a million people existed on Earth (McEvedy and Jones 1978). They sustained themselves through traditional means of production (hunting and gathering, herding, horticulture, and so on), which had evolved over time and were well suited to the natural environments in which they existed. Though populations were susceptible to climate change, natural disasters or disease epidemics that could quickly devastate whole communities, barring such tragedies most groups maintained numerical stability by compensating for high infant mortality through even higher fertility, so that enough children survived to adulthood to reproduce themselves and their society. Natural population increase happened gradually, if at all, when over time a group experienced an excess of births over deaths, though numbers could spike or dip more rapidly if a group gained or lost members through migration.

This pattern shifted as economic development augmented resources, enabling settlements to expand and populations to grow. Generally over time birth and death rates tended to equilibrate, as families eventually adjusted to declining infant mortality in their communities by lowering their fertility. This "demographic transition" from high birth and death rates to low ones could take time, however. In 19th century Europe and the United States, birth and death rates both dropped precipitously, initiating a pattern of low natural population increase that continues to this day. But in much of the rest of the world birth rates stayed high despite significant declines in infant mortality; and because many more women lived to adulthood to have families of their own, their fertility rates compounded to create dramatic upsurges in population numbers in the Global South.[3]

As Thomas Malthus famously predicted three centuries ago, the exponential potential for human reproduction vastly exceeds the expansive potential of agricultural resources, which increase only linearly in the absence of a technological fix. He worried that unless humans exercised a good deal of constraint, they would end up overpopulating their environments and creating pathologies such as disease, famine, and warfare that would act as "natural checks" to bring population numbers back in balance with resource availability. Malthus was not taken seriously in his time—the labor shortages resulting from rapid industrialization were interpreted to mean that the world was *under*populated. Economic liberals had faith that technological advances would right any emerging population-resource imbalances, while many on the political left considered Malthusian concerns about overpopulation to be a purposive strategy to maintain control over numerically weakened populations in the Global South (see Galeano 1973). For the last half-century, though, population trends have led most demographers to conclude that Malthus was basically correct, and that short of massive intervention the world's population numbers could spiral out of control.

Governments and organizations worldwide have tried to decrease fertility by distributing birth control technology and information, and promoting other types of social changes such as advancing women's education to facilitate their ability to control their reproduction. And families have followed market incentives to reduce fertility levels in all but the poorest regions of the world (mostly in sub-Saharan Africa). But during the half-century or so when birth rates vastly exceeded death rates, enough additional members joined the world's population that even with birth rates below replacement levels, the world's population would continue its exponential growth for some time. While technological and economic innovations have helped slow the growing population–resource imbalance, they may be reaching their limits, particularly in the face of the environmental deterioration

---

3   Demographers have generally viewed the demographic transition as an inevitable concomitant of modernization. Modernization is assumed both to fuel the changes that decrease infant mortality and cause families to chose to have fewer children, and to benefit from the increased human capital that can accrue to families able to devote their resources to raising a smaller number of children. However, many demographers have revised their expectations due to empirical trends in much of the Global South, where economic growth is not producing the expected fertility declines.

described above. Forced population transfers and other kinds of dislocations can result from conflicts over scarce resources and other kinds of warfare. But most migrations are for economic reasons, as people feel the "push" of poor or eroding economic conditions in their home communities and the "pull" of (imagined or real) opportunities for financial or social advancement elsewhere, if they are willing to undergo the challenges of relocating in search of a better way of life.

Economically-motivated immigration has been a feature of the world economy for the past 400 years, accelerating with advances in transportation and communication and reflecting the contrast between rich and poor regions that has stimulated geographic mobility in response to differential opportunity structures. Global immigration accelerated as industrialization and economic growth increased labor demand in the 19th and 20th centuries, though it slowed during times of economic crisis such as the Great Depression and during the two world wars. In the past several decades, economic globalization has caused world-wide immigration rates to accelerate rapidly as transportation costs have decreased, wage differentials between sending and receiving communities have widened, and migrant networks have emerged to facilitate members' cross-border movement—with or without official documentation.

Population growth and economic stagnation in much of the Global South (and rapid growth in other parts) have further augmented transnational migration, though the recent recession in the Global North has reduced it to some extent. These trends are combining to make it difficult for destination-country governments to accommodate the large numbers of would-be migrants seeking admission. The gap between migrants' desires for a better way of life and the reality of the restrictive quotas and limited legal options available to many would-be migrants creates a dynamic illicit industry devoted to human smuggling and the promotion of undocumented immigration. The actual or perceived inability of receiving-country governments to absorb the large numbers of people seeking temporary or permanent admission forges the destructive link between migrant smuggling and human trafficking that enables the latter to flourish under the guise of the former.

To compound the pressures posed by rapid demographic growth, populations are stratified by gender, race, class, ethnicity, nationality, citizenship status and other axes of differentiation. Social, economic, and political resources often flow from position in the social hierarchy. When axes overlap to create vulnerable categories of people, particularly in settings marked by resource depletion, poverty, warfare, or environmental crisis, the potential for human trafficking victimization rises precipitously. The vulnerable status of many of the world's women and children makes them grist for the mill of modern-day slavery, particularly in contexts destabilized by conflicts based on ethnicity, race, religion, or other "primordial" or culturally profound dimensions of differentiation.

Population patterns are often shaped by the regulatory attempts of governments that use demographic policies in pursuit of specific ends, interests, or values. Just as some governments try to increase fertility to augment the labor force or the military, others attempt to decrease it to limit population pressures on national resources.

While some party platforms seek to reduce infant mortality and the poverty that underlies it by channeling national resources toward low-income populations, others view both as unavoidable results of natural, social, or transcendental forces that should be allowed to operate without governmental—or any human—intervention. In many cases, the norms and values that underlie national policies show regional variation, with those in the country's capital or power center differing from those in the country's frontier or hinterland. When values and other aspects of culture differ between two geographically adjoining countries, centuries of intermixing can make the frontier regions of both countries more similar to each other than either is to their national capitals. And because many national boundaries were colonial products drawn without consideration for indigenous settlement patterns, they separated what were once organic communities into different nation-states whose border inhabitants share more in common with each other, both culturally and demographically, than with their national centers.

Demographic dynamics represent much more than the biosocial influences that shape human reproductive potential, life expectancy, geographic shifts, and infant and adult mortality. Population patterns also respond to, and in turn shape, the political, economic, and social institutions that organize states, markets, and social arrangements. A group's economy arises as it uses resources from the physical environment to sustain life by creating systems of production, consumption, and exchange. As the following section will demonstrate, the economic dynamics of the past five centuries have promoted a variety of conditions that have fueled the human trade.

Global Economy

Rise of the World Capitalist System

The world economy has steadily progressed toward a single unified system of market exchanges since its inception in the 16th and 17th centuries. As the European economy shifted from mercantilism to capitalism, the growing profitability of trade motivated international exploration and colonial conquest which, over time, came to be organized into a unified network of production and exchange that some have called the "World Capitalist System."[4] At the "core" of the world system

---

4   "World System Theory" as developed by Emmanual Wallerstein (1974) and his colleagues views colonialism in much the same way as the neo-Marxists (Baran 1957), dependency theorists (Cardoso 1979, Frank 1966), post-colonialists (Said 1978) and others who describe the relationship between colonizers and colonized in similarly non-egalitarian terms, even though they may view the colonial system as being less integrated or monolithic than the single-system model of Wallerstein. For the purpose of this narrative I use the concepts "world economy" and "world capitalist system" as Weberian "ideal types" to describe a general tendency toward consolidation that began five centuries ago and

were the European nations and their offshoots in North America and Australia, which developed their economies by extracting natural and human resources from the "peripheral" countries that they either colonized directly or influenced indirectly through economic investment and trade. The driver of the world economy was capitalism, a system of production, consumption and exchange in which profit maximization and market-directed resource allocation were the driving objectives. Of the various resources that make production possible (land, raw materials, inanimate energy and so on) human labor is the most important—though because people have their own minds and motives a steady supply of capable and motivated labor is never a foregone conclusion. Then, as now, creative entrepreneurs developed various institutions to ensure sufficient labor for their mines, farms and factories; since "free" labor was often in short supply in the core countries and their peripheral colonies, indentured servitude, forced migrations and slavery were common strategies to provide enough workers to maintain production. Enslaving and exchanging human beings was an integral aspect of the colonial trade networks that united regions into a single world economy. Although officially outlawed in the 19th century, slavery has remained a common practice in many regions of the world.

The complement to production is consumption—when people use their profits, rents, or wages to purchase commodities that fulfill their needs and wants. Since the dawn of the world economy, consumption has driven production and commerce: products cannot be profitable unless markets exist for them. To maintain the steady consumption that fuels the economy, the range of human needs and wants must continually expand and require fulfillment through an ever-broader array of goods and services. Much of this is achieved by the mass media, via the taste-shaping efforts of advertisers and the public relations industry. In the process, an ever-wider range of human activities has become "commodified"—turned into products or services for market exchange. As the world economy has spread along with a materialist mass culture that measures human worth according to economic purchasing power, an increasing range of human activities has come to be viewed within the market nexus. Love, nurturance, and other emotional experiences that were once confined to the "private" or domestic realm have become subject to commodification, as have the means to fulfill them.

Perhaps the ultimate in commodification is the treatment of human beings as commercial objects to be bought and sold in the marketplace. While slavery has existed as a political and social institution throughout much of human history, with capitalism it assumed a distinctive character because human beings became "productive capital" whose labor was essential for the profits of the enterprise, not simply the success of the household or the subsistence economy. And wealth was generated not just in the work that slaves could do or the services they could

---

continues to this day. But I offer the caveat that such an over-generalized narrative belies the diversity of peoples who strive to maintain their identity and cultural integrity despite being drawn into the global economy.

provide but in the profits accruing from their sale. The profitability of slavery fueled the human trade during the first centuries of the world economy, and since then the trade has waxed and waned with global market forces. While law enforcement efforts have been able to curtail it to some extent, governments have had neither the means nor the motive to eliminate it entirely. As globalization has accelerated communication, transportation, immigration, and capital flows, and has expanded profit-making opportunities across the world economy, the supply- and demand-side factors that regulate international trade have made human trafficking extremely profitable. Experts estimate that the only kind of illicit trade more lucrative than human trafficking is the illegal drug trade, to which it is catching up over time. The commodification of sex, labor, and the human beings who provide them signifies the devaluation of human life that underlies both sex and labor trafficking and modern-day slavery in the 21st century.

Major Trends in the World Economy

Degradation and feminization of labor—Across the world, industrial production is increasingly being organized by global corporations that have segmented the labor process into deskilled operations that can be performed by workers anywhere with minimal training. Much of the world's manufacturing has moved to nations with rock-bottom labor costs and, as often as not, politically repressive regimes that prevent workers from organizing to demand a living wage or workplace rights. In the Global North, where advanced manufacturing sectors have been dismantled through industrial restructuring and overseas investment, little is left of what used to be a vibrant industrial economy with a well-paid, unionized work force. What were once highly-skilled, well-paid manufacturing jobs have become low-skilled, poorly-paid and menial. The industrial workforce has changed its composition as transnational corporations have outsourced their operations to the Global South, leaving in their wake a proliferation of small subcontractors who operate unregulated sweatshops or farm out products for home assembly and employ vulnerable, unorganized, typically female workers to lower production costs. And while corporate investment is helping develop the Global South, governments often have to offer such generous incentives to attract foreign corporate investment that they recoup little of the profits ensuing from the production, and wages are frequently so low that workers benefit little from this prosperity.

Manufacturing is not the only sector to witness a significant decline in the quality and rewards of employment. The automation of mining and farming have dramatically diminished employment opportunities in these sectors, while the service sector is polarizing into a small number of well-paid executives at the top, a growing mass of poorly-paid personal service workers at the bottom, and a dwindling component of mid-level professionals and managers.

Even as the world's population is becoming better educated, many people are reaching working age only to find that their credentials are insufficient to guarantee them a slot within the formal labor force. In the Global South the excess of people needing stable employment relative to the available job opportunities leads to labor surpluses that can be politically destabilizing. Governments resort to various strategies, including encouraging external investment in labor intensive manufacturing or agricultural industries to expand job opportunities, and promoting transnational migration so that wages earned elsewhere can be remitted to family members back home. Both strategies have their downsides. Working conditions in labor-intensive industries are often appalling, particularly if states eager for the investment turn a blind eye to exploitive wages, lousy working conditions or widespread workers' rights violations. And the migrant and guest workers who leave their home countries for foreign jobs may experience exploitive working conditions or find themselves vulnerable to human trafficking and enslavement.

The erosion of working conditions across the global economy has altered the composition of the work force. As International Labor Organization (ILO) economist Guy Standing (1999, 1989) noted in the late 20th century, an increasing proportion of the world's work is being performed by the most marginal sectors of the labor force: women, racial and ethnic minorities, children, and non-citizens, particularly guest workers and undocumented immigrants. These are the workers whose labor market vulnerability and limited employment options leave them little choice but to take whatever jobs they can find, regardless of the wage levels and working conditions. Since the 1960s the corporate relocation from Global North to South has accompanied a specific agenda to target young women for industrial and agribusiness employment because they work for lower wages than men and are believed to be more docile (Tiano 1994, 1987).

The preferential recruitment of women by global corporations has accompanied and reinforced a general upsurge in female employment in most parts of the world. Women's rising economic activity reflects their increased educational attainment, declining fertility and other trends that have expanded their employment options. But economic need plays a key role because with changing global economic conditions women have been forced in growing numbers to take jobs to supplement (or substitute for) the wages of male household members. Between 1960, when researchers first began to examine women's employment cross-nationally[5] and 2011, the proportion of the world's women working for wages surged from 36 to 52 percent (ILO 2011, Tzannatos 1998). Labeling this trend the "feminization of labor," Standing viewed it as more than a demographic reflection of the growing proportion of the world's jobs that are being held by women. For him, "feminization" also characterizes the erosion of working conditions and wages for all workers, male and female, such that the typical global job increasingly comes to resemble the kind of low-skilled, poorly-paid positions in which women have

---

5   Economist Esther Boserup (1970) was the first to compile data on women's global employment trends, which she linked to socioeconomic development and the marginalization it caused many women who were excluded from formal sector jobs due to patriarchal cultural beliefs and practices.

traditionally been relegated in labor markets throughout the world (Tiano 2006, Standing 1989).

To respond to shifting market conditions, employers seek a work force that is "flexible"—available for employment when market demand for their products is high but able to be laid off easily when declining demand forces a drop in production. Women's workforce flexibility reflects gender discrimination and role stereotypes that define women as secondary wage earners with male household members to support them if they lose their jobs. In reality, such traditional (and patriarchal) gender role expectations rarely reflect women's actual circumstances. Rather than relying on family support, women who can't replace jobs in the formal economy are usually forced to generate income by working informally. Women whose age, race, or ethnicity disadvantages them on the labor market are particularly apt to be relegated to the informal sector. There they are likely to encounter another category of "flexible" workers: the immigrants and guest workers whose denial of citizenship often excludes them from workers' rights protections and fair labor standards policies.

The link between feminization, flexibilization and informality across the globalizing economy is a key reason why the surge in women's employment during the last half century has not brought a substantial overall rise in women's well-being. Indeed, it has gone hand in hand with what has been called the "feminization of poverty," the tendency for a growing share of the world's most impoverished inhabitants to be women and girls. In stimulating women's economic activity—and their need for and expectation of employment—without creating sufficient jobs for all the women who require them to support themselves and their families, the transformations in global labor markets that are accompanying globalization are increasing women's vulnerability to human traffickers.

Growth of the informal sector and the underground economy As global production restructures and formal jobs expand too slowly to absorb all the workers needing some means of support, the informal sector helps take up the slack. This sector encompasses those activities that operate beyond the scope of formal governmental regulations such as taxation or worker protection laws. Informal tasks include service provision (housecleaning, child minding, home maintenance), commodity exchange (yard sales, street vending) and informal production (art, crafts, prepared food items). They occur without a labor contract and avoid governmental regulations concerning wage levels and working conditions. Many informal businesses avoid the red tape, fees, and taxes to which governments subject formal sector enterprises by operating under the radar of state regulatory institutions. Workers may prefer informal work because it offers more flexible schedules than the typical 9-to-5 job and better opportunities for increasing income than the fixed daily wage of formal employment. But many people are there because they are unable to secure formal sector jobs.

Historically, the informal sector has been disproportionately populated by women, whether by choice, since informal activities are often more compatible with their childrearing responsibilities, or by necessity, since they often lack formal job opportunities. It was once believed that the informal sector was a remnant of the "traditional" economy that would wither away when economic development sufficiently expanded the formal sector to encompass the full range of workers requiring steady jobs and incomes. Now social scientists recognize that informality is here to stay, due to a variety of factors that are increasing with globalization.

Generally, the informal sector waxes and wanes with the fortunes of the formal economy. In times of economic downturn, when the formal sector shrinks and the jobs that remain fail to ensure economic survival, workers flood into the informal sector. Some have a foot in both sectors, "moonlighting" in a second income-generating activity to supplement their formal-sector job, while others work exclusively in the informal economy. When the formal sector cannot absorb all the men and women who must earn money to support themselves and their families, the informal sector can help take up the slack. But its absorptive capacity is not endless, so emigration may be an important part of a nation's solution to demographic imbalances.

The informal sector is extremely heterogeneous, encompassing a complex array of income-generating activities and industries. What unites them is the fact that in one way or another they exist beyond the perimeters of governmental regulation. Many are too small and marginal to attract it or too numerous to enable it. Others must operate in the shadows because they involve activities that are against social norms or legal statutes. Informal activities span the continuum from legal and socially acceptable practices such as holding garage sales, to illegal and socially unacceptable behaviors such as selling drugs or engaging in prostitution.

The activities that cluster at the illicit end of the continuum might be called the "underground" economy, that shadow part of the informal sector that exists outside the law and resists the criminal justice system's attempts to eradicate it. It has boomed along with the rest of the informal sector (and the formal economy) as globalization has fueled international production and trade. The underground economy involves the production, consumption, and exchange of illicit items—trade that is outlawed to protect the citizenry, preserve a species, uphold a patent or promote other socially valued ends. Guns, drugs, alcohol, pornography, and other restricted items are the most familiar objects of the illicit trade, though the thriving markets for human organs and exotic animals (many consequently threatened with extinction) are gaining notoriety. The common image of the informal sector as constituting small enterprises earning marginal incomes belies the organizational complexity of the underground economy, where the illicit global trade is increasingly being conducted by vast organized crime syndicates that are linking smaller traders into regionally and globally consolidated networks. Those with human cargo often find their victims from among the most dispossessed and vulnerable, who are becoming more numerous as global wealth increasingly concentrates at the top of the economic hierarchy.

Growing economic inequality   Development has brought unprecedented levels of material wealth, but the benefits of growth have not diffused equally within and across the world's nations. Integration into the market economy tends to exacerbate pre-existing inequities based on gender, race, and ethnicity at the same time that it introduces new class-based forms of economic inequality. The earliest forms of socioeconomic organization—hunting and gathering, horticulture, and herding—were generally much more egalitarian than the complex agrarian societies that promoted the accumulation and intergenerational transfer of wealth, or the urban centers that gave birth to the bourgeoisie and their wealth generating system, market capitalism. With capitalism and the achievement-oriented value systems that grew up around it, Protestantism and Liberalism, the accumulation of wealth and property became a virtue and capital investment was encouraged through public policies that enabled entrepreneurs to retain, and motivated them to reinvest, their profits. In theory the resulting wealth and productivity would spread to the rest of the society as jobs were created and wages fueled consumption. But the system at its core needed to be stratified in order to reward innovation and productivity and to motivate people to make the necessary sacrifices of time, money, and effort to get ahead.[6] The result is an economic system in which growth and expansion are inherent and mutually reinforcing; but without built-in mechanisms (such as income and inheritance taxes) to redistribute some of the resulting wealth, it can stay highly concentrated and diffuse very little to those at the bottom of the socio-economic spectrum.

Most social scientists agree that global wealth has become more concentrated since the dawn of world capitalism (McMichael 2008, Wallerstein 1974). The social welfare policies of the mid-20th century that redistributed income to the middle and lower classes temporarily reversed this trend in the United States and Western Europe. But these gains have been undercut since the 1980s by "neoliberal" economic policies that have reduced government spending on social programs in favor of privatized, market-based approaches to providing for the collective good. Unemployment, poverty, and inequality, having burgeoned in the 2008 recession, do not seem to be abating as the economy once again picks up steam.

Unlike the early-to-mid 20th century, when governments in the Global North received a popular mandate to redistribute wealth through income and inheritance taxes, the tax strategies since the 1980s have allowed individuals and corporations

---

6   This rationale is embedded in what is known in sociology as the "Functionalist" theory of social stratification, which justifies inequality as an essential aspect of the modern market economy. Put forth by Kingsley Davis and Wilbert Moore (1945), its goal was to outline the various "positive functions" that social stratification performed for society, particularly in motivating hard work and social achievement. Like all Functionalist theorists, Davis and Moore assumed that if a social practice existed, this was because it contributed to the welfare and equilibrium of the society in which it was embedded. One of Davis's other projects was to outline what he considered to be the various positive functions of prostitution (1937).

to shelter a growing portion of their wealth, while the state has received less to redistribute to the population through social programs. The result, particularly when combined with demographic growth, climate change, and other forces that are changing the population-resource balance throughout the world, is dramatically increasing inequality between the world's richest and poorest inhabitants. When wealth is increasingly monopolized by a relative few and the rest have to share a dwindling portion of what remains, the poor suffer not merely from absolute deprivation (an objective lack of resources) but also from relative deprivation (a subjective deficit in comparison to other people who are better off), which can magnify the psychological and social impacts of objective poverty.

Inequality and poverty promote human trafficking by augmenting the ranks of economically desperate people who feel they have no place to turn for survival, and relatively deprived individuals seeking a better way of life. Not only may they put themselves at risk of victimization, but they may become involved in the trade themselves. Inequality can also feed upper-class demand for enslaved individuals' services because class privilege can generate a sense of entitlement that keeps them from identifying with or feeling guilty about the poor treatment of those forced to provide those services in coercive and exploitative ways.

Weakening regulation and the growing power of corporations Economic globalization has created more expansive opportunities for amassing wealth than the world has ever known. Yet government policy has neither accelerated nor been effective in its efforts to regulate financial transactions in the global economy.

In today's globalizing world, the most powerful economic actors are transnational corporations, some of which amass more wealth and affect the lives of more people than many national governments. Like the international economy that has nurtured them, today's global corporations are able to transcend state and national boundaries to operate in an administrative "grey zone" where their activities are difficult to track and regulate. Through political lobbying and campaign financing, corporations have come to exert considerable influence on states, which have increasingly come to depend on them to supply capital investment, innovative technology, employment opportunities, and other economic inputs that can enable countries to develop and prosper. Even though state regulation is often necessary to prevent global corporations from pursuing economic profits at the expense of human or environmental welfare, many political officials are unwilling to risk the benefits of corporate investment and trade by attempting to regulate corporate activities or negotiate investment terms that are more favorable to local needs than to corporate ones.

This is particularly true of the United States, where the erosion of the regulatory infrastructure during the last 30 years has given the corporate and financial interests that are promoting the global economy considerable autonomy from governmental restrictions. U.S. Supreme Court decisions that view corporations as being entitled to many of the same civil rights as individual citizens have further strengthened their leverage, as have regulatory commissions and presidential cabinets composed of corporate CEOs and their representatives. The result is a system ripe for what one sociologist (Derber 2011) calls "wilding," where tantalizing opportunities for financial gain and limited governmental regulation and law enforcement are systematically encouraging unethical behavior among the corporate and political elite. In nations throughout the world privatization, deregulation, and fiscal crisis have decreased states' ability to monitor and prevent illicit behavior (Naím 2005).

As regulatory control weakens, businesses of all kinds can flourish outside the margins of normatively acceptable enterprise—and within the underground economy that concentrates illicit activity. Criminal trafficking networks are often modeled after the global corporations in which some of their members got their start, and they are able to act with impunity for many of the same economic and political reasons. Like many activities in the global economy, drug smuggling, gun running, and money laundering are becoming corporatized, organized through increasingly complex and large-scale organizations (Naím 2005). Their opportunities for financial gain greatly exceed states' ability to monitor and regulate them. And governments' efforts are hampered when politicians, civil servants, or law enforcement officials are corrupted by the lure of fast profits though participation in illicit commerce and trade. Human trafficking networks, like their counterparts in other illicit sectors of the global economy, flourish in the absence of legal deterrence when the benefits of participation vastly exceed the risks. Inequalities of power can overlap and reinforce those of economic wealth to create a system that perpetuates itself even if individual actors or organizations are apprehended and removed from the game.

In short, various trends in the contemporary global economy are contributing to the human trade. By creating a female labor force compelled by economic need to generate income regardless of the availability of safe and steady jobs, the economic changes of the late 20th and early 21st centuries have made women more vulnerable to sex and labor trafficking. By eroding working conditions and wage levels, and by relaxing the regulatory environment that has protected workers from abuse and exploitation, globalization is paving the way for labor trafficking and forced labor. By denying large sectors of the global population access to resources, growing economic inequality is augmenting the supply of potential trafficking victims by making people's circumstances more precarious. And by promoting the growth of the underground economy, globalization is enabling the human trade to flourish within the growing array of "grey zones" that nurture black market activities. Yet even though economic conditions have created fertile ground for human trafficking, for the human trade to flourish, it requires political contexts that fail to protect people from human traffickers.

Government, Politics and States

During the 17th and 18th centuries, while the world economy was consolidating under capitalism into an increasingly unified system, political power was differentiating into a profusion of states that competed with each other for power and resources (Chirot 1977). States exist to govern their populations, maintain social stability, and protect their territories from external incursion though warfare, colonization, illicit occupation, or unregulated population transfers, including temporary and permanent migration. Political or civil rights depend on citizenship status through birth or naturalization, under conditions that are regulated by the state. States' military, law enforcement, and criminal justice branches are charged with maintaining internal and external security, which among other things involves controlling what comes across the state's borders into its territory.

Such control is often precarious, however. The paradox of a single global economy existing alongside a system of autonomous nation-states creates a situation in which trade reflects global forces of supply and demand that are not easily controlled by the state apparatus and its law enforcement bureaucracy. Such discrepancies tend to magnify in border regions, where jurisdictional divergence between adjacent states and lack of bi-national law enforcement coordination can create "grey zones" where the breakdown of law enforcement and regulation can allow illicit activities to flourish (Naím 2005). The U.S.–Mexico border region provides such a law-enforcement "grey zone," in which dealing in illicit commodities such as drugs and guns runs rampant and is beyond the power of either government to address effectively.

States are also expected to control tourism and immigration, regulating the numbers and categories of persons permitted to enter the country to visit, live, or work, either temporarily or permanently. Evidence that unregulated immigration is taking place beyond a state's control can violate public trust in a government's ability to protect and control its borders. At the same time, state officials may need to appease business interests that benefit from inexpensive immigrant labor. Immigration legislation thus often serves a symbolic function, convincing the public that something is being done about unauthorized immigration, while at the same time permitting the flow of low-waged (and often vulnerable) workers into the economy to accommodate labor demand (Calavita 1989).

For immigration policy to support a country's labor market effectively, it needs to be flexible enough to admit immigrant labor during times of economic expansion when labor demand is high, and to exclude them during times of economic contraction, when declining labor demand augments unemployment. Between the 1880s and the end of the 1920s, for example, 14 million people joined the U.S. population legally and an untold number entered without documents. When the Great Depression of the 1930s drastically reduced labor needs, immigration was dramatically restricted and many international residents were deported or repatriated (Johnson 2005). While these kinds of policies can help balance labor markets, short of draconian solutions like the Berlin Wall they are insufficient to seal borders completely against undocumented migration.

States' ability to regulate undocumented migration flows depends on the resources and technologies available to them to apprehend unauthorized crossers, but even the best equipped states are unable to override completely the economic forces that propel people across borders. Unauthorized migration often persists because the same regional or global economic conditions that stifle labor demand in the receiving countries also reduce employment opportunities in the sending nations. Migrants may continue to come despite restrictive immigration policies and practices because they believe they have no other way to survive. As legal channels shrink and stepped up border enforcement makes it more difficult to cross on their own, economically desperate migrants come to rely on human smugglers ("coyotes" in the U.S.–Mexican borderlands) to sneak them across the border. This makes them more vulnerable to human traffickers with whom the coyotes may be linked, or forced or paid to deliver their human cargo.

The paradoxes of immigration enforcement are compounded in the border zones between sending and receiving countries, where the interests of the sending country in facilitating economic migration as a safety valve for its un- and under-employed population can easily collide with those of the receiving country in controlling its borders to create the illusion, if not the reality, that jobs are being reserved for its citizens. In such a situation the necessary coordination between the two countries that would enable one to enforce the policies of the other may be difficult to achieve. Jurisdictional discrepancies, resource inadequacy, and discord between federal and regional policies and practices can further hinder immigration enforcement and bi-national cooperation. Just as the political economy of the U.S.–Mexico border creates "grey zones" when it comes to criminal law enforcement, it also leads to ambiguity with respect to enforcing immigration laws and policies.

International cooperation to control crime and regulate immigration flows is a desirable but elusive goal of the international state system. Contemporary states maintain an uneasy balance of power, acting autonomously much of the time but also joining forces to create international conventions aimed at regulating complex international issues beyond the scope of any single state or regional coalition. These agreements are a basic foundation for international law even though such conventions are voluntary and compliance among signatories is not easily enforceable. The United Nations protocol addressing Trafficking in Persons, established to coordinate international opposition to this pressing global problem, is such a convention (United Nations 2000).[7] In defining human trafficking, distinguishing it from migrant smuggling, and revealing it to be deeply rooted in the international political economy, the UN Convention has provided a critically important tool for combating the human trade.

---

7   The United Nations Convention against Transnational Organized Crime was adopted in 2000. Two optional protocols—one that addressed human trafficking and another that addressed migrant smuggling—were adopted in 2003 and 2004 respectively.

Social-Cultural Contexts: Community, Family, and Sexuality

Certain social and cultural contexts can insulate people from the economic and political conditions that make them vulnerable to human trafficking. Individuals with strong ties to functioning families receive the social and often the economic support that can insulate them from human traffickers—and the pimps, labor recruiters, and others who may lead them into the traffickers' grip. Even in the absence of family support, people in socially integrated communities can access social networks and service organizations that can cushion the blow of economic hardship or other personal challenges that might otherwise disrupt their lives. Yet the economic dislocations and material deprivations that globalization-related changes are bringing to many households in the world economy are weakening families and communities just when many people's dwindling economic fortunes make such economic and social support more important than ever.

Community Disorganization and Family Breakdown

The rapid social change that accompanies economic development has long been associated with community disorganization. Concern about the destabilizing effects of modernization was one of the motivating factors behind the theoretical reflections of the classical social theorists—Marx, Durkheim, and Weber—and their contemporary counterparts in both the "conflict" and "consensus" theory traditions.[8] Regardless of their affinity for economic development, market capitalism, or other processes associated with modernization, theorists on both sides

---

8   In what Emile Durkheim called "well-integrated" societies, people supported and cared for other members of the community even though they may have been less charitable to outsiders. He worried that rapid social change posed a threat to community integration, particularly if it was accompanied by individualistic value systems that weakened community bonds, and normative breakdown that led to "anomie" (normlessness) and other pathologies such as suicide and lawlessness. Decades before Durkheim, Karl Marx had worried that economic inequality and materialist value systems were antithetical to the cohesive communities that humans need to fulfill what he called their "species being" or their fullest potential. They were not alone in their fear of modernization: Max Weber's worry was that "rationalization"—modernization's cultural driver which impaired inspiration by reducing social life to overly logical ways of thinking and being and overly bureaucratized systems of organization—would destroy both human freedom and social community. Regardless of the mechanisms, all three of the so-called founders of sociology worried that modernization would weaken the social fabric and make people vulnerable to exploitation, devaluation and dehumanization (Allen 2005, Martindale 1960). Contemporary "consensus" theorists share Durkheim's concern for social integration, while "conflict" theorists share the Marxian concern over forces that contribute to political and economic inequality. Despite their contrasting emphases, the two sociological branches are consistent in their conceptions that modernization and its heightened expression under globalization are disorganizing communities.

of the spectrum have emphasized the destabilizing effects of these transformations. As industrialization and urbanization shift populations from countryside to city—where they may or may not find stable jobs, livable housing, and viable neighborhoods—the cultural context is set for what one sociologist (Wirth 1938) called "urbanism as a way of life." In contrast to rural settings in which social bonds forged though face-to-face interaction and shared norms keep communities integrated, even at the expense of social liberties, much of the interaction that occurs in urban settings is between strangers or casual acquaintances whose native languages and cultures may be very different from one another, and who as a result may have difficulty forming cohesive social ties.

Migration itself can be destabilizing, particularly if it involves crossing national borders, so it can lead to interpersonal stress and social strains. And while many migrants may have access to support and assistance through networks of people from their home communities or countries, others may find themselves isolated in their new settings. Cities throughout the Global South have grown so fast that many residents have been forced to crowd into marginal lands, in declining areas of the city, with little or no urban infrastructure or services. Some of these communities are highly organized, but many are not, and in the vacuum of social and political leadership that can characterize rapidly growing, overcrowded and impoverished communities, criminal networks can assume power and reorganize the community to serve their interests. If states are too weakened by national disaster, economic crisis, or civil war to enforce their laws and protect their citizens, regionally based delinquent gangs can morph into or merge with nationally and even internationally powerful criminal networks.

Migrants are not the only urbanites to experience social disruption in the cities, many of which are growing at such an alarming rate that overcrowding, inadequate infrastructure, and shortages of public and social services are diminishing the quality of life. When people, whether migrant or native, are mostly strangers to one another, they are less constrained by gossip, threats of exclusion, and other "informal" strategies that groups in tightly-knit communities normally use to keep their members in line by appealing to their desires for social acceptance and group belonging. The kinds of normative constraints that would typically keep people from committing crimes or hurting each other are not as effective outside the context of well-integrated communities. This increases reliance on the criminal justice system to retard criminal activity, but it faces an uphill struggle dealing with the personal dislocations of rapid social change when religious, political, and social organizations are unable to socially integrate people and supply meaning to their lives.

Community disorganization can happen during economic "good times," particularly when economic growth occurs so rapidly that the cultural context is unable to keep up with the material changes. Or it can occur during economic recessions, when jobs disappear, household resources decline, and some people decide they have little choice but to turn to illicit activities to support themselves and their families. When the economy tanks, effective law enforcement is more important than ever to maintain social order, but it is particularly likely to receive short shrift due to declining municipal budgets. Both boom and bust cycles can promote official corruption, political crime, and "elite deviance" (Simon and Eitzen 1986), all of which are favorable for the emergence of human trafficking cartels and other sorts of organized criminal networks. Such trends are hampering law enforcement in the Global South and with the economic downturn of 2008, increasingly the Global North as well.

The kinds of conditions that have contributed to community disintegration are also promoting family breakdown, particularly in the Global North. Prior to the industrial revolution, families were generally large and extended, encompassing several generations and branching horizontally to include various kinds of relatives related by blood, marriage, or fictive kinship ties. Extended families were well adapted to agrarian life, where many hands were needed on the typical family farm. With industrialization and the rise of the market economy, the nuclear family with one or more parents and their offspring became the modal form. Modern life offers various services such as health care and education that take the place of tasks once produced domestically, so fewer family members are needed to manage the modern urban household. Cultural expectations that grown children should establish their own (nuclear) families, and governmentally provided supports that make it easier for the elderly to live independently, contribute to the nucleation dynamic. Economic crisis, recession, and rising unemployment can make the self-supporting nuclear family more an ideal than a reality, though overall the global trend has been toward smaller families.

Modernization and globalization have not just shrunk families; they have also disintegrated them. Divorce rates have risen rapidly in the last half century, as has the proportion of men and women who are refraining from marriage altogether. Female-headed households are on the rise across the Global North and in much of the Global South. When women are the sole providers for dependent children and have no family support to help them socially or materially, job loss or other financial emergencies can force them to earn money any way they can—which can make them vulnerable to both sex and labor traffickers. The same could be said of men, who without the support of family members could find themselves involved in the human trafficking industry, whether as victims or perpetrators.

Children are the most obvious victims of family disintegration. In countries throughout the world, the number of children living outside nuclear or extended family households and away from the protection of parents or relatives has multiplied in the globalization era. Many communities lack the economic or social resources to accommodate all of the children who are abandoned by or run away from their natal families. The growing phenomenon of children forced by abuse or family disintegration to live "on the street," beyond adult supervision or protection in the most marginal sectors of the city is making them vulnerable to human trafficking. But even if families are still intact, they may be so economically disorganized—or so immersed in cultural norms that denigrate girls—that they knowingly subject their offspring to sex or labor traffickers for economic gain, or they do so inadvertently because they are duped by the recruiters' promises of a better way of life for their children.

Rise of the Desire Industry and the Commodification of Sexuality

The inherent dynamism of the global economy reflects its ability to expand into new geographical regions and economic sectors to access resources that can be turned into commodities for market exchange. The motor of growth in capitalist economies is market expansion. Historically, markets have grown as objects with "use value" (goods produced domestically for household consumption) have been made into or replaced by objects with "exchange value" (commodities produced for market transaction). With the evolution and expansion of the market economy, a growing array of social, environmental, and emotional resources have become commodities to be bought and sold in order to meet consumers' needs. Many of these needs have a biological basis but they are also socially constructed, shaped in the globalization age through advertising and public relations efforts accomplished through an ever-more sophisticated global marketing industry. The world economy requires growing appetites for blue jeans, athletic shoes, and I-pods in order to drive production chains across the world. Consumer tastes are being formed by a multi-billion dollar industry that has perfected the science (and art) of shaping social needs to ensure sufficient consumption to keep the global economy humming along. Materialist value systems that stress conspicuous consumption and evaluate personal worth in terms of economic success help maintain high consumption levels in the Global North—and induce Global Southerners to follow suit as their economies grow.

Commodification has an actual economic dimension in that the product or service is available for purchase once conditions are negotiated to the satisfaction of both parties to the exchange. But it also has a normative aspect, in that processes or products that were once viewed as existing outside the commercial nexus come to be seen as legitimate objects of market exchange. Throughout the 19th and particularly the 20th centuries, an increasing range of phenomena have been encompassed within the market realm. Services originally provided within the domestic arena—child care, education, health care, social support—have been commercialized and made available for sale to buyers able to pay the price. As specialized institutions run by professional staff have replaced the "untrained" mothers and wives who originally provided these services domestically, a growing array of industries has emerged to promote personal transformation and help people maintain social relationships. The market for such services has expanded as family disintegration has impaired members' ability to support each other socially and emotionally, and privatized service providers have stepped in to offer market-based remedies for the isolation and anomie that can accompany the loss of community in contemporary society.

Unsurprisingly, along with the growth of industries tailored to people's emotional needs has come a fluorescence of those for fulfilling their sexual desires.

Sex was an object of economic transactions long before the market economy made money the key medium of exchange. Some would say that sexual exchanges in human societies have always had an economic dimension, with men providing material support for women who nurtured them and their children. Others would object that in societies where women have meaningful productive roles, they do not need to exchange sex for economic survival and can enter into more egalitarian relationships on their own terms, whether within or outside the context of formal marriage. Prostitution, a short-term exchange of sex for economic benefit, is often viewed as the polar opposite of family formation and long-term commitment in the service of biological reproduction, though the two have evolved hand in hand and may actually have reinforced each other. As sociologist Kingsley Davis (1937) has notably argued, prostitution helps shore up marriage by offering philandering husbands a temporary outlet less apt to lead to the complications of pregnancy and emotional attachments than other forms of extramarital sex. And many feminists claim that marriage and prostitution are two sides of the same patriarchal coin that keeps women subordinate to men—even though most uphold women's right to earn income through prostitution and other kinds of sex work.

Regardless of the perceived links between prostitution, family formation and biological reproduction, it appears that until fairly recently in human evolution, sex was considered a "normal" biological function, similar to eating and sleeping. As Foucault (1976) convincingly maintains in his history of sexuality, sex in European culture did not acquire moral overtones until the Catholic Church began regulating sexuality through marriage as a way of influencing parishioners' hearts and minds. By appropriating power over sexuality, the Church could increase contributions to its coffers when "human failings" led to sexual transgressions outside the bounds of Church-sanctioned matrimony, making it necessary for Church officials to intervene to protect families and save souls. The Church maintained its influence over marriage and sexual mores even though secular value systems such as the Victorian ideals of the late 19th century emerged periodically to compete with religious doctrines for control over people's sexuality. The "virgin-whore" dichotomy and the underlying view that female sexuality is for procreation rather than enjoyment was widespread in both religious and secular value systems of the 19th and 20th centuries. These normative systems' intrusion into many couples' sexual ideals and practices may have contributed to the expansion of prostitution and other sexual alternatives to the monogamous nuclear family.

As the market economy expanded to encompass sexuality, entrepreneurs found a diversity of ways to make money from sex. Foucault describes an "explosion" of interest in sex and sexuality in the late-19th century, as science embraced it as a focus for exploration and innovation; the counseling industry emerged to help people work though their (often religiously inspired) confusions over sex; and social reformers tried to shape women's reproduction, whether to encourage their fertility or limit their reproductive contributions to the gene pool. As the 20th century unfolded, the economic profits to be made from sex and sexuality enticed growing numbers of entrepreneurs to enter the business.

Over time the "desire industry" has evolved into one of the most dynamic and profitable sectors of the global economy. It encompasses a variety of branches and includes both illegal and legal behaviors, along with a "grey zone" of questionable but difficult to prosecute activities. Within this zone the boundaries of morality and legality have shifted over time as political debate has been shaped by what sociologist Howard Becker (1963) called "moral entrepreneurs"—people who try to impose their definitions of right and wrong onto everyone else by politicizing ethics in an attempt to legislate morality. The evolution of pornography laws reflects the politics surrounding the desire industry, as do the elaboration and enforcement of anti-prostitution statutes and other attempts to legally regulate sexual mores and behaviors.

The global desire industry has evolved hand in hand with advances in technology that have facilitated access to sexual materials and images for an increasing array of consumers. A century ago, U.S. consumers seeking to purchase a sexual experience had few alternatives to brothels or seedy movie theaters. Today's consumers can access a plethora of erotic materials, often without leaving the privacy of their own homes. This shift has broadened the market for goods and services produced by the desire industry, expanding it across age, social class, and gender lines, and targeting products to "niche markets" to address a broader range of tastes and preferences. The industry's growth reflects the increasing size, scope, and heterogeneity of its consumer base, assuring a stable if not growing demand for its products, which span the continuum from erotica to hard-core porn. Yet even though various erotic products are targeted to women, men are the major market for the desire industry.

Prostitution, too, continues to serve an almost exclusively male clientele. Even though women's increasing buying power would give them the economic wherewithal to purchase sexual services, they are much more apt than men to pursue sexual expression though family and friendship networks. This is also likely true of most men, who generally fulfill their sexual needs in non-market ways—perhaps with some supplementation with pornography or other products of the desire industry. But this still leaves a significant market of male consumers who seek the services of sex workers.

Governments walk a fine line where prostitution is concerned: public sentiment against sex work demands that something be done to protect the public against "vice" and to shore up family values. Yet even if they could abolish prostitution, it's unlikely that they would attempt to do so out fear of possible repercussions from men who depend on sex workers to meet their needs. This political ambivalence puts prostitution in a law-enforcement "grey zone," curbed but never eliminated and driven by steady demand for sex workers' services. Sex work itself forms a complex hierarchy ranging from well-paid escorts of wealthy patrons to street prostitutes serving their johns in rent-by-the-hour motel rooms and automobile backseats—so workers at the top of the hierarchy would obviously enjoy better working conditions than their peers farther down the ladder. No doubt if prostitution were legalized and sex workers protected rather than punished for their work, working conditions would improve across the industry and jobs would become more attractive to potential workers. As things currently stand, however, the demand for sex workers' services, particularly at the lower levels of the hierarchy, is apt to exceed the supply of workers willing and able to participate in the industry. The fact that a sex worker's career span is usually shorter than those of women in less physically demanding jobs may also limit the availability of sex workers. If a voluntary labor force cannot be enticed into sex work, enslavement and human trafficking are apt to flourish to meet the demand of male consumers.

Since desire is often sparked by a change of scenery or an adventure in a foreign land, the global desire industry has evolved hand in hand with the global sex tourism industry, where a region's women and youth become the primary attraction for the mostly male tourists who vacation there. Various cities (Amsterdam, Bangkok, and 1950s Havana) have distinguished themselves as favored sex tourism sites, marketing themselves as vacation destinations that fulfill emotional as well as sexual needs. Many sex tourism locations have grown up around military bases and have shifted to a broader international clientele as their industry has expanded. While the sex workers in such vacation spots are often local residents, many are international workers in a range of circumstances, including having been trafficked and enslaved.

Both the desire industry and the sex tourism industry it nurtures are fed by the economic and cultural changes wrought by globalization. The worldviews and value systems instilled by the global corporate media (materialism, individualism, mass consumption) are as central to globalization as the economic, technological, and organizational changes that are integrating the world's regions into the global economy—and making it easier for workers and consumers to travel the world more effortlessly. Thus, one of the most important ways that globalization is fueling sex trafficking is by enabling the global desire industry to flourish. While part of this industry is the realm of legitimate business enterprise, much takes place in the underground economy and the "grey zone" between the two, where organized crime networks are morphing in response to the vast opportunities for profit-making.

Organizations and Networks: Regional and Global Crime Cartels

Since the beginning of the world economy, criminal enterprises have acted individually or collectively to reap profits by exchanging illegal goods and services or trading licit products in illicit ways. Their operations have waxed and waned in rhythm with shifting governmental policies attempting to influence the behaviors of consumers and suppliers—even though, as an unintended consequence, their regulatory efforts have often increased the profitability of the illicit products by limiting their supply in the face of continuing demand. A well-known example is the burgeoning of organized crime syndicates in the United States when Congress enacted the Volstead Act of 1920 in what turned out to be a futile attempt to prohibit alcohol consumption. The Harrison Act of 1914, which outlawed cocaine, opiates, and other psychoactive substances that had been in conventional use during the 19th century, provided a further incentive to organized crime networks within and outside the United States. With some exceptions, such as the British government's purposeful expansion of the 19th century opium trade, the general tendency over time has been for states to try to restrict the use of mind-altering substances that were originally sold freely in the legitimate marketplace, and for criminal networks to emerge to meet the consumer demand that persisted after the substance was outlawed.

On occasion states have reversed this trend by relaxing restrictions—as did the U.S. government in 1933, when it struck down the Volstead Act in the hopes that legalizing alcohol would eliminate the incentives to organized crime created by its prohibition (Goode 1972). Once the genie is out of the bottle, however, it's not easily enticed back in. When alcohol was legalized criminal networks simply shifted to drugs, pornography, and other illicit items and continued to grow in influence and profitability. Their experience is not unusual. Once created, criminal organizations can simply switch to other products if the deregulation or legalization of their mainstay reduces the economic incentives to its illicit distribution. The "War on Drugs" initiated by then-President Richard Nixon in 1973 has vastly exceeded the Volstead Act as an incentive to criminal networks within and outside the United States. And psychoactive substances such as drugs and alcohol are but one of the many kinds of products that have become more rather than less lucrative with government regulation. They have typically followed what may be called an "illegal product life-cycle" in which products are introduced, appetites are whetted, supply networks evolve to meet the growing demand, governmental attempts at regulation make the products more profitable, and the illicit industry expands to reap the resulting profits. The shifting terrain between licit and illicit products as laws and regulations are enacted, enforced, and rescinded creates law enforcement "grey zones" that can enable the illicit trade to flourish within their shadows.

This is not to imply that the United States, whose clash between its Puritan historical roots and its Madison-Avenue spawned appetites has enabled the desire industry to flourish along with ever-more expansive law enforcement attempts to control it, is typical of the entire Global North. Various European governments have adopted a less schizophrenic approach to regulating the desire industry. Yet throughout the 20th and early 21st centuries, the global underground economy has experienced a similar set of trends. Criminal organizations have generally been able to benefit from a steady increase in profitable illicit products, as (1) technological innovations have expanded the range of ways for people to enjoy themselves through activities that challenge conventional morality; (2) moral entrepreneurs have influenced politicians to outlaw such activities in an attempt to enforce conventional norms by legislating morality; (3) criminal organizations have extended themselves to supply the now-illicit demand; and (4) law enforcement efforts attempting to suppress them have been unable to counteract the market pressures that entice newcomers into the industry to fill the void left by their incarcerated competitors.

During most of the 20th century, law enforcement agencies were able to achieve a rough equilibrium with organized crime syndicates, keeping them in check despite being unable to defeat them entirely. One of the factors contributing to their (partial) success was that the organizational structures of the criminal networks were predictable: their hierarchical, top-down decision-making and highly controlled rank and file made it possible to weaken the organization by "decapitating" it (Naím 2005).

All this changed drastically in the 1990s, when globalization transformed the illicit global trade and the criminal organizations that perpetuate it. As policies promoting free trade and investment expanded the world economy, one of the unintended consequences was the growth of the underground economy, with its illicit trade in illegal and regulated products and services. According to the "Washington Consensus"[9] that supported these policies, global trade was hampered not only by taxes and tariffs that increased the cost of trans-border transport, but by regulations and practices that demanded careful inspection and documentation of goods and transport vessels. Disparate regulatory regimes between countries were "harmonized" by loosening tight controls to bring them in line with less restrictive ones. The weakening of trade regulations, and the reduced funding for customs and other border control agencies charged with implementing them, has occurred at the same time that global trends have drastically increased the flow of products throughout the global system and across national borders—leaving fewer inspectors to process a much higher volume of incoming goods. Traffickers and smugglers have availed themselves of this discrepancy to step up the illicit global trade. Yet while trade controls have generally been harmonized across borders to facilitate product entry, political and law enforcement regimes have not followed suit, leading to jurisdictional discrepancies that have complicated cross-border investigation and apprehension of illicit traders. Aided by technological advances that have enabled them to monitor cross-border shipments and coordinate supply chains from a safe distance, and abetted by corrupt officials attempting to supplement their eroding salaries through bribes and kickbacks, traffickers and

---

9   The neo-liberal ideology that came to be called the "Washington Consensus" was based on the free-market principles emphasized by Fredrick Hayeck and popularized by Ayn Rand, who viewed economic investment, corporate regulation, and support for public welfare as illegitimate functions of government (Rand 1964, 1957). One of the chief architects of the Washington Consensus was Rand-advocate Alan Greenspan, who ran the U.S. federal reserve bank between 1987, when he was installed by then-President Ronald Reagan, and 2006, when he retired from public life. In this capacity, his policies transcended the U.S. economy to promote free-market principles worldwide. Greenspan famously stated that the "market" was sufficient to regulate all commercial activity, including preventing fraudulent behavior, and that government's efforts to enact and enforce laws against fraud were unnecessary and implicitly illegitimate. In 2008, as a troubled U.S. Congress investigated the corporate underpinnings of the financial crisis, Greenspan admitted that events had proven him wrong (Andrews 2008).

smugglers have decreased their risk of apprehension at the same that the economic benefits of the illicit trade have never been greater (Naím 2005).

To take advantage of these incentives, criminal organizations have changed their structure to make them more flexible and better able to accommodate shifting economic and political conditions. As former *Foreign Policy* editor Moisés Naím (2005) described in his path-breaking book on the illicit global trade, the top-down, vertically integrated organizations that concentrated power and centralized decision making in the hands of a few "godfather" figures were an early-to-mid 20th century adaptation to the need for large-scale coordination when communications technologies were in their infancy. The organizational trade-off was that such bureaucratic systems are unwieldy, slow to adapt to changing conditions and opportunities, and difficult to network over time and space.

Criminal organizations in the globalization era have increased their adaptability to quickly changing conditions by flattening their hierarchies, decentralizing their decision-making, and elongating their horizontal connections across supply chains to make them more flexible and better able to respond to emerging opportunities. Advances in communication technologies have facilitated coordination among these loosely integrated networks, which can now link across industries and product lines to forge complex interregional chains of supply and transportation. This structural innovation has made organized crime networks more flexible, more adaptable, and better able to take advantage of new product niches and supply lines. It has also made them better able to conceal their activities and resist detection—and to replace network members who are apprehended by crime fighting agencies without suffering damage to the network's operations.

This organizational structure has given illicit trade networks an advantage over the governmental agencies charged with apprehending and prosecuting them because the latter continue to retain the inflexible bureaucratic forms common to the organizations of the previous century. The difficulties posed by their unwieldy organizations are compounded in border regions when two or more law enforcement bureaucracies are required to coordinate their activities and harmonize their contrasting regulatory and enforcement regimes across national borders. These organizational differences compound the political obstacles facing cross-border law enforcement to further reduce the illegal traders' risk of apprehension.

The crime-promoting incentive structure is particularly unbalanced in what political scientists refer to as "weak" or "failed" states that lack the capacity to carry out the basic governmental functions of collecting taxes, enforcing laws and regulations, maintaining internal order, and controlling their borders. When governments are weakened through economic crisis, political conflict, or social upheaval, organized crime networks can gain influence over the state apparatus in ways that enable them to manipulate border control and law enforcement agencies to their advantage (Naím 2005). Structural vulnerabilities of states are often most pronounced in the border or frontier regions that are farthest from the centers of whatever power and legitimacy the government is able to marshal.

When such power vacuums emerge, states are ripe for "colonization" or "capture" by organized crime networks that are able to use them as staging areas for smuggling and trafficking operations with little threat of apprehension by the state's crippled law enforcement authorities (Naím 2005). Many analysts view Mexico as a "weak" state on its way to becoming a "failed" one due to its increasingly violent confrontations with drug cartels, which are murdering politicians and law enforcement agents along with ordinary citizens in an attempt to disrupt Mexican politics and society (Grayson 2010). While pockets of lawlessness exist throughout the country, the northern border region has become particularly ungovernable—a situation that is presenting huge challenges to U.S. officials trying to retard the flow of illicit goods and services across the U.S.–Mexico border.

Human traffickers have adopted the same loosely structured networks as their counterparts in other branches of the illicit trade. In previous eras, when human smuggling was the norm and most transnational moves involved crossing a single border, it was easier for coyotes to operate independently and to ferry people across borders voluntarily. Today's human smugglers are often integrated into complex trafficking networks that span the globe, moving their human cargo through complicated transportation routes and across multiple series of borders, and blurring the distinction between voluntary human smuggling and coercive human trafficking.

The U.S.–Mexican borderlands are a fertile area for human trafficking networks. The consistent demand for inexpensive and vulnerable workers in the United States, the constant supply of migrants hoping for a better way of life but unable to access U.S. labor markets legally, and the difficulty of policing the vast expanse of the borderlands create huge incentives for traffickers. Ironically, as efforts of U.S. border control agents to deter undocumented immigration have increased over time, making it more difficult for aspiring migrants to cross the border on their own and forcing them to contract the services of smugglers who are increasingly aligned with trafficking networks, the volume of trafficked persons has risen proportionately. In 2005, an estimated 300 human trafficking networks were operating in the U.S.–Mexico borderlands (Naím 2005: 98), a number that has likely increased over time as efforts to restrict undocumented immigration into the United States have increased the cost to would-be migrants, and have in turn expanded the profit margins of smugglers and traffickers.

Human trafficking networks have been proactive in responding to the growing opportunities for profiting from the human trade. Governments, whose regulatory powers, budgets, and personnel have been greatly decreased by neo-liberal politics and policies, have been unable to stem the tide. This mismatch has been exacerbated by the change in their organizational structures: ironically, just as human trafficking networks, like other kinds of illicit organizations, have become less hierarchal, more flexible, and more adaptable to changing circumstances, law enforcement agencies have often coped with their decreasing political and budgetary fortunes by becoming more bureaucratic and less suitable for interagency cooperation (Naím 2005). The fact that border control, one of the few areas in which U.S. law enforcement budgets have been strengthened in the economic downturn, actually contributes to human trafficking by forcing growing numbers of would-be migrants into the hands smugglers who pass them on to human traffickers, only deepens the paradox.

Globalization is thus fanning the flames of human trafficking by augmenting its economic incentives, decreasing the risks of apprehension, and transforming the organizational structures that both fuel and impede the human trade. These contradictions are magnified along international borders and in frontier zones on the perimeters of governmental influence, public regulation, and law enforcement efficacy. They are especially pronounced in the U.S.–Mexico borderlands, where the world's richest economy abuts a region whose growth in the globalization era has been slowed by rising inequality, inadequate economic opportunities for its growing population, and a protracted "war" on national and foreign drug kingpins that is weakening the state and civil society. As human trafficking grows in the 21st century, its regional manifestation along the U.S.–Mexico border is likely to skyrocket.

Summary: Theorizing Human Trafficking in the Borderlands

The essence of globalization is the accelerated flow of capital, technology, goods and ideas across national borders and throughout the global economy. Earlier patterns of trade and investment have morphed into complex chains of commodity production and exchange that have reorganized the global economy. These changes are most obvious in the formal economy, where states and intergovernmental organizations monitor and regulate financial transactions, albeit to a more limited extent under the "deregulationist" free market principles and policies that have guided globalization. Less perceptible but in many ways equally important to the global economy is the informal sector, which operates alongside the formal economy to absorb its surplus workforce and to accelerate the flow of products and services by eliminating the bureaucratic "red tape" of laws and regulations.

"Informality" need not imply "illegality," of course; while informal activities are generally unregulated, only some violate legal statute or pose the risk of jail time for those who engage in them. The "underground" branch of the informal economy encompasses products and services whose production and exchange are prohibited by national and international law. The illicit nature of these goods tends to limit their supply and thereby drive up profits for the entrepreneurs and organizations that deal in them. Globalization has augmented the economic incentives to the illicit trade at the same time that it has diminished states' ability to enforce their laws and apprehend lawbreakers. This imbalance has enabled the illicit trade and the criminal networks that engage in it to flourish in the globalization era. The underground nature of these activities makes them hard to track, but by all estimates human trafficking ranks second behind the illegal drug trade as a source of profits for criminal enterprises in the underground economy. More people are being bought and sold into slavery today than at any other time in human history.

Yet modern-day slavery is so antithetical to liberal Western values and historical narratives that most people are blind to its occurrence. Only recently has it begun to be defined as a pressing social problem whose causes must be understood and ameliorated if we are to have any chance of combating it.

The global human trade reflects a complex conjunction of economic, cultural, and social dynamics that are converging in contemporary times to augment both the supply and demand for illegally procured laborers and sex workers. To ensure a ready supply of victims, traffickers may forcefully overpower and abduct people, but the transportation process is easier if victims go "voluntarily" through subterfuge and manipulation. Recruiters play upon the only-too-human desire for a better way of life for oneself and one's children. Those most vulnerable to their appeals are often the individuals who feel the strongest sense of deprivation, if not in absolute terms, then in relative ones. Worldwide, aspirations have risen as the global media have promoted the modern middle-class family, with its emphasis on individual achievement and material consumption, as the cultural ideal. Yet while personal aspirations for material improvement have risen throughout the world, the conditions for their fulfillment have not kept pace, and have often moved in the opposite direction.

Globalization has meant winners and losers because the benefits of growth have not diffused equally and periods of remarkable economic expansion have been punctuated by economic downturns, recessions and crises that have threatened the subsistence of countless households in the Global North and South. Gender-based inequities that limit women's employment opportunities, social status, and household decision-making power—and race-based inequalities that expose minorities to discrimination and marginalization—reinforce the economic hardships faced by many people. Migration is one of the only survival strategies available when livelihoods are threatened and rising aspirations dashed. It is often so expensive and difficult that recruiters who promise to help with financial and logistical arrangements may have great appeal to would-be migrants who, in their desperation, ignore niggling fears that the recruiters' promises may be too good to be true. And international migration is often so tightly regulated that many migrants are unable to access legal channels and end up paying smugglers to ferry them to intended destinations—a choice that puts them at risk of being delivered into the hands of human traffickers.

Societies wracked by civil conflict and those in which individual freedoms are constrained by authoritarian regimes are particularly fertile areas for human traders who prey upon the uprooted and the oppressed. Perhaps paradoxically, countries that shift radically from planned to free-market economies can experience such pronounced economic dislocations that their citizens become vulnerable to human trafficking even though—and in part because—they now have broader individual freedoms to choose occupations and physical locations. Societies in which rapid population growth has vastly exceeded the necessary expansion of job opportunities and social services to sustain their citizens are especially vulnerable to the human trade. Ones whose natural environments have been depleted through resource extraction, unregulated development or overly rapid population growth contribute more than their share of victims. Fueled by the lure of economic and social opportunity and the desire to escape the constraints of financial need, social marginalization, or political conflict or oppression, the global pool of potential and actual victims is continually replenished.

Just as the global supply of humans vulnerable to trafficking and enslavement has never been so vast, the global demand for the illicitly procured labor and sexual services of enslaved human beings has never been greater. At a most basic level, slavery, whether for labor, sex, or both, can only flourish in a cultural context in which social solidarity and the respect for human life are so limited that humans can come to be seen as simply one more kind of commodity for market exchange. In such conditions, so many people fail to develop the moral compass to keep them from victimizing others when the lure of financial gain or personal benefit is sufficiently enticing, that the society can no longer protect its members from exploitation and victimization. If governments are sufficiently motivated, resourced, and capable, they may be able to counteract the inadequate internal social control among the populace with consistent and effective external social control on the part of regulators or law enforcement personnel. If states are so weakened by widespread corruption or fiscal inadequacy that officials are unwilling or unable to enforce the state's laws and regulations, they unquestionably will lack the authority and efficacy to enforce anti-trafficking and anti-slavery laws. By privatizing government functions, eroding state budgets, and promoting neoliberal ideologies that view markets, rather than governments, as the only legitimate way to shape economic behavior, globalization has weakened the internal and external controls that might otherwise dampen demand for illicit labor or sex workers.

Beyond their shared roots in the weakening of regulatory and law enforcement regimes that could diminish the demand for slaves by hobbling their employers and customers, labor and sex trafficking are fueled by different dynamics that maintain the demand for their victims' services. Working for a living is not against the law; what drives illicit employers underground is their desire to avoid worker-protection regulations in order to exploit the workforce more effectively. Obeying labor laws that regulate working conditions and pay scales drives up the cost of labor by limiting the length of the work day, circumscribing the range of tasks, requiring sometimes-costly health and safety protections, and maintaining minimum wage levels, all of which increase operating expenses and drive down profits. Employers who want a cheap, docile, and vulnerable labor force at any cost cannot do much better than enslaving the people who work for them. Whether they are forced into mines, farms or factories to extract resources or produce commodities for market exchange, or are made to do household and childcare tasks within the confines of the private household, enslaved laborers lower the cost of reproduction and production in a way that can stimulate demand for their services in the absence of moral or legal imperatives against such hyper-exploitation of labor power.

Enslaving women as sex workers, by contrast, is not all about reducing the costs of doing business, though that might be an added incentive. The illegal status of the sex industry, the social taboos associated with prostitution, and the difficult nature of the working conditions all combine to limit the supply of workers available to enter the industry. In most markets the labor pool is pared down still further because workers need to meet qualifications such as youth and physical attractiveness which are not just scarce but fleeting, further contributing to high turnover in the sex industry. Labor shortages are not an inevitable feature of the sex industry, particularly in "high end" sectors with attractive wages and working conditions. But the conditions of sex work along much of the rest of the continuum may be sufficiently non-enticing to even the most economically desperate that enslavement is the only way to recruit a sufficient workforce to meet customer demand. While some might expect the prostitution industry to suffer from competition from the pornography industry, expanding as it has with globalization-related technologies such as the Internet, this does not seem to have been the case. "Virtual" women have not replaced real ones as objects of desire; instead, the forces of social disorganization, human commodification, and the rise of the desire industry appear to be stimulating the market for sex workers, even if human trafficking and enslavement are the only reliable ways to meet that demand.

Two distinct but related features of the borderlands make them particularly susceptible to trafficking in illicit goods, including human beings. On the one hand, the purpose of international borders—demarcating and differentiating the territories of two adjoining countries while facilitating or impeding the movements of people and goods between them—makes border regions the obvious focus of illicit transport from one national context to the other. The U.S.–Mexico border, where one of the world's richest nations abuts a country that has struggled economically and politically (some would say because of, rather than in spite of, Mexico's physical proximity to the United States), models the kinds of regional disparities that can stimulate the osmotic flow of goods and people from one context to the other. On the other hand, the status of borderlands as frontier regions that are often physically and symbolically distant from the centers of national power can limit their integration into the rest of the nation and make it difficult for states to enforce their laws and policies in the borderlands.

Perversely, even though their function as transit sites for commodity flows makes borderlands vulnerable to smugglers and traffickers, their distance from the centers of national power and influence in their respective nations can limit their ability to secure the resources necessary to combat the illegal trade. The U.S. image of its "wild west" as an ungovernable, lawless context has its parallels in Mexico, where many see their northern borderlands as the domain of outlaws, revolutionaries, and—particularly since Mexican President Calderón's recent crime fighting efforts have given them national notoriety—drug cartels. Whether as an international boundary region or a pair of peripheral frontiers, the U.S.–Mexico borderlands epitomize the dynamics that make border regions vulnerable to human trafficking, all of which have become more pronounced with globalization.

International borders highlight the mismatch between an increasingly unified global economy and the multitude of autonomous nation states that vie to shape economic exchanges to promote their political interests. Borders focus, stimulate, and symbolize the accelerated flow of information, products, and investment that is the hallmark of globalization. At the same time, they represent and magnify the challenges facing national governments in their efforts to control their territories despite neoliberal international policies that reduce state revenues and discredit and dismantle national regulatory regimes. Borders also heighten the contradictions of immigration, which in today's world generally flows from Global South to North. Absolute deprivation (stemming from overpopulation, economic crises, political wars and conflicts, and environmental upheavals) and relative deprivation (reflecting rising but unfilled aspirations due to the spread of materialist culture) have led increasing numbers to attempt to migrate at any cost, even if it means placing their fates in the hands of coyotes who are linked to human trafficking networks.

Migrants' dilemma demonstrates a key contradiction of globalization. The expansion of the global economy has stimulated the exchange of all the factors of production, including the human capital or labor power embodied in human beings. Yet while free-trade policies have promoted the flow of natural resources, investment capital, and entrepreneurial expertise—not to mention the resulting products—they have done little to facilitate migration. Instead, migration policies have been left to the various nation-states, which have formulated them to promote national interests. So-called "sending countries" have used them to stimulate out-migration as a safety valve for underemployed populations, while "destination countries" have authored them to regulate or restrict in-migration to more closely attune migration flows to shifting economic circumstances. When labor demand is high and in-migration is encouraged, the two kinds of national policies can complement one another. But when economic downturns reduce labor demand and stimulate restrictive policies, the two kinds of policies move out of alignment. This policy disjuncture—and the contrasting motives of those charged with enforcing the discrepant policy agendas—can impair cross-border cooperation in apprehending undocumented migrants.

These kinds of challenges are endemic to the U.S.–Mexico borderlands, whose history of unimpeded flow of goods and people across what is still seen by many border residents as an artificial boundary, has set a local precedent that limits motivation to enforce national policy imposed from politicians in Washington D.C. or Mexico City. The challenges to bi-national cooperation are not limited to immigration policy; enforcement of criminal and civil laws in the borderlands has also been impeded by contrasting regulatory regimes and law enforcement cultures between the adjoining nations. Though the United States and Mexico have often joined forces to apprehend and punish human traffickers and other illicit traders, they have been unable to combat the globalization-related forces that are stimulating human trafficking across their shared border. The fate of the victims of 21st-century slavery in the U.S.–Mexico borderlands, as elsewhere in the world, will depend on concerted policies to transform the environmental, demographic, economic, political, socio-cultural, and organizational factors that are stimulating the practice that is condemning them to abuse and exploitation.

Bibliography

Allen, K. 2005. *Explorations in Classical Sociological Theory*. Thousand Oaks, CA: Pine Forge Press.

Andrews, E. 2008. Greenspan Concedes Error on Regulation. *New York Times*, October 23.

Baran, P.1957. *The Political Economy of Growth*. Monthly Review Press: New York.

Bales, K., Trodd, Z., and Williamson, A.K. 2009. *Modern Slavery: The Secret World of 27 Million People*. Great Britain: Oneworld Publications.

Becker, H.S.1963. *Outsiders: Studies in the Sociology of Deviance*. New York: The Free Press.

Boserup, E. 1970. *Women's Role in Economic Development*. England: Earthscan; reprinted 2007, England: Cromwell Press.

Calavita, K. 1989. The Contradictions of Immigration Lawmaking: The Immigration Reform and Control Act of 1986. *Law & Policy*, 11(1),17–47.

Calavita, K. 1996. The New Politics of Immigration: 'Balanced-Budget Conservatism' and the Symbolism of Proposition 18. *Social Problems*, 43(3), 284–305.

Cardoso, F.H. and Faletto, E. 1979. *Dependency and Development in Latin América*. Berkley and Los Angeles, California: University of California Press.

Chirot, D. 1977. *Social Change in the Twentieth Century*. New York: Harcourt Brace Jovanovich.

Davis, K. 1937. The Sociology of Prostitution. *American Sociological Review*, 2(5), 744–755.

Davis, K. and Moore W.E. 1945. Some Principles of Stratification. *American Sociological Review*, 10(2), 242–249.

Derber, C.2011. *The Wilding of America: Money, Mayhem, and the New American Dream*. Fifth Edition. New York: Worth Publishers.

Eitzen, S. and Simon, D. 1982. *Elite Deviance*. Boston: Allyn and Bacon.

Foucault, M. 1976. *The History of Sexuality, Volume 1: The Will to Knowledge*. Paris: Editions Gallimard; reprinted 1998, London: Penguin.

Frank, A.G. 1972. The Development of Underdevelopment, in Dependence and Underdevelopment: Latin America's Political Economy, edited by J.D. Cockcroft, A.G. Franke, and D.L. Hohnson. Garden City, NY: Anchor Books, 3–18.

Galeano, E.1973. *Open Veins of Latin America: Five Centuries of the Pillage of a Continent*. English edition.

Goode, E. 1972. *Drugs in American Society*. New York: Knopf.

Grayson,G. 2010. Mexico: *Narco-violence and a Failed State*. New Brunswick, N.J.: Transaction Publishers. 267.

International Labor Organization (ILO). 2011. Global Employment Trends 2011: The challenge of jobs recovery. International Labour Office [Online]. Available at: http://www.ilo.org/wcmsp5/groups/public/@dgreports/@dcomm/@publ/documents/publication/wcms_150440.pdf [accessed: November 28, 2011].

Martindale, D. 1960. *The Nature and Types of Sociological Theory*. Boston: Houghton Mifflin Company.

McEvedy, C. and Jones, R. 1978. *Atlas of World Population History*. Auckland: Penguin Books.

McMichael, P. 2008. *Development and Social Change: A Global Perspective*, Fourth Edition, Thousand Oaks, CA: Pine Forge Press.

Naím, M. 2005. *Illicit: How Smugglers, Traffickers and Copycats are Hijacking the Global Economy*. New York: Anchor Books.

Said, E. 1978. *Orientalism*. Vintage Books.

Simon, D. and Eitzen, D.S. 1986. *Elite Deviance*. Allyn and Bacon.

Siskin, A. and Wyler, L.A. 2010. Trafficking in Persons: U.S. Policy and Issues for Congress [Online, Congressional Research Service]. Available at: http://www.fas.org/sgp/crs/misc/RL34317.pdf [accessed: November 28, 2011].

Standing, G. 1999. Global Feminization through Flexible Labor: A Theme Revisited. *World Development*, 27(3), 583–602.

Standing, G. 1989. Global Feminization through Flexible Labor. *World Development*, 17(7), 1077–1095.

Rand, A. 1957. *Atlas Shrugged*. New York: Random House.

Rand, A. 1964. *The Virtue of Selfishness*. New York: New American Library.

Tiano, S. 1994. *Patriarchy on the Line: Labor, Gender, and Ideology in the Mexican Maquila Industry*. Philadelphia: Temple University Press.

Tiano, S.1987. Maquiladoras in Mexicali: Integration or Exploitation?, in *Women on the U.S.–Mexico Border: Responses to Change*, edited by V. Ruiz and S. Tiano. Boston: Allen and Unwin; reprinted 1991, Boulder: Westview Press, 77–101.

Tiano, S. 2006. The Changing Gender Composition of the Maquila Work Force Along the U.S.–Mexico Border, in *Women and Change at the U.S. Mexico Border: Mobility, Labor, and Activism,* edited by D. Mattingly and E. Hansen. Tucson: University of Arizona Press, 73–90.

Tzannatos, Z. 1998. Women and labor market changes in the global economy: growth helps, inequalities hurt and public policy matters [Online, April]. Available at: http://www.siteresources.worldbank.org/INTGENDER/Resources/tradezafiris.pdf [accessed: November 28, 2011].

UN.GIFT (Global Initiative to Fight Human Trafficking). Human Trafficking the Facts [Online]. Available at: http://www.unglobalcompact.org/docs/issues_doc/labour/Forced_labour/HUMAN_TRAFFICKING_-_THE_FACTS_-_final.pdf [accessed: November 28, 2011).

United Nations. 2000. Protocol to Prevent, Suppress and Punish Trafficking in Persons, especially Women and Children [Online]. Available at: http://www. unhcr.org/refworld/docid/472070660.html [accessed: November 28, 2011].

Wirth, L.1938. Urbanism as a Way of Life. *American Journal of Sociology*, 44(1), 1–24; reprinted in *Louis Wirth on Cities and Social Life: Selected Papers*, edited by A. Reiss Jr. Chicago: University of Chicago Press.

Wallerstein, I. 1974. *The Modern World-System*, vol.1*: Capitalist Agriculture and the Origins of the European World-Economy in the Sixteenth Century*. New York/London: Academic Press.

Chapter 3

Migration: The Forgotten Link in the Nexus between Freedom from Want and Freedom from Fear[1]

Sandro Calvani and Olivia Jung
(in collaboration with Vittoria Luda di Cortemiglia)

In 2005, as he assessed global progress toward the United Nations Millennium Development goals formulated five years previously, then-UN Secretary Kofi Annan emphasized three key freedoms: freedom from want (economic welfare); freedom from fear (collective security); and freedom to live in dignity (human rights). Annan emphasized the inextricable connection between these three kinds of freedoms when he explained, "Not only are development, security and human rights all imperative; they also reinforce each other. This relationship has only been strengthened in our era of rapid technological advances, increasing economic interdependence, globalization and dramatic geopolitical change. [...] We will not enjoy development without security, we will not enjoy security without development, and we will not enjoy either without respect for human rights." (Annan 2005: paragraph 16)

Migration is intimately connected to all three kinds of freedoms. People often move for economic reasons, hoping to improve their financial circumstances by availing themselves of the improved economic opportunities in their destination context. But they also may be forced to move to escape what Annan considered to be the major threats to security in the 21st century: "not just international war and conflict, but terrorism, weapons of mass destruction, organized crime and civil violence." (United Nations 2005: Executive Summary) And many also migrate to escape authoritarian regimes, oppression, torture, or other circumstances that erode the rule of law and violate their human rights. Migration is not merely a way

---

1   This chapter is based on a talk given by Sandro Calvani, UNICRI Director, at the University of New Mexico on April 2, 2009, during the international conference "*Modern-day Slavery in the Americas: A Regional Approach to a Global Epidemic*" sponsored by the University of New Mexico's Latin American and Iberian Institute, UNICRI, and the Mexican Consulate of Albuquerque, New Mexico. UNICRI, the United Nations Interregional Crime and Justice Research Institute, has led the United Nations' efforts to combat human trafficking.

to further human freedom; it is a fundamental engine for promoting the positive trends of globalization and encouraging dialog among civilizations.

In our time, branded by globalization and featuring extensive international flows of goods, services, information, and people, population movements have intensified. Much of this international migration takes place in licit ways that follow national laws and regulations, but much of it occurs through illegal channels and in situations that fuel criminal associations. Unfortunately, public perception and political discourse have been so focused on the two types of illicit migration, migrant smuggling and human trafficking, that many people resent and fear all migratory flows and the individuals who engage in them. As a result, they often institutionalize their fears in misguided policies that reduce the benefits of licit migration while heightening the pitfalls of illicit flows, particularly those of forced migration and human trafficking. A more nuanced view of the complexities of migration is essential to reverse this trend. As Demetrius G. Papademetriou, co-founder of the Migration Policy Institute of Washington D.C. puts it, "There are few more urgent 21st-century challenges for policy-makers than to communicate the benefits of immigration while containing its more negative consequences. Success requires three foundations: law and regulations grounded in a realistic policy vision; an acute sensitivity to domestic requirements; and clarity about international obligations and objectives." (Papademetriou 2003)

World Population Trends From 1750–2000

Over the past several centuries the rapid growth of the world's population has stimulated the constant movement of people around the globe. Less than 300 years ago fewer than a billion people inhabited the planet. As the industrial, medical and technological revolutions made their appearance on the global stage, their combined effects led to an unprecedented rate of population growth. From a relatively gradual increase in the 18th and 19th centuries, population growth has surged exponentially to augment the size of the global population from just over a billion and a half people at the beginning of the 20th century to over 6 billion at the end (http://www.geohive.com/earth/default.aspx). Today, five new babies are born every two seconds; every minute there are 150 more people, and, at the end of the day, there are 215,875 more people in the world. Such population growth and the socioeconomic changes that have propelled it have accelerated global migration flows as growing numbers of the world's people have sought to expand their opportunities and to escape from want and fear.

Human Migration

Migration is an essential aspect of human existence which has shaped the course of human history. Population growth has occurred hand in hand with population redistribution, as groups have outgrown their territories and ventured into new lands in search of sustenance and survival. Starting in Africa, the cradle of human existence, successive waves of humans have fanned out to progressively inhabit the world's continents.

In modern times, globalization has accelerated the pace of migratory flows. Between 1990 and 2005, the world gained 36 million international migrants. By 2005 the number of international migrants in the world had reached almost 191 million, which represented about 3 percent of the global workforce. Developed countries absorbed most of the increase in the number of international migrants between 1990 and 2005 (33 out of 36 million). As a result, international migrants have been increasingly concentrated in the developed world (Appave and Cholewiński 2008).

According to the *World Migration Report of 2008* issued by the International Organization for Migration (Appave and Cholewiński 2008), only about half of the world's migrant population has moved to countries in the Global North: about a third to Europe and another one-quarter to North America. Restrictive immigration policies in these popular destination regions have meant that most of the rest of the world's migrants are moving from one developing country to another. Most of the labor migration flows consist of low-skilled workers, though the number of high-skilled workers is increasing over time. The latter are more apt than their lower-skilled counterparts to move to or within the developed world.

The Americas region is predominantly characterized by South-North migratory patterns, which account for 87 percent of total migration in the region (IOM 2008). Of the 51.1 million migrants in the Americas, over half of them (55 percent) had come from another country in the American region, and the remaining 45 percent were from a country outside the hemisphere. The vast majority of these migrants (44.5 million) were in North America, with 38.3 million in the United States and 6.2 million in Canada. The other 6.6 million migrants lived in Latin America—particularly Argentina, Venezuela, Brazil, Costa Rica, and Chile—and the Caribbean, especially Puerto Rico. Their major countries of origin were Mexico, Colombia, Cuba, Brazil, El Salvador, Dominican Republic and Haiti (Ratha and Silwal 2010, Appave and Cholewiński 2008).

The desire for freedom from want and fear are driving forces behind these flows, given that these intra-regional migration patterns have been influenced by economic crises and disparities, social conflict, violence, economic and political change, and environmental disasters.

Brain Drain vs. Brain Gain in Development

Those who are willing to leave their homes and communities to search for a better way of life are often the "best and the brightest"—on average younger, more entrepreneurial, better educated and more highly skilled than those who remain in their home communities. Their migration represents a loss of human capital for the sending community (a "brain drain"), and a net inflow of human capital for the community that receives them (a "brain gain"). Yet if the volume of migrant flows is too heavy for the receiving community to integrate the newcomers into the work force, their skills and talents may go to waste. The resulting imbalance between "brain drain" and "brain gain" can hamper sustainable development. It can also lead to misplaced fears about the effects of migration. Public opinion in developed countries may come to see migration as the cause of deteriorating job opportunities and labor conditions, while public anxieties in developing nations may focus exclusively on the "brain drain" and the loss of the nation's human capital. Both views neglect migration's substantial benefits. On balance, we maintain, the gains of migration significantly outweigh its disadvantages.

Two trends are characterizing developed countries. The increasing age of their population and the shrinking size of their workforce are contributing to a growing demand for labor. Also, as developed countries invest more resources in higher education and training to capacitate their labor forces, national workers tend to prefer higher-skill employment opportunities. The resulting demand for low-skill labor is often filled by migrant workers.

An examination of inflows of higher-skilled migrants suggests that these migrants are not exactly "stealing" national jobs. Instead they are filling a specialized niche that often opens new opportunities locally and promotes trade and investment within the global market by utilizing the foreign workers' knowledge of different languages and transnational networks. Moreover, many highly-skilled immigrants open new businesses: rather than taking existing jobs away from national workers, they are actually creating new jobs and generating wealth.

These trends can be observed in the Information Technology (IT) sector in California's Silicon Valley, where Chinese and Korean engineers often rely on ethnic strategies to enhance entrepreneurial opportunities. Using social and professional networks to mobilize information, know-how, skills and capital, they are able to start new technology firms, many of which conduct business with their countries of origin. In this way they are "strengthening the economic infrastructure in the U.S. while providing new opportunities to peripheral regions of the world economy." (Saxenian 2002)

A growing number of "brains" eventually return home. This is partly due to the dynamism of emerging economies in Asia and elsewhere that are drawing back skilled workers, turning the "brain drain" into "brain circulation." (Saxenian, 2002) Even lower-skill migrants can significantly contribute to both countries of origin and those of destination. They do so through transnational ties with their home countries that promote economic development by increasing demand for goods and services in both origin and destination countries. Called by some the "5 T's," they include (Orozco et al. 2005):

- **Tourism** (migrants returning home to visit relatives can become the focus of an emerging tourist sector)
- **Transportation** (migrants' visits to relatives back home or family members

abroad contribute to the transportation sector)
- **Telecommunications** (migrants' increasing volume of phone calls to home countries offer opportunities for expanding the communication infrastructure)
- **Trade** (migrants' growing demand for products from their home countries promotes opportunities for commerce in local and regional export products)
- **Transfer of Remittances** (migrants sending earnings to the home country can be a key source of income and foreign exchange).

Remittances as an Engine of Development

Migrants' remittances make a significant contribution to economic development. According to the World Bank, migrant remittances sent through official channels amounted to US $305 billion in 2008, of which $145 billion went to developing countries. Between 2002 and 2008, the amount of remittances sent to developing countries almost tripled (Ratha et al. 2010). These figures vastly underestimate the real value of migrant remittances because they are limited to official transfers; the amounts sent through informal channels likely equal or exceed those sent through formal ones. Migrant remittances are a major source of foreign exchange earnings as well as an important addition to the gross domestic product.

East Asia and the Pacific received the largest volume of remittances of all the world's regions in 2008, with Europe and Central Asia ranking second, and Latin America and the Caribbean ranking third. Comparing across countries, India and China received the largest amount of remittances from migrants working elsewhere, with Mexico running a close third (Ratha et al. 2010). In many developing countries inflows of remittances are a more important source of funds and their volume is often larger than either foreign direct investment or official development assistance. Latin American nations, on average, receive eight times more money from remittances than from official assistance (Ratha et al. 2010). Receivers of remittances are predominantly women, who typically spend the funds to meet basic needs of their households. Some recipients find ways to save or invest the funds, particularly with the assistance of micro-credit programmes. Both kinds of expenditures foster human development in receiving countries.

Migrations are a Global Public Good

The developmental effects of migration are not limited to remittances. Migration is conducive to the formation of human capital, becoming "a harbinger of net capital gain, rather than a culprit of human capital drain." (Stark 2003) The bottom line seems to be that migration benefits both the countries of destination and those of origin. By creating jobs, enhancing trade and investment flows, generating wealth and promoting human development, migration can improve economic welfare on a global scale.

Increasingly, governments of receiving countries have been recognizing these aggregate benefits of migration. In particular they have encouraged flows of skilled labor and have created temporary worker programmes to address their labor shortages. To facilitate labor movements they have concluded numerous bilateral agreements (UNDESA 2006) as well as several regional ones (such as the Caribbean Community agreement, CARICOM) and tentatively, global ones (i.e. the General Agreement on Trade and Services).

Illicit Migrations Come in Two Bad Varieties: Smuggling and Trafficking in Persons

Despite its many positive impacts, migration also has its downside. Much of the global movement of people occurs not through official channels but through the illicit forms of smuggling and trafficking. Smuggling in human beings refers to "the procurement in order to obtain (directly or indirectly) a financial or other material benefit, from the illegal entry of a person into a state of which the person is not a national or a permanent resident." (United Nations 2000a)

Trafficking in persons refers to "the recruitment, transportation, transfer, harbouring or receipt of persons, by means of threat or use of force or other forms of coercion, of abduction, of fraud, of deception, of the abuse of power or of a position of vulnerability or of the giving or receiving of payments or benefits to achieve consent of a person having control over another person for the purpose of exploitation." (United Nations 2000b) Human trafficking is probably the worst abuse of human dignity on Earth: it is about selling hopes at very high prices and then stealing dreams on the cheap.

As highlighted in the newly released UNODC Global Report on Human Trafficking, the term "trafficking in persons" can be misleading since it emphasizes "the transaction aspects of a crime that is more accurately described as enslavement:" it is a *de facto* "exploitation of people, day after day, for years on end." (UNODC 2009)

A Failure of Global Governance

Data on forced labor well reveal one of the gravest failures of modern global governance. The International Labour Organization (ILO) has estimated that at any given time at least 2.45 million people worldwide are victims of forced labor (including sexual exploitation) as a result of human trafficking (Belser 2005). This figure includes both transnational and internal trafficking.

The destination region ranking first in this ILO study is Asia-Pacific, with an estimated 1.36 million victims of trafficking for forced labor. About 270,000 people are trafficked to industrial countries, 250,000 to Latin America and the Caribbean, and around 230,000 people to the Middle East and North Africa. The ILO researchers attribute the lower estimates for Africa (130,000) and for transition economies (200,000) to the fact that many people from these regions are trafficked towards other regions, including industrial countries.

While the smuggling of human beings is always across borders, human trafficking flows take place along three geographical dimensions: trans-regional, intra-regional and domestic. Domestic trafficking affects victims who are citizens of the country in which they are exploited. Intra-regional trafficking occurs between different countries within the same region. This includes cross-border trafficking and trafficking between countries geographically close to one another. In trans-regional trafficking, victims are trafficked from one region to another. This could be trans-continental trafficking, but it could also involve trafficking flows to neighboring regions of the same continent (e.g. from Eastern Europe to Western and Central Europe, or from Central to North America). Perhaps unexpectedly, most forms of exploitation actually take place close to home: the data show that intra-regional and domestic trafficking are the predominant forms of trafficking in persons.

The purpose of trafficking is illicit enrichment. Human trafficking occurs for several exploitative purposes: labor, sexual, begging, employment in criminal activities or armed conflict, forced marriage, illicit adoption and even removal of organs.

According to the newly released UNODC Global Report,[2] "the most common form of human trafficking (79 percent) is sexual exploitation."[3] The victims of sexual exploitation are predominantly women and girls. While it remains likely that labor exploitation and male victims are relatively under-detected, the predominance of sexually exploited women is true across regions, even in countries where other forms of trafficking are routinely detected. The second most common form of human trafficking is forced labor (18 percent), although this may be an underestimate or misrepresentation because forced labor is less frequently detected and reported than trafficking for sexual exploitation (UNODC 2009).

Traffickers are a Heterogeneous Group

Far less information is available on offenders than on their victims. Traffickers can perform various functions (serving, for example, as recruiters, transporters, exploiters or "managers") and may engage in various activities during the different stages of the process (including forging documents, pacifying victims, or

---

2   UNODC Global Report on Human Trafficking is based on data from 155 countries and territories, collected over a few months in 2007 and 2008. With a few notable exceptions, nearly all of the larger states participated.

3   In the 52 countries' reports where the form of exploitation was specified, 79 percent of the victims were subjected to sexual exploitation.

maintaining relations with corrupt officials). Human trafficking organizations span the spectrum from small networks connected through family ties or shared ethnicity, to highly organized transnational criminal networks operating internationally and overseeing the entire operation from recruitment to exploitation.

One might assume that human trafficking, which is characterized by violence and threats, would mostly be carried out by men. However, the data gathered by UNODC in 46 countries on the gender of offenders suggests that women are increasingly playing key roles in trafficking worldwide, particularly in Eastern Europe and in Central Asia. Female traffickers are actively engaged both in recruitment (particularly as the emphasis shifts from impersonal advertisements to recruitment through personal networks) and in managing the exploitation (acting as managers, receptionists and money launderers). Many traffickers are former victims themselves. For instance, a "Madam" in a destination country might supervise and organize girls and women trafficked for sexual exploitation, coordinating their activities and collecting their earnings. Many of these "Madams" are themselves former victims who, once their "debt" was paid off to their own "Madam," started using this same method to make money (Kangaspunta 2006).

Since almost every country is a country of origin, transit and/or destination, traffickers can be of any nationality. Knowledge of both the countries in which they operate and their home country may offer insight into their roles and ways of operating. For instance, recruiting victims may be easier if the recruiter shares their language and cultural background, so it's not surprising that in several countries, the majority of offenders are nationals of the country in which the trafficking case is investigated (EUROPOL 2008).

Victims are the Weakest Part of Affected Communities

Identifying global trends in the number of victims detected is not straightforward. Countries have contrasting laws and definitions of trafficking in persons, and few have the quality of data that would allow for the identification of clear trends. And official data are inexact because a substantial portion of trafficking cases goes unreported due to victims' fear of retribution by traffickers, or arrest and deportation by government officials.

Nonetheless data collected by UNODC can offer some tentative insights into the profile of the victims. In 2006, among the 111 countries reporting victim data for that year, over 21,400 victims were identified. Victims were identified through the criminal justice process and through victims' assistance organizations. The profile of the victims was strongly influenced by local laws and priorities, which often focus on child victims and victims of sexual exploitation, who are usually women. Bearing this caveat in mind, in the 61 countries where the gender and age of the victim were specified, two thirds of the identified victims were women and 13 percent were girls. Less than a quarter of identified victims were men or boys (UNODC 2006). Twenty-two percent of identified victims in the UNODC study were children, which may under-represent their actual proportions in some places such as the Mekong region where children predominate, or in West Africa where almost all trafficking victims are children. According to the IOM Counter-Trafficking database, the age group most apt to receive assistance is between 18 and 24. Many victims have at least middle-level education (IOM 2000).

Human Trafficking is a Truly Global Phenomenon

Research on human trafficking demonstrates a clear geographical division of labor among sending and receiving regions. The main destination regions for trafficked victims are Western Europe, North America, Western Asia, Turkey and Oceania. Regions of origin are typically Africa, Asia, Latin America and the Caribbean, and Central and South Eastern Europe where, after the break-up of the Soviet Union, the Commonwealth of Independent States became a source region for human trafficking. Transit areas have been identified in Central and South Eastern Europe, Asia, Africa and Western Europe.

Such patterns may indicate either intra-regional trafficking (in the case of Central and South Eastern Europe, Asia and Africa), or the use of certain countries and sub-regions mainly as transit areas intermediate to the final destination (most often Western Europe). There are also significant differences between sub-regions. And trafficking routes may depart from the more common pattern of "from poor to rich," as in the case of migratory flows from Benin to Nigeria and from Nigeria to Togo.

The Sexual Exploitation Industry is Ubiquitous in Latin America

The Latin American and Caribbean region is mainly a region of origin, but to a lesser extent it is also a destination region. Political instability and social unrest in some parts of the region have created an environment conducive to traffickers. Since Asia began taking measures to reduce sex tourism, traffickers have broadened their horizons and have started targeting Latin America, resulting in increased human trafficking activities in that region.

Two thirds of trafficking in this region is for sexual exploitation, with the remaining third involving labor exploitation. Thus, more than 50,000 women from Brazil, Colombia, Guatemala, Mexico and the Dominican Republic are trafficked abroad each year to work in the sex industry in North America, Western Europe and Eastern Asia (Japan) (Phinney 2001). At the same time, according to a UNODC study, increasing numbers of men and boys are being recorded as victims of human trafficking for forced labor in Argentina, Brazil, Colombia, Venezuela and, episodically, in Bolivia (UNODC 2009). The same study reveals a growing problem of intra-regional human trafficking in Latin America. Victims from across the region are being trafficked into Costa Rica, Mexico, El Salvador, and Guatemala. For example, about 2,000 children annually are sexually exploited in the brothels of Guatemala City, which are estimated to number over 600.

Transnational Organized Crime is a Protagonist of Human Trafficking

Transnational organized crime (TOC) is the major force behind global human trafficking. It is responsible for turning migrants' aspirations into the reality of modern slavery, crushing their hopes for freedom from fear and severely impinging on their pursuit of freedom from want.

In the last decade, organized crime has evolved rapidly, propelled by the opening of new markets, facilitated by new communication technologies and pressured by law enforcement strikes. In a number of countries a nexus has emerged between organized crime, corruption and terrorism. Since the end of the cold war, countries with economies in transition have become particularly vulnerable to the growth of organized crime. In many regions conflicts and instability have been intimately associated with the growth of powerful criminal organizations. War not only generates the kind of instability in which organized crime thrives, but it also provides opportunities for illicit enrichment by creating profitable markets for smuggled goods.

A significant trend in the last decade is the expansion of criminal organizations into a widening array of illicit activities. Many organized criminal groups have diversified their activities and new groups have emerged in several new and specialized sectors. Trafficking in persons has developed into a multibillion-dollar enterprise. Criminal groups now also engage in trafficking in firearms, cultural objects and natural resources.

Organized crime is known for its diversity, flexibility and ability to take advantage of new opportunities quickly. As one UN document (United Nations 1994) aptly states:

> Transnational criminal organizations are diverse in structure, outlook and membership, but all of them operate across national borders with great ease and provide formidable challenges to law enforcement at both the national and international levels ...Because such organizations are highly fluid and have a loose structure, they are able to respond rapidly to law enforcement challenges.

The current nature of organized crime requires a concerted global response through increased international cooperation. First and foremost, an effective collective response to organized crime depends on the consolidation and strengthening of the international treaty framework.

The United Nations Convention against Transnational Organized Crime

The primary international instrument for combating TOC is the United Nations Convention against Transnational Organized Crime and its Protocols, which entered into force on September 29, 2003, and requires member states to take action to increase their capacities through effective coordination and cooperation.

This Convention is further supplemented by two Protocols targeting specific areas and manifestations of organized crime, strongly emphasizing the protection of victims:

- The Protocol to Prevent, Suppress and Punish Trafficking in Persons, Especially Women and Children, which was entered into force on December 25, 2003, and
- The Protocol against the Smuggling of Migrants by Land, Sea and Air, which was entered into force on January 28, 2004.

These instruments are extremely important because they provide a solid foundation for fighting transnational organized crime. They offer clear definitions of the relevant concepts, and they provide a broadly comprehensive approach that includes identification and prevention of crimes, protection of victims' human rights, specification of essential research and data collection, training of criminal justice and social service professionals, and enhanced international cooperation through extradition, crime control mechanisms, and law-enforcement legal assistance.

Licit and Illicit Migrations Should Become a Key Priority for Effective Global Governance

As international migration has moved to the forefront of the international agenda, the United Nations system has addressed various dimensions of this increasingly complex phenomenon. Among the suggestions for policy makers emerging from international research and practice, the following seven recommendations by Demetrios G. Papademetriou, co-founder of the Migration Policy Institute, might be taken into consideration (Papademetriou 2003):

- Recapture control of migration from the two groups that are threatening this valuable instrument of progress: the demagogues who are riding the issue for political advantage, and the international criminal syndicates whose interests subjugate those of their helpless victims and the societies in which their "cargo" ends up.
- Be more truthful and transparent. Wilful distortions and outright lies about immigration by politicians and spin-doctors play directly into the hands of immigration opponents.
- Explain to the public what they are doing and why through a national debate

making the case for immigration policies that maximize benefits while minimizing costs. Consistently applied rules-based actions and predictable outcomes are essential to building public confidence in complex and divisive policy realms.

- Build robust migration management systems, fund them properly, review and adjust them frequently, and carefully monitor delivery (since most systems stumble during implementation). Building and maintaining capacity in migration management should become a policy priority for all immigrant destination countries.
- Understand that single-purpose policies, like single-cause explanations, are weak policy tools for such complex issues.
- Make immigration decisions part of the central policy arena across domains and responsibilities. The consequences of immigration are multifaceted and cut across many policy domains: public order, social welfare, education, training, and foreign and development policies. Migration policies are stronger when they are considered holistically and are accordingly implemented across multiple policy domains.
- Turn two of the most determined "critics" of migration—the market and organized civil society—into partners collaborating in a common effort to create win-win situations in managing migration. Working against, rather than with, the market is often an exercise in futility. Working on complex issues without the benefit of civil society, a system's main stakeholders, makes the task of governance tougher than it needs to be. Working with critics on difficult issues makes it possible to share responsibility for what succeeds rather than always being blamed for what fails.

Human Rights-based Approach to Migration and Development

In 2004 the UN Secretary-General's High Level Panel on Threats, Challenges and Change issued a report titled, *In a More Secure World: Our Shared Responsibility* (United Nations 2004). As the report clearly highlighted,

> We live in world of new and evolving threats, threats that could not have been anticipated when the UN was founded in 1945. New threats have risen, like environmental degradation, State collapse, terrorism and transnational organized crime, all of which can undermine States as the basic unit of the international system. Collective security today depends on accepting that the threats, which each region of the world perceives as most urgent, are in fact equally so for all.

The threats we face are deeply interconnected. We must therefore establish a new security consensus, the first article of which must be that all human beings are entitled to freedom from fear (Annan 2005). The new consensus should also be based on interdependence among democracy, security, development and human welfare. Emphasis should be put on prevention, respect for the rule of law, and human rights. Transnational partnerships and cooperation among the international community, the UN, regional organizations, and member states is paramount in addressing the issue of migration.

The UN-NGO Committee on Migration has emphasized the need for a human rights-based approach to migration, highlighting a few suggestions and good practices (UN-NGO Committee on Migration 2008):

- International migration, development, and human rights are intrinsically interrelated and interdependent. Human rights and the root causes of migration must be dealt with as cross-cutting issues.
- Receiving states should recognize migrant workers' contributions to their economies. States should respect migrant workers' human rights (as recognized in the *Universal Declaration of Human Rights* and ILO Conventions) and grant them the opportunity to remain with regular status and to integrate into the society.
- States should ratify the *International Convention on the Protection of the Rights of All Migrant Workers and Members of Their Families*, and should comply with existing UN instruments and agreements to develop effective institutional and policy coherence regarding migration and development.
- States should reduce the root causes of worldwide migration by eliminating discriminatory trade and economic policies in the industrialized North that prevent sustainable development in the sending countries, undermine economic stability, and exacerbate outward migration.
- Migrants and the organizations speaking for them should be given the space to participate systematically in the process of developing effective institutional and policy coherence regarding migration and development.

According to UDHR Article 13, everyone has the right to leave any country. The words of former U.N. Secretary-General Kofi Annan[4] underscore the role of migration in the globalized economy as well as the opportunities and challenges caused by it:

> Migration is a courageous expression of an individual's will to overcome adversity and live a better life. Over the past decade, globalization has increased the number of people with the desire and capacity to move to other places. This new era of mobility has created opportunities for societies throughout the world, as well as new challenges, underscoring the strong linkages between international migration and development.

---

4 Presented during the High-Level Dialogue of the General Assembly on "International Migration and Development," held in New York on September 14, 2006.

The most effective path to sustainable global development and human security is to enable people to express their right to migrate. Without this basic freedom the benefits of migration will be overshadowed by the detrimental effects of human smuggling, and increasingly, human trafficking.

Bibliography

Annan, K. 2005. *In Larger Freedom: Towards Security, Development, and Human Rights for All*. Report to the Secretary General of the UN. New York: United Nations.

Appave, G. and Cholewinski, R. (editors-in-chief). 2008. World Migration Report 2008: Managing Labour Mobility in the Evolving Global Economy. Volume 4. Geneva: International Organizations for Migration.

Belser, P. 2005. Minimum Estimate of Forced Labour in the World. Geneva: International Labour Organization, 4,5. [Online]. Available at: http://www.ilo.org/wcmsp5/groups/public/---ed_norm/---declaration/documents/publication/wcms_081913.pdf [accessed: August 25, 2008].

EUROPOL. 2008. The Threat from Organised Crime [Online]. Available at: http://www.eurpol.europa.eu [accessed on: September 30, 2008].

Footnote 20: International Organization for Migration. 2000. IOM Counter-Trafficking Database. [Online]. Available at: http://www.iom.int/jahia/page748.html [accessed: August 28, 2008].

IOM 2008. World Migration Report 2008. [Online, International Organization for Migration]. Available at: http://www.publications.iom/int/bookstore/free_1.pdf [accessed: September 15, 2001].

Kangaspunta, K. 2006. Trafficking in Persons: Global Patterns. Presented to: International Symposium on International Migration and Development, Turin, June 28–30. Anti-Trafficking Unit: United Nations Office on Drugs and Crime.

Orozco, M., Lowell, B., Bump, M., and Fedewa, R. 2005. *Transnational Engagement, Remittances and their Relationship to Development in Latin America and in the Caribbea*. Institute for the study of International Migration Georgetown University.

Papademetriou, D.G. 2003. Managing Migration for Everyone: the 21st Century Challenge [Online, openDemocracy]. Available at: http://www.opendemocracy.net/people-migrationeurope/article_1601.jsp [accessed: September 30, 2008].

Phinney, A. 2001. Trafficking of Women and Children for Sexual Exploitation in the Americas Fact Sheet. Prepared for Inter-American Commission of Women and Women, Health and Development Program [Online]. Available at: http://www.paho.org/english/hdp/hdw/traffickingfactsheeteng.pdf [accessed: September 28, 2008].

Ratha, D., Mohapatra, S., and Silwal, A. 2010. Migration and Remittances Factbook. Washington D.C.: The World Bank.

Saxenian, A. 2002. Brain Circulation: How High Skill Immigration Makes Everyone Better off. *The Bookings Review*, 20(1), 28–31.

Stark,O. 2003. Rethinking the Brain Drain. *World Development*, 32(1), 15–22.

United Nations. 1994. Problems and Dangers posed by Organized Crime in the Various Regions of the World. United Nations, Economic and Social Council, and World Ministerial Conference on Organized Transnational Crime, Vienna.

United Nations. 2000a. Protocol against the Smuggling of Migrants by Land, Sea and Air Supplementing the UN Convention against Transnational Organized Crime. United Nations, Annex III, Art 3(a).

United Nations. 2000b. Protocol to Prevent, Suppress and Punish Trafficking in Persons, Especially Women and Children. United Nations, Annex II, Art 3(a).

United Nations. 2004. A more secure world: Our shared responsibility. United Nations.

United Nations, Department of Economic and Social Affairs, Population Division. 2009. International Migration Report 2006: a Global Assessment. New York: United Nations [Online]. Available at: http://www.un.org/esa/population/publications/2006_MigrationRep/exec_sum.pdf [accessed: September 20, 2008].

United Nations Office on Drugs and Crime.2009. Global Report of Human Trafficking in Persons. 54–55. [Online, UNODC]. Available at: http://www.unodc.org/documents/Global_Report_on_TIP.pdf [accessed: September 24, 2008].

UN-NGO Committee on Migration. 2008. A Call for a Human Rights-Based Approach to Migration and Development. In occasion of the High-Level Dialogue of the General Assembly on *International Migration And Development,* held in New York [Online, September 2006]. Available at: http://www.un.org/esa/population/meetings/seventhcoord2008/P18_NGO.pdf on September 14, 2006 [accessed: September 14, 2008].

Chapter 4

Trafficking in Women and Girls: Commodification for Profit

Kathryn Farr

As a young teen in Cambodia, Somaly Mam was sold into prostitution by an older male relative. Enslaved in one or another of Phnom Penh's brothels for a number of years, she was repeatedly beaten, raped and tortured by a string of traffickers and customers (Gupta 2009). Mam, who is not sure of her birth year, grew up in a small village near Cambodia's border with Vietnam, where her family, along with others, struggled to make ends meet. When Mam was still a young child, Pol Pot's Khmer Rouge took control of Cambodia and began its murderous campaign against Cambodian civilians. Mam's early experiences with entrepreneurial predators, then, occurred against a backdrop of personal and country-wide poverty and extreme state violence.

Mam escaped her enslavement and fled to France in 1993. As actor and activist Angelina Jolie (2009) wrote in her recommendation that Mam be on *Time* magazine's list of outstanding people of the year, "The fact that she [Mam] escaped makes her unique, but what makes her truly extraordinary is that she went back." In 1996, Mam returned to Cambodia and, with her then-husband, founded the NGO *Agir pour les Femmes en Situation Précaire*, or AFESIP (in English, Acting for Women in Distressing Situations). The organization, which now runs several shelters, has extended its reach into Cambodia, Vietnam, Laos, and Thailand. A parallel effort, the Somaly Mam Foundation, operates in the United States and in South-east Asia and is an active fund-raiser with rising political support. Noting that girls as young as four have been in her shelters, Mam says that among some in Cambodia, the belief that sex with a virgin will better one's health and vitality, even cure HIV/AIDS, justifies coercive sex with very young girls (Ng 2009). In this regard, Cambodia is certainly not unique; similar beliefs circulate in countries all around the world and are most likely a factor in the drop in the average age of girls trafficked into prostitution.

Today, more than 15 years after Mam's escape, millions of women and girls, mainly from developing and transitional countries, are, like Mam, enslaved in prostitution or other forced labor, victims of abduction, recruitment deception, or sale by friends or family members. Counting the number of persons trafficked into sexual or other forced labor, like the counting of any intentionally-hidden behavior, is problematic to say the least, but all counts indicate a substantial problem. Commonly-cited estimates of the number of people trafficked across national borders annually range from 700,000 to two million (a few place the number at four million); millions more are trafficked each year within their own country (see, for example, UNESCO 2009, U.S. Department of State 2007, UNIFEM 2007). According to Ann Veneman, executive director of UNICEF, over one million of those trafficked either internationally or internally are children (UNICEF 2007). Overall, reports the International Labour Organization (2009), some 12.3 million people world-wide are enslaved in sexual or other forced labor at any given time. Women and girls account for some 70–80 percent of those trafficked across international borders, and the majority of them are trafficked for commercial sexual exploitation (U.S. Department of State 2007).

Trafficking in Persons, Especially Women and Children

The parameters of trafficking as a criminal act are not fully resolved. However, the 2000 United Nations Protocol to Prevent, Suppress and Punish Trafficking in Persons, especially Women and Children (United Nations 2000: 3), often used as a criminality guideline for countries' legislative efforts, defines trafficking in persons as:

> the recruitment, transportation, transfer, harbouring or receipt of persons, by means of the threat or use of force or other forms of coercion, of abduction, of fraud, or deception, of the abuse of power or of a position of vulnerability or of the giving or receiving payments or benefits to achieve the consent of a person having control over another person, for the purpose of exploitation. Exploitation shall include, at a minimum, the exploitation of the prostitution of others or other forms of sexual exploitation, forced labour or services, slavery or practices similar to slavery, servitude or the removal of organs.

In this definition, trafficking is identified as an endeavor to take control of another person for purposes of exploitation, and the means of control range from force (or even its threat), to some form of deceit, to payment in exchange for consent. That is, human trafficking is forbidden by international protocol even in a case in which a person knows she is to be trafficked and accepts payment in exchange for her consent. It should also be noted that human trafficking, whether for sexual or other labor, is different from human smuggling. In the latter, would-be migrants pay a price for the smuggling service. Yet, because "providers" of smuggling services to poor and desperate migrants hold the transactional power, they can turn a "customer" into a trafficking commodity at any time in the smuggling process. Of related importance is the recognition of migration as separate from either smuggling or trafficking; the former is a legitimate, world-wide phenomenon, whereas the latter two are illegitimate and exploitative industries.

In cases in which women and men are trafficked into domestic, agricultural or industrial labor, it is their services that are sold for profit. However, in the trafficking of women and girls into commercial sex, it is the actual person who is the commodity. This phenomenon probably causes little cognitive dissonance, as the economic commodification of women is consistent with the cultural objectification of women's bodies as sexual objects. The sex sector of human trafficking, which relies on institutionalized gender relations as well as advances in transnational trade operations, provides an important example of how the trafficking industry profits from human commodification. In this chapter, I examine this commodification with a description of the sex trafficking process and experience; the organization of the sex trafficking industry and patterns of trade; and circumstances that facilitate the trade in women and girls, including not only socio-economic factors, but also the less-examined role of armed conflict. I begin, however, with a discussion of contested constructions of sex trafficking itself.

Choice and Consent: Constructions of Sex Trafficking

While many women are unknowingly and unwillingly trafficked into commercial sex, others voluntarily migrate, perhaps even aided by traffickers, to another city or country to work in the sex industry. It is around these issues of choice and consent that some of the fiercest feminist debates about sex trafficking have occurred. For some (Farley 2004, Raymond 2003, Barry 1995), prostitution itself constitutes violence against women and thus cannot be constructed as simply one legitimate "choice" among many. From this perspective, women in prostitution are "prostituted women," victims, rather than autonomous agents in charge of their destinies. This designation leads to a related understanding of sex trafficking as part of the "prostituting" of women and girls, regardless of whether the "victim" knows of the trafficking intent. The goal, then, is not just the elimination of trafficking, but the abolition of prostitution itself. Major targets are the traffickers and pimps who prostitute women.

For others (Doezema 2001, 2002, Kempadoo 1998), prostitution is best understood as labor—as indicated by the term "sex work." Although admittedly their alternatives may be limited, some women, it is argued, make a choice to do sex work. From this perspective, only some cases, namely those involving traffickers' fraudulent or forced recruitment and movement of people into enslaved sexual labor, qualify as (illegitimate) sex trafficking. Moreover, as Jo Doezema notes, a singular focus on the "acts of violent traffickers (as reprehensible as these are)," ignores "state oppression of sex workers," especially that by the police (Murphy and Ringheim 2002: 14). Solutions are aimed at the strengthening and enforcement of the civil, labor and legal rights of sex workers, as well the implementation of safe and legal migration practices more generally.

Whereas the abolitionists strongly support campaigns to rescue and free all/ enslaved prostitutes, the labor rights activists note that many sex workers do not want to be "rescued," and may view such efforts as interfering with their livelihood, invading their rights to privacy, and depriving them of personal agency. The often-hostile debate includes labor rights activist claims that the (Western) abolitionists' constructions of prostitutes from the global South as "wounded" victims in need of feminist liberation are not only racist, but they reflect a hegemonic agenda for, "advancing certain feminist interests, which cannot be assumed to be those of third world sex workers themselves." (Doezema 2002: 20) A further concern is that an excessive focus on sex trafficking "masks" the substantial trafficking of women and girls into industries other than commercial sex, as well as the trafficking of men and boys into forced labor (for examples of these trafficking forms, see Cameron 2008). For their part, abolitionists claim that the labor rights activists disregard not only the pervasiveness of sexual violence against women and girls, but also the worldwide hegemony of patriarchal structures of dominance that sustain such violence. Furthermore, the concern of labor rights activists that a focus on sex trafficking ignores the trafficking of men and boys into forced labor sounds a bit to some abolitionists like criticism of a women's studies course for failing to address men's issues.

There are alternatives to such polarization in understandings of sex trafficking. For example, the abolitionist and labor rights frameworks can be examined for their relevance to particular groups of women and girls at certain sites, situations and times. As suggested by Susan Tiano (1994: 47) in her examination of the fit and usefulness of oppositional theories of the effect of globalized development on women working in the Mexican maquila industry, "commonalities and divergences" in particular "perspectives" can "provide a useful theoretical basis for an empirically grounded portrait" of the phenomenon under study. Indeed, Tiano's empirical work showed that two oppositional maquila theories (integration and exploitation) were each applicable under certain circumstances. Such a grounded theoretical endeavor can also provide the basis for implementing targeted policies. Moreover, policies emanating from oppositional perspectives are not necessarily incompatible—certainly, efforts to provide legal and civil rights to women in the commercial sex industry (whether viewed as workers or victims) can co-exist with efforts to provide ways out of/escapes from the industry by those who seek exit from/are enslaved in it.

Testimonial data do indicate that whether individuals are labor-trafficked "willingly" or coercively—whether they are viewed as workers or victims—to the extent that they are ultimately labor-*enslaved*, the experience is typically horrific. The monetary success of sex traffickers depends on keeping the commodity in their possession and under their control—trading and re-using her until she is no longer of value. Toward this end, the traffickers employ ruthless tactics for keeping her powerless, isolated, and sometimes literally under lock and key. Controlling the commodity also reduces trafficking risks, such as exposure to law enforcement or immigration officials.

The Sex Trafficking Process and Experience

Recruitment and Debt Bondage

Women and girls trafficked into the sex industry are most commonly recruited by deceit or fraud; frequently the promise is that a legitimate job, for example, as a nanny, waitress, or hostess, is awaiting them in a different city or country. Recruiters may make the offer directly to the woman or, in the case of young girls, to her family, who may be given a small sum for her sale. Less commonly, women and girls are outright abducted and sold into the industry. Those who are told that the job to which they will be delivered is in the sex industry rarely know how exploitative and unsafe the living and working conditions are likely to be. Some are told in advance that they will be charged a fee to cover the costs of travel documents, transportation, and the arrangement of employment. What most do not know is that trafficking into the commercial sex industry typically occurs through a debt bondage system. That is, recruits are told, often only after arriving at their destination, that they owe a sizeable debt (commonly much higher than any fee amount they might have been quoted during recruitment), which they will have to work off as a prostitute. Traffickers told Phan, a Thai woman trafficked to Japan, for example, that her travel and job fees would come to $4,000, but once she had been delivered to her destination, she was told that she owed close to $30,000 (Human Rights Watch 2000a). Earnings are usually kept by the employer and allegedly applied to the debt, but room and board is virtually always deducted, and new fines or fees are frequently added; often the woman is not told how much remains of her debt at any given time. Moreover, she may be re-sold into a new brothel at any time, thus acquiring a new debt.

The debt bondage system provides ample income for traffickers at each stage of the process—from the initial recruiter to a transporter, to a document forger, to a broker, to a first employer, a second employer, and so on. Debts for Southeast Asian women trafficked to Japan, the United States and Canada tend to be high, typically from $20,000 to $40,000 (France 2000, Human Rights Watch 2000a). Debts for trafficking within regions, particularly from and to developing countries, are usually much less. One study, for example, found the average debt of Nepali girls trafficked to India to be about $1,800 (Friedman 1996). Yet, debt amounts don't always follow a particular regional pattern. In another investigation, Nigerian girls trafficked into Western Europe were found to have debts of varying amounts, some as high as $50,000 (Pannell 2001).

Conditions

Living and working conditions for women trafficked into the sex industry tend to be dismal. The women usually live in crowded and unclean quarters, sometimes in the very spaces in which they work. A police officer who took part in a raid on a brothel in New York City using women trafficked to the United States from the Czech Republic described the women's living quarters as "unspeakable," crawling with cockroaches and empty except for "kitchen equipment, a table and a few chairs." (Rayman 2001) In his investigation of the trafficking of women from Russia and Ukraine into the sex industry in Israel, journalist Michael Specter (1998) noted that the women were "held in apartments, bars and makeshift brothels" and often slept "in shifts, four to a bed." Reports from women who have been trafficked into enslaved prostitution also indicate grueling work shifts and heavy customer loads. Only 15 when she was trafficked from her village in Mexico into enslaved prostitution in Florida, Maria testified following her release through an FBI raid that her traffickers made the girls work six days a week, servicing 25 to 30 men each day (Gardiner and Mohan 2001). Studies in London and Brussels found similar customer loads—from 20 to 30 men daily—for women trafficked to brothels in these cities from former Soviet Republics (also referred to as the Newly Independent States, or NIS[1]) and Eastern Europe (Kennedy, Tendler, and Philipps 2002, Ukranian: film warns. 1998). One study of girls trafficked from Nepal to India found that an average daily customer load was 15, and the girls worked an average of 13 hours a day (International Labour Organization/ International Programme on the Elimination of Child Labour 2001).

Control

As indicated earlier, control of the commodity is essential to the success of the sex trafficking industry. Many of the control mechanisms work to create dependency. Traffickers begin with a clear advantage over the women and girls who are trafficked across national borders, who typically don't speak the language of their destination country, are unfamiliar with the culture, are in the country illegally, know no one there, and are engaging in work that may be against the law. Traffickers further the women's isolation by restricting their space and movement, disallowing communication with family back home, and holding their earnings as well as their passports or other identification documents. Guards are often employed to oversee the behavior of the women. The use and threat of violence serve a variety of control purposes: breaking-in violence, including rape and beatings, breaks down the women's resistance in preparation for their enslaved sex work; routine and unpredictable violence destabilizes the women psychologically and keeps them off guard and easier to control; and retributive violence, including murder, is used as punishment for infractions or as a general deterrent to prevent disobedience by other women.

---

1   Following the breakup of the Soviet Union in 1991, the former Soviet Republics— Armenia, Azerbaijan, Belarus, Georgia, Kazakhstan, Kyrgyzstan, Moldova, Russia, Turkmenistan, Tajikistan, Ukraine and Uzbekistan—were referred to as the Newly Independent States (NIS). In early December of 1991, Belarus, Russia and Ukraine formed the Commonwealth of Independent States (CIS), which the other republics soon joined. Thus, the NIS are also referred to as the CIS.

Conditions Vary

Conditions for women trafficked into the sex industry do vary—sometimes substantially. However, the situations described above are frighteningly common. Testimony attesting to brutal living and working conditions comes from women trafficked from and to all regions of the world. At the same time, some women travel willingly with the aid of traffickers to work in sex industries in other countries and report that their experiences have been at least tolerable (see, for example, research by Rodriguez, Guven-Lisaniler and Uoural 2001, on foreign sex workers in North Cyprus). The quality and length of a trafficked woman's experience in the global sex trade varies in accordance with factors such as her age and economic status, the nature of her recruitment, protections in or from the source country, immigration and prostitution policies in the destination country, and the power and ruthlessness of particular trafficking groups and employers.

The Sex Trafficking Industry

Aided by the very globalization developments that have increased opportunities and profits for many legitimate businesses—opening up of borders, de-regulation of trade, introduction of special export processing zones, greater access to cross-national transportation and money transfers, growth of the Internet and its capacity for transnational communication, including mass advertising—the human trafficking industry has become an even higher profit-lower cost industry than it was in its earlier years. The International Labour Organization (ILO) reported in its 2005 Global Report that profits from forced labor totaled some US $43.3 billion annually, and that of that sum, US $31.6 billion came from trafficking victims (Belser 2005, International Labour Organization 2005). The most sizeable annual profits—over US $15 billion—came from workers trafficked to countries in the global north. In a 2009 follow-up report, the ILO estimated that the "opportunity cost" (workers' lost earnings) of coercive and abusive labor practices amounted to more than US $20 billion.

The most commonly-cited estimates of annual profits from the trafficking of women for commercial sex range from US $7 to 12 billion. Some suggest that even this higher end number is a conservative one. What does seem to be clear is that around the world, commercial sex industries have expanded since the beginning of the 1990s (Williams 2008), facilitated by advances in transnational transportation and the increasing sophistication of criminal groups involved in sex trafficking, as well as by growth in demand.

The sex trafficking industry flourishes through flexible and ever-changing networks that adapt to meet new challenges from law enforcement. Entities within the networks vary in size, organizational form, level of professionalism, and other characteristics. What binds them is the transnational character of their connections. In organized crime expert Phil Williams' (2008) typology, trafficking groups include opportunistic amateurs (some of which can be thought of as "mom and pop" businesses), transnational criminal organizations, traditional criminal organizations, ethnically-based trafficking organizations, and criminal-controlled businesses. Also critical to the success of the industry are what I refer to elsewhere (Farr 2005) as "corrupt guardians," that is, officials in positions of public trust such as police officers, border guards, immigration or embassy agents, and political operatives. In some instances, the involvement is systemic (involving a whole or at least a part of an agency); in other cases, individuals profit on their own without the knowledge of their employer. Proactive involvement in trafficking is complemented by supportive inaction on the part of public officials, who might look the other way at a suspicious border crossing, or fail to act on a reported document forgery. Also, direct connections often exist between organized criminal trafficking groups and legitimate governmental units. Investigations in Russia in the mid-1990s, for example, uncovered "serious allegations of government complicity" in the sex trafficking business there (Caldwell, Galster, and Steinzor 1997).

Finally, the sex trafficking and sex industries rely on high demand—an ongoing supply of customers. Here too, proliferation has occurred. Sex industry customers include military and civilian men stationed or working away from home as well as local civilian men and the increasingly common groups of male sex tourists for whom entire "vacations" are organized around sex services.

Circumstances that Facilitate Human Trafficking, Especially of Women and Girls into the Sex Industry: The Case of the Soviet Union

While poor young women in many countries, especially in the global south, are chronically vulnerable to exploitation, several situations or events have actually increased the pool of at-risk women and girls. One such event was the early 1990s collapse of the Soviet Union, which ushered in a period of economic stagnation and joblessness in the Soviet republics. While wages overall declined, women's income plummeted, going in Russia, for example, from 70 percent of men's income in 1989 to just 40 percent of men's income in 1995 (Hunt 1998). Moreover, women in Russia constituted over 70 percent of the officially unemployed by the mid-1990s (Marsh 1996). Along with the severe downturn in economies in the region (e.g. Russia's GDP declined by 34 percent between 1991 and 1995), the considerable political instability led to massive infrastructure breakdown and in many places, a climate of lawlessness. As the NIS experimented with fledgling market economies, opportunities increased for already well-established organized crime groups to exploit profitable markets, one of which was the trafficking of women into high-demand sex industries in Western Europe, Middle East Gulf countries, the United States, Japan and Thailand. The influx of NIS women into foreign sex industries was notable in the 1990s and into the 2000s: for example, of the 400 women arrested in Israeli brothels in 2000, all but one were from former Soviet countries—almost half from Ukraine alone (Trafficking in Persons 2001);

in 1995, police in the Philippines arrested from 50 to 100 Russian women who had been trafficked and were in the Philippines in transit to sex industries in Japan (Ukrainian women say 1995); and, by the end of the 1990s, some 15,000 women from the NIS and Eastern Europe were working in brothels in Germany (Caldwell, Galster, and Steinzor 1997).

The fall of the Soviet Union and the ensuing plight of its republics and neighboring bloc countries highlight several conditions that lead to an increase in the trafficking supply pool: economic stagnation, along with declining incomes and joblessness (particularly among women); state instability or failure and accompanying infrastructure breakdown; and the presence of local or migratory organized crime. Many of the above conditions found in countries undergoing traumatic transition are chronic in a number of developing countries, and thus help explain the latter's role as sources of women trafficked for profit to wealthier, high-demand countries.

Regional Variations in Sex Trafficking Patterns

The former Soviet states continue to be prominent sources of women trafficked into commercial sex, and the number of both women and men from the region trafficked into other forms of forced labor has also increased in recent years (International Labour Organization 2009). Especially vulnerable to trafficking into enslaved sexual or domestic labor are women from the poorest countries in the region, such as Moldova, today a huge source country. From Moldova, women and girls are heavily trafficked through Ukraine into a number of Western European countries, as well as to Russia, Turkey and Middle Eastern Gulf countries (Calandruccio 2005, U.S. Department of State 2009).

Three categories of countries serve as major destinations. Of those, the most frequent recipients of international trafficking victims are affluent countries from the global north, notably the United States, Canada and Western European countries. Increasing recognition has also been given to a sizeable internal trafficking problem in many of these countries.[2] The second category consists of the relatively wealthy Gulf nations, principal among which are Israel, Qatar, the

---

2 In the United States, attention to the internal or domestic sex trafficking problem reflects the ongoing definitional debate. Based upon their construction of all women and girls recruited into prostitution by pimps (also broadly defined) as victims of sex trafficking, abolitionists report internal sex trafficking to be far more pervasive than would be the case if a narrower construction were used. For this abolitionist perspective on internal sex trafficking in the United States, see Snow, 2009; Raymond and Hughes, 2001. Websites of organizations whose work in the United States is compatible with the abolitionist view include www.freetheslaves.net; www.polarisproject; www.sharedhope.org. For criticisms of the abolitionist description of sex trafficking in the United States, see Gozdziak and Collett, 2005.

United Arab Emirates and Kuwait. Large numbers of women are trafficked across borders into these countries for domestic labor as well as exploitative sex. The third category is made up of wealthier East Asian destinations, such as Japan, Hong Kong and Singapore, all of which are major tourist sites.

With thriving sex industries, boosted by high soldier demand during World War II and the Korean and Vietnam Wars, other East Asian countries are today also heavily involved in the sex trade. Thailand, for example, is a major hub, with women and girls trafficked from, through and to the country. Surrounding countries, such as Myanmar, Cambodia, Laos and China, provide an ongoing pool for Thai sex markets. Sex industries in Okinawa and the Philippines also rose to meet high military demand during the earlier wars, relying in part on domestic and cross-border trafficking of women and girls. Today, with the U.S. bases there largely closed down, the Philippines is a major source of women trafficked to the Asian destination countries, as well as to countries in Africa, the Middle East and Western Europe. Okinawa's still militarized sex industry uses women trafficked from the Philippines and elsewhere (U.S. Department of State 2009).

In South Asia, India has for some time been another trafficking hub, with women routinely trafficked from, to and through the country. Nepal is an important source of women trafficked into sex markets in India, as well as through India to Pakistan and Gulf countries.

As elsewhere, though, new sources and markets for trafficked women are emerging, or at least being uncovered, in Asia. Due in part to the heavily-publicized arrests of U.S. journalists Laura Ling and Euna Lee in North Korea, greater attention has been focused on the trafficking of North Korean women into China. While still a small part of the worldwide trafficking phenomenon, one estimate is that between 80 and 90 percent of Korean women refugees in China are trafficking victims (Yuh 2009). Other sources claim that women from North Korea and Vietnam are increasingly being trafficked to China as part of a widespread bride-selling enterprise (U.S. Department of State 2009).

Reliable trafficking data are less forthcoming from Latin America and Africa, but there are several well-documented older, as well as emerging, patterns. Colombia, for example, has long been a major source of women trafficked across international borders for sexual exploitation and other forced labor; the destinations of Colombian women are far-reaching and include other Latin American countries, Western Europe, East Asia, the Middle East and the U.S. (U.S. Department of State 2009). With a flourishing sex industry and an emphasis on sex tourism, Guatemala has emerged over the last decade or so as a trafficking hub—a source of women and children trafficked to Mexico and the United States and a destination for women and children trafficked from other Central American countries, most notably, El Salvador, Honduras and Nicaragua (U.S. Department of State 2009).

Africa—particularly sub-Saharan Africa—has long had, in Aderanti Adepoju's words, a complex "variety of migration patterns, including cross-border movements; contract workers; labour migrants; and the migration of skilled professionals, refugees, and displaced persons." (2005: 76) In many countries, children have traditionally been part of these migrations, sent by families to other towns or neighboring countries to supplement income for the family through domestic or agricultural work, or to help finance a son's education. In recent years, however, the trafficking of women and children into enslaved labor, including commercial sex, has been recognized as a growing problem. As in other parts of the world, traffickers have recognized the recruitment potential in the abundant pool of (particularly sub-Saharan) African people desperate for work, in a region in which internal migration has been a legitimate part of that search. Trafficking in Africa is diverse and subject to change, but there are some current patterns. In West Africa, Ghana, Nigeria and Senegal serve as important source, transit and destination countries for women and children. Trafficked across international borders are a relatively large number of Nigerian women, sent (sometimes through Ghana) to countries in Western Europe such as Italy, Germany and the Netherlands. In East Africa, women from Uganda and Ethiopia are trafficked for sex and domestic labor into the Gulf states (UNICEF 2003). Kenya has also become a significant player in the trafficking of women and girls for sexual exploitation—as a source for Western European countries, as a transit area for Ethiopian women trafficked on to Europe and the Gulf states, and as a destination for young girls from India and other parts of South Asia to help fill the demand for Kenya's growing tourism and sex industries (Adepoju 2005, Butegwa 1997). And South Africa, with now well-established tourism and sex industries, is a major destination for women and girls trafficked from a number of countries in Africa, as well as from Thailand, China and Eastern Europe (Martens, Pieczkowski, and van Vuuren-Smyth 2003).

The trafficking of African women and children for sexual exploitation has been advanced by the plight of civilians displaced by ongoing armed conflicts. Here, as in other places, armed conflicts today are characterized by considerable violence against civilians generally and sexual violence against women and girls specifically. While militarized rape has long been a regular part of war, certain features of today's wars, I argue, also contribute to a growing and ruthless trade in women and girls, increasing the risks for all civilian women living in places with ongoing or recently-ended armed conflicts (Farr 2009a).

Militarization, Armed Conflict and Assaults on Women and Children

Militarized rape is ubiquitous, pervasive across time and cultures and firmly situated within a staunchly-patriarchal institution. If patriarchy is understood as an organizational system or set of relations with supporting norms, that a) is hierarchical, with a small, elite group of men at the top; b) dominates and discriminates against all women (some groups of women more so than others) and some lower-status men; c) devalues all that is feminine and actively engages the masculine; and d) gains or maintains control by violence or the threat of violence, then the military certainly fits the ideal type. But virtually all societies maintain unequal gender relations in some way, and patriarchal norms and beliefs remain active in cultural repertoires around the world. The lesser status of women, as well as men's sexual entitlement to them, is clearly nothing to be learned anew by soldiers *or* civilian men anywhere.

War rape, as many have argued, serves a variety of military purposes: it is part of soldiers' socialization into and acceptance of a militarized masculinity, in which violence against and control over women and all that is feminine/weak is heralded; it is a war strategy to weaken and humiliate the enemy by raping (taking) his property (women); it is a post-victory reward, as in "to the victor goes the spoils." Similar functions are assigned to soldiers' use of prostitution services away from combat. Soldiers' rest and recreation ("r and r") has regularly featured prostitution services, perceived as useful in building male camaraderie and spirit, celebrating patriarchal masculinity, and providing soldiers with a time-out reward for having done battle and then having to return to it. In World War II, the Korean War and the Vietnam War, prostitution services were either tolerated or intentionally organized by the military on or near bases and in common "r and r" destinations. The contradiction between chivalry, in this case going to war to protect women and children, and the exploitation of women for sexual purposes is resolved by a sub-theme of patriarchy—the tired distinction between "good" and "bad" women. While men may feel entitled to control both types, overt sexual exploitation is often reserved for the second category. For militarized as well as civilian exploitations, the racial, ethnic or class identities of women are commonly employed as part of the good-bad categorization scheme.

The basic realities of militarized rape and sexual exploitation remain the same across time and conflicts. However, a closer examination of today's largely intrastate wars reveals certain features that intensify and shape war-related gender violence and advance the trade in women and girls.

Features of Today's Armed Conflicts that Intensify and Shape War-related Violence against Women

At any given time, some 30 armed civil conflicts are active around the world today. While they occur primarily in developing and transitional countries, they are heavily impacted by neighboring, regional and/or international involvement in them. Counting all war-related (not just battlefield) deaths, civilians constitute the vast majority of victims in most of today's civil wars.[3] Ongoing war-related

---

3   "New wars" theorists (e.g. Kaldor 2002, Duffield 2001) have argued that violence against civilians is greater and civilian death rates higher (absolutely and in proportion to military deaths) in today's wars than in earlier ones. Others (e.g. Melander, Oberg and Hall 2009, Lacina and Gleditsch 2005), comparing "battle death" data across years, particularly for pre- and post- Cold war intrastate wars, refute these claims. According to Leitenberg (2006: 3), data on deaths in wars and conflicts "vary widely in quality and reliability" and

adversities, such as illness and a lack of medical resources, and an absence of adequate food and housing impact civilians not only during but often for years following active conflict. The important U.N. Security Council Resolution 1325 (2000) noted that women and children are particularly hard hit by the devastations of war: "Civilians, particularly women and children, account for the vast majority of those adversely affected by armed conflict, including as refugees and internally displaced persons, and increasingly are targeted by combatants and armed elements." These post-World War II, largely intrastate wars are fought not on designated battlefields but rather in and around towns and villages, even inside the homes of civilians. In fact, women civilians are targeted in their homes by both government and insurgent combatants, often because they are thought to be related to members of, or supportive of, an enemy combatant group; in other cases, their targeting is part of a deliberate war strategy aimed at terrorizing and demoralizing an enemy group by attacking its women. Home invasions also allow for opportunistic, often gang, rapes. Additionally these wars have extremely high population displacement rates, as people flee the violence in their communities. The great majority of those in flight and seeking refuge are women and their children, without either the support of male relatives (many of whom have been conscripted or detained) or their now-disbanded community. Sexual assaults on women routinely occur while they are in flight and are literally open targets.

Survivors of sexual assaults are often unsure of the affiliation of their attackers, enhancing the likelihood that the group responsible will remain unknown. These wars almost always involve multiple combatant groups, including government

---

"at times display enormous variance." Part of the variability is due to differences in the operationalization of "war deaths." Some data sets are of battle deaths only and do not count war deaths from such acts as forced starvation or the withholding of medical supplies, let alone deaths from war-related effects such as disease and homelessness. Although standard, the use of mortality as a sole measure of war violence can be criticized as well; most of today's intrastate wars are notable for pervasive, intentional and severe assaults on civilians. As for the recording of the combatant status of the victim, it can also be argued that distinctions between soldiers and civilians have become increasingly blurred in many of the civil wars of the 1990s and 2000s. Definitions of intrastate war also vary, so that lists of wars are themselves not uniform. Furthermore, time distinctions between "old wars" and "new wars" vary among researchers—a few refer to the beginning of the 20th century as the dividing point, more use the end of World War II, and even more set the division at the 1990 demise of the Soviet Union (a proxy for the end of the Cold War). Relatedly problematic is the bifurcation of time periods (set at a single year, as in pre- and post-Cold War), particularly when the argument is made that socio-economic changes that actually took place over a relatively long period of time distinguish the two periods. Finally, as Newman (2004: 174) suggests, the effort to "identify common patterns among all contemporary civil conflicts ignores differences among them." Nevertheless, even though their universal claims about past vs. current intrastate wars can be questioned, the "new wars" theorists have provided deeper analytical insight into intrastate wars *per se* (2004: 174), as well as the considerable violence against civilians committed in them.

forces, private militias, large and small insurgent groups, neighboring and sometimes international forces, local and neighboring bandits, and peace or security (including localized defense) troops. To make matters more confusing, combatants sometimes change positions; for example, a government soldier might become a member of a private militia or even a rebel group. Of all armed groups, private militias may operate with the freest reign. Consider, for example, the Janjaweed militia in Sudan, responsible for so much of the violence against African Darfurians, particularly women. Although most certainly supported by the Sudanese government, the Janjaweed have no formal connection to the government, making it easier for them to rape and pillage with impunity. Or, take the more than 180,000 private contractors in Iraq on the U.S. Defense payroll, some number of whom have taken on combatant roles and have also committed acts of violence against civilians, including rape (Miller 2007). Because these wars tend to take place in countries with already unstable or failing states or where the war has itself caused state breakdown, authorities often lack the power or resources to hold combatant groups accountable.

The instability and lawlessness that pervades armed conflict also renders the reporting of assaults of any kind problematic. There may simply be no one—or no one who is reliable—to whom civilians can report militarized assaults, and no place set up for victims to seek aid. For sexually-assaulted women and girls the reporting dilemma is much more challenging. All too often, war rape victims are shunned and rejected by their families and communities. Although local women's and humanitarian groups in war-torn countries have had some successes in bringing about reconciliations, most of the literally millions of victims still find themselves on their own.

Rape Prevalence in Today's Wars: Some Examples[4]

From studies counting only the reported cases (thought to represent merely the "tip of the iceberg" by many researchers and on-the-ground aid workers) to extrapolations based on reported cases, the numbers are astounding. Some of the most extensive rapings have occurred over very short periods of time. During the 1994 Rwandan genocide, several hundred thousand, largely Tutsi, women and girls were raped by rampaging militia and civilian men. In the 1998 anti-Kurdish campaign in northern Afghanistan, an estimated 100,000 women were raped; in 2006 alone, 2,000 cases of sexual assault were registered in Afghanistan. Over a one-year period in Kosovo, 23,000 to 45,000 women were raped, largely but not exclusively by Serbian military troops. In the 4-year Bosnian armed conflict 50,000 women were sexually assaulted. In Colombia, forensic reports gathered from 2000–2002 identified sexual assaults in over 40,000 cases of women. Over

---

4   For individual citations for each of the cases described below, as well as for additional prevalence studies, see Farr, 2009b, "Appendix."

the 2-year period following the overthrow of President Aristide in Haiti, some 35,000 women are thought to have been sexually assaulted. Other numbers are spread over longer periods of armed conflict, and under-counts are thought to be considerable: over 50 percent of women in Liberia are believed to have been raped during that country's 14-year civil war; over 11 years of war, some 200,000 women and girls were sexually assaulted in Sierra Leone. Recalling their lives in combat areas of war-torn Myanmar, 75 percent of ethnic Burmese women told Refugees International that they knew someone who had been raped.

Apart from their frequency, the brutality of sexual assault is another feature that terrorizes and terrifies women *en masse*. Due in part to patriarchal license, but also to features of today's wars described above, many of the sexual assaults in today's wars constitute what I have called elsewhere "extreme rape," that is,

> regularized, war-normative acts of sexual violence accompanied by intentional serious harm, including physical injury, physical and psychological torture, kidnap and, all too often, murder. Perpetrators intentionally harm their victims by means such as penetration with foreign objects and substances; multiple and sequential rapings (including long-term sexual enslavement) and multiple rapists (gang-raping); and amputation, stabbing and cutting (including symbolic or territorial markings on the women's body). Perpetrators commit psychological torture by a number of methods, but among the most brutal are raping (and then sometimes kidnapping or killing) family members in front of other family members, or forcing family members to rape family members. (Farr 2009b: 6)

The women and girls who survive these rapes have shown tremendous courage in their willingness to continue to seek safety for themselves and their children. But as indicated, they are often in flight on their own and thus are highly susceptible to further exploitation.

Enslavement and Trafficking Risks for War-Affected Women and Children

Some members of all types of combatant groups—government, militia and insurgent—meet their sexual demands through the abduction of civilian women and girls. Whether for use by the group or to be given to particular high-ranking commanders as euphemistic "wives," women and girls are often abducted and taken to a group's encampment, where they are repeatedly raped and sexually enslaved for months, sometimes years. In Sierra Leone, for instance, of an estimated 10,000 women and girls living with the Revolutionary United Front (RUF) rebels, almost all (some 9,500) are believed to have been kidnapped (Bah 1997). After the war, with nowhere to go, many of the women stayed with their rebel "husbands;" of those who did leave, most were not registered for a re-integration program, and many became prostitutes (Rehn and Johnson 2002).

Combatant groups have high demand for a variety of other forms of war-related labor. Abducted and enslaved women and children are forced to do much of the group's domestic work and serve also as farmers, look-outs, looters, couriers and porters (e.g. of ammunition, stolen goods), and combatants. In one situation, in the late 1990s the government of Burundi placed civilians in so-called "protection sites," or "regroupment camps," and from these places recruited children to do war-related work such as spying and looting (Human Rights Watch 2000b).

Many government and insurgent groups abduct or coercively recruit children to be soldiers. Indeed, an estimated 300,000 children are currently serving as soldiers for armed groups. The top number is in Myanmar, where 70,000 of the army's 350,000 soldiers are children (Human Rights Watch 2002). While the majority are boys, girls are also coercively conscripted, and often their military duties include forced sex. In Colombia, with over 11,000 child soldiers, girls have been sent by rebel groups to have sex with government soldiers in order to obtain war-related information from them (Watchlist on Children and Armed Conflict 2004). In a continuation of their militarized sex and labor enslavement histories, children are also sold into civilian markets. Child prostitution rings abound in war-torn Colombia, for example, where over 3 and a half million people remain internally displaced. An estimated 35,000 children, many of whom have been displaced by the conflict, work as prostitutes in Colombia (Leech 2002).

Refugee and internal displacement camps, the majority of whose residents are women and children, serve as major sites for abduction or recruitment into exploited sex. Among this vulnerable "captive" pool, resources are in short supply, and women often have no way to support themselves and their children. Within and on the periphery of the camps, women may engage in "survival sex," exchanging their bodies for food or other subsistence supplies. Women are also trafficked from the camps into domestic and international prostitution. Refugee camps along the Myanmar-Thailand border, for instance, where 100,000 or more people have fled past and current violence in Myanmar, have become a major source site for traffickers (Archavanitkul 2000). Another example is that of Kosovar women, who have been abducted from refugee camps by Albanian organized-crime groups and sold into prostitution in Italy and other Western European countries (Montgomery 1999). Refugee and emergency IDP camps are often set up along borders, hastily constructed when a spike in violence results in a mass civilian exodus. Illegal crossings are facilitated by guards, soldiers, immigration officials, or other authorities in exchange for money or other goods and services.

The recognition that there is money to be made has increasingly led combatants to sell war-enslaved women and girls to military or civilian traffickers. Armed militants in Algeria, for example, are said to regularly traffic women for sex or domestic labor (Algeria n.d.). Similarly, Sierra Leonean combatant groups sell kidnapped women into high-demand markets in Western Europe and the Middle East Gulf countries (Wolte 2004). During their 1980s war, Afghan mujahidin purportedly sold Afghan women to traffickers; and in the early 1990s, women were kidnapped at or near the Afghanistan-Pakistan border and sold there to criminal traders (Amnesty International 1995). A women's NGO in Iraq claims that about 3,500 Iraqi women have disappeared since the 2003 beginning of the U.S.-led war, and many of them are thought to have been sex-trafficked, largely to the Gulf states (Iraq-Syria-United Arab Emirates: Sex traffickers. 2006). In the aftermath of the 1990s war in Bosnia, employees of DynCorp, a Virginia-based private contractor firm hired by the U.N. to provide policing services in the country, were implicated there in a prostitution ring that bought and sold girls as young as twelve (Isenberg 2003). For women in war-affected areas, the sexual violence and exploitation that occurs during armed conflict segues seamlessly into sex and forced labor trafficking.

Concluding Comments

The trafficking of people into forced and enslaved labor in a variety of markets is a growing transnational problem that violates the most basic human rights and standards of decency. Efforts to prevent and curtail such trafficking have deepened, but so have the innovative tactics of the traffickers as they have striven to build up business and advance profits. This chapter has focused on the trafficking of women and girls into one market, commercial sex, as an example of the commodification of humans for profit. In this market, I argue, trafficking strategies play upon the culturally-normative objectification of women and girls as well as the real-life vulnerabilities that women encounter worldwide, but especially in developing and transition countries. Concerns over the sometimes sensationalized or moralistic orientation of sex trafficking rescue should not impede thorough gender analyses of coercive or deceptive trafficking for sexual exploitation. The sex sector of the larger human trafficking industry clearly exploits women as sexualized "other," independent of the choices or motives of the individual women on whose commodification the industry relies. A woman-centered approach to such exploitation should incorporate the voices and views of women with diverse experiences in and around the trafficking industry into any plan to a) aid or support women prior to, during or after an abusive trafficking experience; b) derail the exploitative trafficking industry itself; and c) provide safe and legitimate migration passages for women and men.

Bibliography

Adepoju, A. 2005. Review of research and data on human trafficking in sub-Saharan Africa. Data and research on human trafficking: A global survey. *International Migration*, 43(1/2), 75–98.

Algeria. n.d. *Nation Master - Transnational issues — trafficking in persons — current situation by country* [Online]. Available at: http://www.nationmaster.com/graph [accessed: September 28, 2008].

Amnesty International.1995. *Women in Afghanistan: A human rights catastrophe* [Online]. Available at: http://www.amnesty.org/library [accessed: May 20, 2008].

Archavanitkul, K. 2000 [updated], 1998. *Combatting the trafficking in children and their exploitation, prostitution and other intolerable forms of child labor in Mekong Basin countries.* Bangkok: Institute for Population and Social Research, Mahidol University.

Bah, K.A. 1997. *Rural women and girls in the war in Sierra Leone* [Online, Conciliation Resources]. Available at: http://www.c-r.org/resources/occasional-papers/rural-women-sierra-leone.php [accessed: May 25, 2008].

Barry, K. 1995. *The prostitution of sexuality.* New York: New York University Press.

Belser, P. 2005. Forced labour and human trafficking: Estimating the profits. Working paper 42, March. International Labour Office, Geneva.

Butegwa, F. 1997. *Trafficking in women in Africa: A regional report*: Global Alliance Against Trafficking in Women—Canada. Prevention through awareness and activities North American regional consultative forum on trafficking in women: Victoria, Canada, April 30–May 3.

Calandruccio, G. 2005. A review of recent research on human trafficking in the Middle East. *International Migration,* 43(1/2), 267–299.

Caldwell, G., Gastler, S., and Steinzor, N. 1997. *Crime & servitude: An expose of the traffic in women for prostitution from the Newly Independent States.* Washington, DC: Global Survival Network.

Cameron, S. 2008. Trafficking of women for prostitution, in *Trafficking in Humans: Social, cultural and political dimensions*, edited by S. Cameron and E. Newman. New York: United Nations University Press, 80–110.

Doezema, J. 2002. Who gets to choose? Coercion, consent, and the UN Trafficking Protocol. *Gender and Development,* 10(1), 20–27.

Doezema, J. 2001. Ouch? Western feminists' 'wounded attachment' to the 'third world prostitute'. *Feminist Review,* 67(Spring), 16–38.

Duffield, M. 2001. *Global governance and the new wars: The merging of development and security.* London: Zed.

Farley, M. 2004. 'Bad for the body, bad for the heart': Prostitution harms women even if legalized or decriminalized. *Violence Against Women,* 10, 1087–1125.

Farr, K. 2009a. Armed conflict, war rape, and the commercial trade in women and children's labour. *Pakistan Journal of Women's Studies,* 16(1–2), 1–31.

Farr, K. 2009b. Extreme war rape in today's civil-war-torn states: A contextual and comparative analysis. *Gender Issues,* 26(1), 1–41.

Farr, K. 2005. *Sex trafficking: The global market in women and children* [Contemporary social issues, series ed., George Ritzer]. New York: Worth.

France, D. 2000. Slavery's new face. *Newsweek* [Online, 17 December]. Available at: http://www.newesweek.com [accessed: June 15, 2010].

Friedman, R. I. 1996. India's shame: Sexual slavery and political corruption are leading to an AIDS catastrophe. *The Nation,* 8 April, 10.

Gardiner, S. and Mohan, G. 2001. The sex slaves from Mexico: Teen-agers tell of forced prostitution. *Newsday* [Online, 12 March]. Available at: http:///www. newsday.com/news/local/newyork/ny-smuggled-mexico.story [accessed: May 10, 2010].

Gozdziak, E.M. and Collett, E.A. 2005. Research on human trafficking in North America: A review of the literature. *International Migration*, 43(1/2), 99–128.

Gupta, A. 2009. One woman's journey to save child slaves. *Smithsonian* [Online, January 12]. Available at: http://www.Smithsonian.com [accessed: July 15, 2010].

Human Rights Watch. 2000a. Owed justice: Thai women trafficked into debt bondage in Japan September [Online]. Available at: http://www.hrw.org/ legacy/reports/2000/japan [accessed: May 20, 2010].

Human Rights Watch. 2000b. Emptying the hills: Regroupement camps in Burundi [Online, July]. Available at: http://www.hrw.org/fr/news/2000/07/18/ regroupement-camps/burundi [accessed: July 2010].

Human Rights Watch. 2002. My gun was as tall as me: Child soldiers in Burma [Online, July]. Available at: http://www.chidsdream.org/general/ ChildSoldier_02.pdf [accessed: May 18, 2010].

Hunt, S. 1998. For east bloc women, a dearth of democracy. *International Herald Tribune*, July 7.

International Labour Organization. 2005. *A global alliance against forced labour Report IB* (Global Report under the follow-up to the ILO Declaration on Fundamental Principles and Rights at Work). Paper to the: International Labour Conference ILC, 93rd session, Geneva.

International Labour Organization. 2009. *The cost of coercion. Global Report under the follow-up to the ILO Declaration on Fundamental Principles and Rights at Work Report IB*. Paper to the: International Labour Conference ILC, 98th session, Geneva.

International Labour Organization/International Programme on the Elimination of Child Labour. 2001. *Nepal: trafficking in girls with special reference to prostitution: A rapid assessment*. Geneva.

Iraq-Syria-United Arab Emirates: Sex traffickers target women in war-torn Iraq. 2006. *IRIN* [Online, October 26]. Available at: http://www.alertnet.org/ thenews/newsdesk/IRIN [accessed: July 25, 2010].

Isenberg, D. 2003. Security for sale in Afghanistan. *Asia Times* [Online]. Available at: http://www.atimes.com [accessed: June 10, 2010].

Jolie, A. 2009. Somaly Mam. *Time* [Online 30 April]. Available at: http://www. time.com [accessed: July 23, 2010].

Kaldor, M. 2002. *New and old wars: Organized violence in a global era*, 2nd ed. Cambridge: Polity Press.

Kempadoo, K. 1998. Introduction: Globalizing sex workers' rights, in *Global sex workers: Rights, resistance and redefinition*, edited by K. Kempadoo and J. Doezema. New York: Routledge, 1–33.

Kennedy, D., Tendler, S. and Philipps, J. 2002. Times: Albanian gangs corner Britain's sex trade. *Reality Macedoni* [Online, July 6]. Available at: http://www.realitymacedonia.org/mk [accessed: July 15, 2010].

Lacina, B. and Gleditsch, P.E. 2005. Monitoring trends in global combat: A new dataset of battle deaths. *European Journal of Population,* 21(2–3), 145–166.

Leech, G. 2002. Combating child prostitution in Colombia. *Colombia Report* [Online]. Available at: http://www.colombiajournal.org/combating-child-prostituion-in-colombia.htm. [accessed: July 15, 2010].

Leitenberg, M. 2006. *Deaths in wars and conflicts in the 20th century,* 3rd ed. Cornell University Peace Studies Program, Occasional paper # 29.

Marsh, R. 1996. Introduction: Women's studies and women's issues in Russia, Ukraine and the post-Soviet states, in *Women and Ukraine,* edited by R. Marsh. Cambridge: Cambridge University Press, 1–28.

Martens, J., Pieczkowski, M. and van Vuuren-Smyth, B. 2003. Seduction, sale and slavery: Trafficking in women and children for sexual exploitation in southern Africa. International Organization for Migration [Online, May]. Available at: http://www.sarpn.org/documents/d0001633/P1960-IOM [accessed: July 14, 2010].

Melander, E., Oberg, M. & and Hall, J. 2009. Are 'new wars' more atrocious? Battle severity, civilians killed and forced migration before and after the end of the cold war. *European Journal of International Relations,* 15, 505–536.

Miller, T.C. 2007. Iraq: Private contractors outnumber U.S. troops in Iraq. *The Los Angeles Times,* July 4, A-1.

Montgomery, L. 1999. Albanians sell Kosovo women into prostitution. *Miami Herald* [Online, May 30]. Available at: http://www.miamiherald.com [accessed: July 15, 2010].

Murphy, E. and Ringheim, K. 2002. An interview with Jo Doezema, of the Network of Sex Work Projects: Does attention to trafficking adversely affect sex workers' rights? *Reproductive health and rights — Reaching the hardly reached,* edited by Murphy, E. Washington D.C., 13–15.

Newman, E. 2004. The 'New wars' debate: A historical perspective is needed. *Security Dialogue,* 35, 173–189.

Ng, C. 2009. *Sex slaves! Crusader battles pimps, credit crisis* [Online]. Available at: http://www.Reuters.com [accessed: May 26, 2010].

Pannell, I. 2001. Trafficking nightmare for Nigerian children. *BBC News* [Online, January 10]. Available at: http://www.news.bbc.co.uk/2/hi/world/africa/841928.stm [accessed: May 25, 2010].

Rayman, G. 2001. Stripped of their dignity: Czech women lured to work at NYC sex clubs. *Newsday* [Online, March 16]. Available at: http://www.newsday.com/local/newyork/ny-smuggled-easteurope [accessed: August 5, 2010].

Raymond, J.G. 2003. Ten reasons for not legalizing prostitution and a legal response to the demand for prostitution. *Journal of Trauma Practice,* 2, 315–332.

Raymond, J.G. and Hughes, D.H. 2001. *Sex trafficking of women in the United States: International and domestic trends.* Research report submitted to the U.S. Department of Justice Coalition Against Trafficking in Women.

Rehn, E. and Johnson S., E. 2002. Women, war and peace: The independent experts' assessment on the impact of armed conflict on women and women's role in peace-building. New York: UNIFEM.

Rodriguez, L., Guven-Lisaniler, F. and Uoural, S. 2001. Foreign sex workers and state regulations in North Cyprus. Paper to the: European Association for Evolutionary Political Economy, Siena, Italy, November 8–11.

Snow, M. 2009. Domestic minor sex trafficking. *Charities USA Magazine* [Online, Summer 22–23]. Available at: http://www.catholiccharities.usci.org/ NetCommunity [accessed: August 5, 2010].

Specter, M. 1998. Traffickers' new cargo: Naive Slavic women. *The New York Times,* 11 January, 1, 6.

Tiano, S. 1994. *Patriarchy on the line: Labor, gender, and ideology in the Mexican Maquila Industry.* Philadelphia: Temple University Press.

Trafficking in persons for the purpose of prostitution in Israel. 2001. Hotline for migrant workers, June [cited in The Protection Project. 2002. Israel, *Human rights report on trafficking in persons, especially women and children: A country-by-country report on a contemporary form of slavery,* 2nd ed. Washington D.C.: The Paul H. Nitze School of Advanced International Studies, John Hopkins University].

Ukraine: Film warns of forcible prostitution abroad. 1998. *Russia Today,* July 1.

Ukranian woman says Russian prostitutes working in Philippines. 1995. Deutsche Presse-Agentur, July.

UNESCO Trafficking Statistics Project. 2009. [Online]. Available at: http://www. unescobkk.org [accessed: July 14, 2010].

UNICEF. 2003. Trafficking in human beings, especially women and children in Africa. Florence: UNICEF Innocenti Research Centre.

UNICEF 2007. *UNICEF calls for increased efforts to prevent trafficking of children.* UNICEF Press Release [Online, June 16]. Available at: http://www. unicef.org/media/media_40002.html?q=primtime [accessed: August 1, 2010].

UNIFEM (United Nations Development Fund for Women). 2007. Trafficking in women and girls. *Facts and figures in VAW* [Online]. Available at: http:// www.unifem.org/gender_issues/violence_against_women/facts_figures.php [accessed: August 6, 2010].

United Nations Security Council. 2000. Resolution 1325 adopted at 4213th meeting, 00-72018 (E), October 3.

United Nations. 2000. Protocol to Prevent, Suppress and Punish Trafficking in Persons, especially Women and Children [Online]. Available at: http://www. unhcr.org/refworld/docid/472070660.html [accessed: August17, 2010].

U.S. Department of State. 2007. Victims of Trafficking and Violence Protection Act: Trafficking in persons report *2007.* Washington, D.C.: Office to Monitor and Combat Trafficking in Persons.

U.S. Department of State. 2009. Victims of Trafficking and Violence Protection Act: Trafficking in persons report 2009. Washington, D.C.: Office to Monitor and Combat Trafficking in Persons.

Watchlist on Children and Armed Conflict. 2004. Colombia's war on children. New York.

Williams, P. 2008. Trafficking in women: The role of transnational organized crime, in *Trafficking in humans: Social, cultural and political dimensions*, edited by S. Cameron and E. Newman. New York: United Nations University Press, 126–157.

Wolte, S. 2004. Armed conflict and trafficking in women: Desk study. Sector Project against Trafficking in Women. Eschborn: Deutsche Gesellschaft fur Technische Zusammenarbeit (GTZ) GmbH.

Yuh, J. 2009. What were Laura Ling and Euna Lee looking for in North Korea? [Online, Women's Media Center]. Available at: http://www.womensmediacenter.com/ [accessed: August 10, 2010].

PART II
Human Trafficking in Mexico

Chapter 5

Trata de Personas: Mexico's Efforts[1]

Gustavo de Unánue Aguirre

Human Trafficking

The United Nations defines human trafficking as the capture, transport, harboring, reception, or delivery of people by means of violence or the threat of violence. This may involve abduction, fraud, trickery, abuse of power, exploitation of a precarious situation, receiving or giving out payments or favors to persons in positions of power over other individuals, or other forms of coercion for the purpose of exploitation. Victims may be exploited through prostitution and other forms of sexual exploitation, forced labor, slavery, servitude or the extraction of body parts (Protocol 55/25 2001).

It is important distinguish between human smuggling and human trafficking. In cases of human trafficking, the contact between the traffickers and the victim is a result of deception and abuse, in contrast to human smuggling where the migrant has voluntarily established direct contact with the smuggler. The relationship between the victim–trafficker and the migrant–smuggler is another key area of distinction between the two. The trafficker–victim relationship is continual and often long-term, marked by abuse of power and frequently generating a dependency that deepens the enslavement. By contrast, the migrant–smuggler relationship is ended as soon as the migrant reaches his or her destination. Smuggling implies crossing (usually international) borders in exchange for a monetary payment, while human trafficking does not necessitate the crossing of borders. The risks to health and life involved in human smuggling are often present, but may not be apparent, whereas the risks to life and health associated with human trafficking, including protracted physical and psychological abuse, are obvious and long-term. Human trafficking is a crime against individuals that compromises human dignity.

The International Organization for Migration (IOM) estimates that annually more than two million people worldwide are captured, kidnapped, ensnared, or trapped through deception and/or force in order to be exploited. Deprived of their liberty and their rights, they are forced to labor or render services for the benefit of others. The lives of these trafficked persons are transformed through a web of illegal and lucrative businesses that generate close to US $30 million a year worldwide. Human trafficking is a mounting global issue that is increasingly

---

1   The editors are indebted to Dr. Makram Haluani for translating this chapter. "*Trata de personas*" translated into English means human trafficking.

affecting the Americas. The United States plays a distinctive role in the region as a primary destination country for trafficked victims. In a 2007 report to the U.S. Congress, the Attorney General's Office estimated that between 14,500 and 17,500 people, mostly women and children, are trafficked each year into the United States.[2] Other countries in the region play various roles in this burgeoning industry. Between 50,000 and 70,000 women from the Dominican Republic work abroad in prostitution (IOM 1996), as do another 75,000 women from Brazil (U.S. DOS 2001). In 2002, more than 2,000 Central American children of both sexes, the majority of them migrants, were found in brothels in Guatemala (Pratt 2001). Many Colombian, Dominican and Filipina teenagers are transported every year to Costa Rica to work as prostitutes in that country's well-known sex tourism sector (Calcetas-Santos 2000). Each year, 35,000 Colombian women are victims of human trafficking (Dimenstein 1992).

Mexico and Human Trafficking

Mexico is not free from the horrors of human trafficking. It can serve as a source, conduit, or destination country for victims of sex or labor trafficking (U.S. DOS 2010). The majority of the human trafficking victims in Mexico are foreigners. Those exploited sexually for commercial reasons often come from Central America, particularly Guatemala, Honduras, and El Salvador. Their exploitation in Mexico often happens during a "lay over" on their way to being trafficked to the United States or, less frequently, to Canada or Western Europe. An equally pressing problem is the exploitation of Mexican children and youth in the country's sex tourism industry, estimated to average more than 20,000 annually. This is particularly pronounced in cities such as Acapulco and Cancún as well as northern border cities such as Tijuana and Ciudad Juárez, which are frequently visited by foreign tourists from the United States, Canada and Western Europe.

According to the diagnostic "Human Trafficking Assessment Tool" implemented in Mexico by the American Bar Association (ABA) (discussed in Chapter 8 by Brenner Allen in this volume), some 47 cartels dedicated to labor and sex trafficking operate in Mexico (HTAT 2009). The areas where this illegal activity is most likely to occur are Mexico City, Baja California, Chiapas, Chihuahua, Guerrero, Oaxaca, Tlaxcala and Quintana Roo. In addition to women and children, indigenous persons and undocumented migrants are also especially vulnerable. Mexico is a "bridge-country" (*país puente*) for both human trafficking and migrant smuggling into the United States. Despite the previously-noted distinctions between trafficking and smuggling, the two are interrelated. An individual may agree to be smuggled across the international border only to end up against his or her will as part of a prostitution ring.

---

2   http://www.humantrafficking.org/countries/united_states_of_america.

Undoubtedly, smuggling and trafficking have evolved into lucrative endeavors. At any given time there are roughly a million persons attempting to cross the border and willing to pay the bands of smugglers (known as "coyotes" or "*polleros*") an average of US $1,800 per person to cross the border (Cornelius 2009). The Council of Europe estimates that in the last decade human smuggling organizations have netted some US $42.5 billion in profits (Statement 2007). An unknown but significant number of people smuggled across the border end up in the hands of human traffickers.

Certainly it is worthwhile contemplating whether the profits from smuggling and trafficking are shared with border authorities on either side of the Mexico–U.S. border. Though little data exist on profit sharing of this sort, given the importance of the human smuggling business as well as its large profit margin, it would be safe to assume that at least some officials do receive economic benefit from it.

The Mexican government is attempting to combat the problem and has made some important steps both to stop the spread of human trafficking and to provide services and support for identified victims. In 2007, the legislative branch approved a new law called the *Law for Preventing and Sanctioning Human Trafficking* (LPSHT) which, "established the mechanism to provide protection, care and assistance to victims of human trafficking and potential victims of human trafficking and to safeguard the free development of the personality, integrity and human rights of the victims or persons threatened by human trafficking." The law initiated a program to repatriate trafficking victims and requires, per Section A of Fraction 1 of Article 13, that migratory orientation as well as translation services be provided together with the provision of housing, transportation, and communication services. This specific section of LPSHT prohibits the housing of victims in migration stations or facilities of that nature. In cases where repatriation is requested by the victim, LPSHT provides the means and security to transport the victim safely back to the home country.

Mexico's *Instituto Nacional de Migración (INM)* (National Institute of Migration) also provides various kinds of migratory assistance to victims of human trafficking. Forms of assistance include repatriation of adults and children, regulation of the migratory situation of adults and children, and refugee services. For victims who wish to be repatriated there are specific procedures to expedite departure from the country, and for those who wish to stay in Mexico there are measures to facilitate the approval of their legal status as migrants or refugees (HTAT 2009).

Other autonomous public institutions and non-governmental organizations have been carrying out specific actions to fight trafficking and aid its victims. For example, in September 2009 the National Commission for Human Rights installed the National Observatory against Trafficking in Persons to complement the National Program against Trafficking in Persons, which was established in September 2007. As a result of the 2007 program, regional committees have formed in diverse areas of the country to fight trafficking through a network of inter-institutional and inter-disciplinary teams. Various organizations, such as End Child Prostitution, Child Pornography and Trafficking of Children for

Sexual Purposes (ECPAT) and *Centro de Estudios e Investigación en Desarrollo y Asistencia Social* (CEIDAS) (The Center for Study and Research on Development and Social Assistance) are also united in combating this crime.

In addition to domestic actions designed to combat human trafficking and protect the rights of victims and potential victims, in the international arena Mexico has joined other countries in fighting human trafficking through international agreements, protocols and conventions. The international instruments to which Mexico is a party include:

- Fight against the Crime of Human Trafficking, Especially Women, Adolescents, and Children (October 31, 2002).
- Protocol to Prevent, Suppress and Sanction Human Trafficking, Especially Women and Children (December 4, 2000).
- United Nations Convention against Transnational Organized Crime (November 15, 2000).
- Convention on the Rights of the Child. Approved by the U.N. General Assembly, 1989.
- Convention on Elimination of All Forms of Discrimination against Women (CEDAW). Adopted by the U.N. General Assembly, 1979.
- Convention on Consent for Marriage, Minimum Age for Marriage, and Marriage Registry. Approved by the U.N. General Assembly, 1962.
- Convention on Nationality of Married Women. Adopted by the U.N. General Assembly, 1957.
- Convention on Political Rights for Women. Approved by the U.N. General Assembly, 1952.
- Convention 110 of the International Labour Organization (ILO) on Equal Remuneration, ILO, 1951.
- Convention 89 of the International Labour Organization (ILO) on Night Work (Women), ILO, 1948.
- Convention Related to Forced or Obligatory Labor. International Labour Organization, ILO, 1930.

In working to combat this crime at the international, state and regional levels, Mexico and the other signatories to these conventions are maximizing our chances of success because criminal networks operate on all of these levels. Success is most likely when governments cooperate across levels in the fight against human trafficking.

The following case provides an example of international cooperation between Mexican and U.S. authorities which resulted in the dismantling of a trafficking organization.

The Flores-Carreto Case

The Victims

Documented cases involve nine women between 14 and 19 years of age. Poor, with little or no education, and suffering from low self-esteem, they hailed from various peripheral regions of Mexico. They had come to urban zones, Tenancingo, Tlaxcala and Mexico City, to look for a better way of life. They were typical of other women victimized by the Carreto network, which operated between 1991 and 2004.

Modus Operandi

In some of these documented cases, Gerardo Carreto, Josué Flores Carreto, Daniel Pérez Alonso, and Eliú Carreto Fernández used seduction and deceit, partial or total, to recruit their victims and force them into prostitution. In other cases, kidnapping, rape and physical violence were used to keep the victims under control. Many times the traffickers had established intimate relations with their victims prior to trafficking them. Some even married their victims in order to obtain information about their families and to establish close relationships with the victims and their families. The emotional and sentimental bonds to the victims facilitated the perpetrators' ability to manipulate and threaten them.

Once "hooked," the victims were taken to live in the house of Consuelo Carreto, Josué's and Gerado's mother, in Tenancingo, who along with her daughter-in-law María de los Ángeles Velásquez kept the women isolated and under strict surveillance. Carreto and Velásquez took care of the children that some of the victims had with the traffickers. It was in Consuelo's house that the women's exploitation began, when they were raped, beaten, and forced to prostitute themselves.

During the first phase of their exploitation, almost all the victims were forced to prostitute themselves in various parts of the country (Tenancingo, Federal District, Puebla, Irapuato and Tijuana). Later they were taken illegally to Queens, New York, where they were forced to serve an average of 30 men a day. Although the charge was between $25 and $35 a client, the women could keep none of the money they earned. Upon threat of severe beatings if they refused, they gave part of their earnings to the brothel owners and the rest to the Carretos, who sent the money to Consuelo and other family members in Mexico. The Carreto family amassed huge profits by exploiting their victims. Investigations revealed that each of the victims was earning between $800 and $1,600 weekly for the Carreto family in Mexico.

The Investigation

Apart from the evidence presented by the nine victims who agreed to testify in this case, U.S. authorities had a "cooperative witness" who was intimately related to the family and had on many occasions watched over the victims and accompanied the accused traffickers during their operations.

In addition, in January 2004, U.S. agents of the Immigration and Customs Enforcement (ICE) raided the two apartments that the Carretos and their victims shared in Queens, New York. There the agents found a considerable amount of evidence, including addresses and phone numbers of brothels, massage parlors, and strip clubs; a price list and profit entries for the women's work; sleeping bags, condoms, lubricants and other articles for sexual use; and letters, photos, receipts of money transfers, and other types of documents.

A day after the raid, on January 5, 2004, Josué Flores Carreto, Gerardo Carreto and Daniel Pérez Alonso were arrested. As part of the joint operation, in February 2004 in Tenancingo, Mexican authorities arrested Consuelo Carreto Valencia and María de los Ángeles Velásquez Reyes. Additionally, Edith Mosquera de Flores, owner of the brothel in Tenancingo, pleaded guilty to the charge of profiting economically from forced prostitution.

Among the accusations leveled against the Carreto family were conspiracy, trafficking for sexual exploitation, forced labor, illegal trafficking for prostitution, conspiracy to import foreigners for immoral purposes, trafficking in persons and smuggling.

This case did not proceed through the full trial process because all of the accused pleaded guilty on the first day of the court proceedings. Yet it is one of the most important trafficking in persons cases to be brought to the U.S. courts since the Protection of Trafficking Victims Act went into effect. Josué Flores Carreto and Gerardo Carreto each received a 50-year sentence, while Daniel Pérez Alonso was sentenced to 25 years. Some years after her sons were sentenced—in November 2009—Consuelo Carreto Valencia was sentenced to 121 months for her role in the organization (U.S. Department of Justice 2009).

Conclusion

As this case suggests, apprehension and prosecution of human traffickers can occur most effectively through international cooperation. The laws are in place to prosecute perpetrators, though they will require more effective administration and enforcement to end the scourge of human trafficking. Known today as "twenty-first century slavery," it is a crime that violates all human rights because it infringes on the very essence of the person: life, liberty, integrity and human dignity. The practice is unlikely to diminish as long as the demand for sexual services, particularly those of minors, continues to flourish, so it must be deterred by concerted governmental action within and across national borders. Without coordinated international cooperation and without similar legislation across countries, eliminating the crime will be very difficult.

In my personal opinion, a central factor that facilitates criminal bands involved in human smuggling and trafficking is corruption at the borders. How and why can arms enter a country in a clandestine manner? How and why can drugs enter a country in a clandestine manner? How and why can people enter a country in a clandestine manner? How and why are there international networks of human trafficking? All of this continues in the face of legal impediments to trafficking in drugs, arms, and persons. Borders are porous despite the administrative, regulatory, and legislative attempts to seal them when officials are economically motivated to turn a blind eye to the illicit, trans-border transport of goods and people. If our aim is to do away with trafficking and other related crimes against individuals, one element that should be investigated and more severely sanctioned is corruption at the international border between the United States and Mexico.

Bibliography

Calcetas-Santos, O. 2000. Report on the mission to Guatemala. Report of the Special Rapporteur on the sale of children, child prostitution and child pornography. United Nations Commission on Human Rights (E/CN.4/2000/73/Add2), as cited by A. Phinney (2001), in Trafficking of Women and Children for Sexual Exploitation in the America, *Inter-American Commission of Women; Women Health and Development Program.* Organization of American States; Pan-American Health Organization [Online]. Available at: http://www.oas.org/en/ cim/docs/Trafficking-Paper%5BEN%5D.pdf [accessed: July 28, 2010].

Cornelius, W., et al. 2009. *Mexican Migration and the U.S. Economic Crisis: A Transnational Perspective.* La Jolla, CA: Center for Comparative Immigration Studies.

Dimenstein, G. 1992. *Meninas da Noite: a Prostituição de Meninas- escrivas no Brasil.* Editora Atica, S.A. São Paulo: CECRIA, as cited by A. Phinney (2001), in Trafficking of Women and Children for Sexual Exploitation in the America. *Inter-American Commission of Women: Women Health and Development Program.* Organization of American States; Pan-American Health Organization [Online]. Available at: http://www.oas.org/en/cim/docs/ Trafficking-Paper%5BEN%5D.pdf [accessed: July 28, 2010].

Human Trafficking Assessment Tool Report for Mexico. 2009. *American Bar Association Rule of Law Initiative.* American Bar Association [Online]. Available at: http://www.apps.americanbar.org/rol/publications/mexico_2009_ htat_en.pdf [accessed: August 4, 2010].

International Organization for Migration. 1996. *Trafficking in Women from the Dominican Republic for Sexual Exploitation.* Geneva: International Organization for Migration, as cited by A. Phinney (2001), in Trafficking of Women and Children for Sexual Exploitation in the America. *Inter-American Commission of Women; Women Health and Development Program.* Organization of American States; Pan-American Health Organization [Online]. Available at: http://www.oas.org/en/cim/docs/Trafficking-Paper%5BEN%5D. pdf [accessed: July 28, 2010].

Pratt, T. 2001. Sex slavery racket a growing concern in Latin America. *The Christian Science Monitor*, as cited by A. Phinney (2001), in Trafficking of Women and Children for Sexual Exploitation in the America. *Inter-American Commission of Women; Women Health and Development Program.* Organization of American States; Pan-American Health Organization [Online, January 11, 2001]. Available at: http://www.oas.org/en/cim/docs/Trafficking-Paper%5BEN%5D.pdf [accessed: July 28, 2010].

Protocol to Prevent, Suppress and Punish Trafficking in Persons, especially Women and Children (Trafficking Protocol; Palermo Protocol). 2001. U.N. General Assembly, 55th session. (A/Res/55/25).

Richard, A.O. 1999. International Trafficking in Women to the United States: A Contemporary Manifestation of Slavery and Organized Crime. *DCI Exceptional Intelligence Analyst Program An Intelligence Monograph* [Online, Center for the Study of Intelligence]. Available at: https://www.cia.gov/library/center-for-the-study-of-intelligence/csi-publications/books-and-monographs/trafficking.pdf [accessed: August 4, 2010].

Statement on Cyprus Seminar on Convention on Action against Trafficking in Human Beings. 2007. Press Release 088. *Council of Europe Press Division.* Council of Europe [Online]. Available at: https://www.wcd.coe.int/ViewDoc.jsp?id=1092417&Site=COE [accessed: July 28, 2010].

U.S. Department of Justice. 2009. Women Sentenced to 10 Years for Running NY Sex Slavery Ring. Criminal Section Selected Case Summaries [Online]. Available at: http://www.justice.gov/crt/about/crm/selcases.php#humantrafficking [accessed: August 4, 2010].

U.S. Department of State. 2010. *Trafficking in Person Report* [Online]. Available at: http://www.state.gov/documents/organization/142979.pdf [accessed: August 4, 2010].

U.S. Department of State. 2001. Victims of Trafficking and Violence Protection Act of 2000: Trafficking in Persons Report [Online]. Available at: http://www.state.gov/g/inl/rls/tiprpt/2001/, as cited by A. Phinney (2001), in Trafficking of Women and Children for Sexual Exploitation in the America. *Inter-American Commission of Women; Women Health and Development Program.* Organization of American States; Pan-American Health Organization [Online]. Available at: http://www.oas.org/en/cim/docs/Trafficking-Paper%5BEN%5D.pdf [accessed: July 28, 2010].

Chapter 6

Corazón Azul: A Hope for the Vulnerable

Roberto Rodríquez Hernández

Thousands of men, women and children are victims of human trafficking every day. Statistics are unreliable; in fact, no one knows exactly how many cases occur each year. What we are sure about is that the problem is increasing due to factors such as poverty, inequality, inadequate education, and above all prostitution and other black market activities linked to organized crime networks that often use profits from the human trade to subsidize other illicit activities.

Human trafficking is more than just a crime; it is a life that is taken away, it is freedom pulled away in chains, it is a tear in a world sewed with order and perfection. Every day we hear about global trafficking: in drugs, animals, merchandise, and even money. The most horrifying and shocking of them all is human trafficking. This transnational problem is not new, but it is getting worse. Even though more cases are being identified each year, this is just the tip of the iceberg. One of our most important tasks of the 21st century is to improve our ability to identify human trafficking so we can accelerate our efforts to combat it.

According to the United Nations, although most trafficking victims are between 18 and 24 years of age (ILO 1999), an estimated 1.2 million children are trafficked each year (UNICEF 2003). Of these, 43 percent are forced into commercial, physical and/or sexual violence.

In Mexico, according to the Coalition against Trafficking Women and Girls in Latin America and the Caribbean, there are currently some 1,200,000 victims of human trafficking (CATWIN). To combat this scourge, the United Nations created the Blue Heart Campaign. This chapter outlines Mexico's efforts as the first country to launch the campaign in Latin America. It describes the initiatives presented by President Calderón's administration and presents the story of Flor, a girl born in Ciudad Juárez who at the age of 15 was forced into sexual exploitation and experienced physical and sexual violence.[1]

The Blue Heart Campaign

In March 2008, The United Nations Office on Drugs and Crime (UNODC), guardian of the United Nations Convention against Transnational Organized

---

1   This chapter expresses the views of the author and by no means represents the view of the Mexican Government.

Crime (UNTOC) and the related Protocols, created the international Blue Heart Campaign in Vienna, Austria. The Blue Heart project is intended to create awareness of human trafficking and its impact on society, and to combat all forms of the practice. It assists States around the world in their efforts to implement the Protocol to Prevent, Suppress and Punish Trafficking in Persons (United Nations 2000). It aims to encourage social participation and public dialogue to help eradicate this heinous crime.

As a global initiative, Blue Heart promotes coordinated efforts between the signatories to the Palermo Protocol[2] against human trafficking. A related objective is to reduce the vulnerability of potential victims by promoting public awareness. Blue Heart is a campaign shaped to inspire and move the masses, as well as to raise awareness and show solidarity with the victims.

In addition, with the help of governments, intergovernmental and non-governmental organizations, the Blue Heart Campaign supports the continuous call for contributions to the UN Voluntary Trust Fund for Victims of Human Trafficking to protect and support trafficking victims (Blue Heart Campaign). This fund was established in July 2010, by the General Assembly of the United Nations Global Plan of Action to Combat Trafficking in Persons. One of its missions is to help governments to coordinate action plans to combat this illicit activity and to adopt an approach consistent with a human rights framework.

The blue heart represents the sadness of the victims who are trafficked; it represents and reminds every person who wears it of the callousness of the traffickers. The color blue represents the United Nations' commitment to combat this crime and to encourage the public-at-large to show solidarity with victims of the human trade. One of the simplest ways in which the public can join the fight against modern-day slavery is simply to wear a blue heart, and to use the logo in social networks to encourage others to use it and to participate in awareness-raising activities around the world.

The Government of Mexico launched the Blue Heart Campaign (*Corazón Azul* in Spanish) in Mexico City on April 14, 2010, becoming the first country in the world to officially adopt the campaign. With this initiative, Mexico intends to develop various programs to prevent cases of trafficking. Since the principle aim of this campaign is to eradicate the problem worldwide, government officials must understand that this is a shared problem with no limits or borders. Human trafficking is a crime that involves everyone, so we all have a collective responsibility to put an end to it and to protect those who can't protect themselves. The movement in Mexico, in partnership with the UNODC, has the objective of mobilizing all sectors of Mexican society, private and public, collective and individual, to ensure that every human being understands the characteristics, modalities and impacts of this illicit activity. Ultimately, it aims to build a

---

2   Otherwise known as the "Protocol to Prevent, Suppress and Punish Trafficking in Persons."

collective culture that denounces the human trade and is conscious of its global consequences.

When he initiated the campaign, President Felipe Calderón Hinojosa emphatically stated, "I applaud the leadership of the Mexican citizens, the media, and the community leaders who have opened their hearts. Today Mexico joins the Blue Heart Campaign with determination, an example that must be followed by others." With this statement, Mexico's Chief Executive reaffirmed the commitment of the Mexican State to support the United Nations in its fight against all forms of human trafficking. On this same day, over a dozen emblematic buildings were lit up in blue all over Mexico City as a symbolic act to raise awareness of the campaign.

With the launch of this campaign, Mexico positioned itself as a regional leader in the prevention of human trafficking and as a platform from which to launch the campaign in Latin America. Through this initiative, Mexico has demonstrated not only its democratic character, but its commitment to assure that a constitutional order is based on respect and full recognition of human rights.

Corazón Azul developed a pact which lists ten points that serve as principles for those who wish to join the campaign. This pact has been translated into English and can be found on the website of the Blue Heart Campaign.

Pact with My Heart:

- I will categorically reject all forms of exploitation that come from human trafficking.
- I will inform myself about all forms of human trafficking and share this information with my family, my community and in my work place.
- I will not involve myself in activities that may indirectly or directly be involved with sexual or labor exploitation or other forms of human trafficking.
- I will not obtain or consume products or services from people or establishments that keep others in slavery.
- I will provide assistance to a victim or potential victim of trafficking in the case that I have contact with that person.
- I will tell the proper authorities about any activity that could be related to human trafficking.
- I will promote all activities whose objective is to sensitize, inform, make aware and educate about the grave crime of human trafficking.
- I will participate in the Blue Heart Campaign activities that are organized in my community.
- To demonstrate my solidarity with victims of trafficking, I will display the Blue Heart in the products and services that I offer, and will promote the campaign to my networks and contacts.
- I will spread the message, "Human beings are not for sale."

The Trafficking of Minors is a Growing Problem in Mexico

Worldwide, organized criminal networks such as drug cartels are increasingly recruiting minors for their illicit activities. In Mexico drug cartels and related kinds of organized crime networks have enlisted thousands of children to transport drugs and commit other crimes. According to the Attorney General's Office, between December 2006 and April 2010, 3,664 juveniles were detained in investigations, busts, and other kinds of operations. Coming from poor backgrounds with no opportunities for success and from families that were too impoverished or too disorganized to protect them, the children and youth had been enticed, manipulated, deceived, or coerced into participating in the illicit activities. Most had entered under coercive conditions that had forced their recruitment so they should not be considered criminally responsible. Rather than being punished for working in illegal activities, as often happens, youth in such circumstances should be considered human trafficking victims and treated as such.

Mexican children and youth are exploited in other ways as well. Researchers and members of non-governmental organizations believe that sexual tourism involving minors continues to grow in Mexico, especially in tourist regions such as Cancún, Acapulco and border cities like Tijuana and Ciudad Juárez. Girls are particularly likely to be trafficked into the sex tourism industry, but boys are also victimized in considerable numbers. Victims may be Mexican natives but they are equally or more apt to have been transported from other countries in Latin America or elsewhere in the world. While the vulnerability of children makes the trafficking of minors particularly pernicious, adults are equally or more likely to be victims of the human trade that is on the rise in Mexico as it is throughout the globe.

It might be argued that in Mexico as elsewhere, success in fighting human trafficking is elusive. Nevertheless, it is important to give credit to those authorities, organizations and offices that devote their hard work, day in and day out, to combat slavery and exploitation.

Mexico's Initiatives

The Government of Mexico is well aware of the problems that exist in our country and around the world. In January 2007, Mexico enacted a National Program to Prevent and Sanction Human Traffickers. Elaborated by a special commission, the program contains 58 lines of action to sensitize government and business officials and members of the general society about the nature of this crime, and to motivate and teach them how to formulate complaints. A related objective is to develop a universal data base with information for tracing missing persons.

In compliance with our own legislation, Mexico was the first country to initiate an alliance in collaboration with the United Nations. With this established, the Government was able to enhance the legal framework necessary to undergird the actions of its judicial institutions. On 2007, Mexico published the Law to Prevent and Sanction Human Trafficking, which establishes harsh punishments for those who commit this crime and mandates up to 18 years of incarceration for those convicted of the offense.

In July 2008, the Mexican Government installed the Inter-secretarial Commission to Prevent and Sanction Human Trafficking. This agency coordinates the Federal Government's initiatives to establish prevention programs, and to assist and protect the victims. In addition to this effort, the Special Prosecutor for Crimes of Violence against Women and Human Trafficking (FEVIMTRA, in Spanish) was created to investigate these crimes. Today, FEVIMTRA has developed an important database of information about gender violence and human trafficking in Mexico.

President Calderón's administration has developed many initiatives to assist victims of trafficking. Special offices have been established that specialize in handling the cases and protecting the victims by offering them physical shelter, medical assistance, psychological attention, and social case work management. Since January 2009, more than 4,000 victims have been treated in these programs to help them overcome the negative effects of the destructive circumstances into which they were forced (El Presidente Calderón 2010).

The Mexican Ministry of the interior (*Secretaría de Gobernación*), through the National Institute of Migration (*Instituto Nacional de Migración*) and the National Commission for Human Rights, has launched an initiative to combat human trafficking on a national level. The objective of this initiative is to train personnel to identify and support victims of human trafficking.

The Consulate General of Mexico in El Paso, Texas, is working with diverse authorities on both sides of the border to combat this transnational problem. With the help of the Federal Bureau of Investigation, personnel of this Consulate have acquired training to help them recognize victims of human trafficking when they are interviewed after a detention. All juveniles who are detained by Border Patrol or Customs and Border Protection are interviewed by our officers. Such training makes it easier for officials to locate and identify persons in need of help and legal assistance.

The Ministry of Foreign Affairs, through its Embassy and Consulates, is working diligently to ensure that all victims who approach these offices have legal and economic aid with the support and the commitment of the Mexican Government to protect the rights and interests of the Mexican community abroad. The Department of Citizen Services is charged with helping anyone living abroad who is in distress, especially possible victims of human trafficking.

Initiatives at the Border

Mexican and U.S. officials often encounter situations in which they must work across borders to combat trafficking and assist victims. Regardless of the victim's immigration status the availability of relief is determined by the circumstances surrounding the victimization and the specific eligibility requirements for the type of relief required (USCIS 2008). These situations are handled on a case-by-case basis according to the individual's circumstances in order to provide the proper help, in accordance with the provisions of U.S. and Mexican human trafficking laws.

On the U.S. side, the victim may be eligible to apply for a T or U non-immigrant visa, which is reserved for victims of domestic violence, human trafficking, and physical or mental abuse. This type of visa allows eligible trafficking victims to remain in the United States for up to four years.

The Mexican Consulate in El Paso offers protection to victims in cases such as these through the department of Citizen Services. The Consulate works with many organizations who are dedicated to assisting victims of human trafficking. When a case is referred to the Consulate, the following steps are taken: (Consulate General Office)

1. If the victim is in danger, shelter is offered with the help of several organizations: Center against Family Violence (CAFV), Diocesan and Migrant and Refugee Services and/or Texas Civil Rights Project.
2. If the victim is not in immediate danger, an interview is arranged with the resource center for her or his evaluation, or the person is referred to various organizations that work with the Consulate.
3. The victim is then explained the procedure and is recommended to obtain police reports, testimonies, pictures and a detailed explanation of what happened.
4. Legal as well as civil and migratory assistance is offered. The cases are supported with economic help from the Consulate and with representation of consulting lawyers, to obtain a divorce, if needed, and to retain custody of children.
5. In cases requiring medical support, victims are referred to the Thomason Hospital, La Fe Clinic, and the Saint Vincent Clinic.
6. If necessary, the victim is offered economic help for other types of medical expenses including medicines and medical needs.

In this region, the Secretary of Interior and the National Institute of Migration have developed an inter-institutional committee for attending to human trafficking victims. The objective of this committee is to encourage the collective participation of federal, state and municipal authorities as well as non-governmental organizations in workshops convened every two or three months. The overall mission is to ensure that all possible cases of human trafficking are addressed properly within the jurisdiction of the committee. From 2007 to 2010, 18 meetings took place in the state of Chihuahua. Among the committee's achievements is National Migration Week, when films about human trafficking are shown to juveniles in order to sensitize them to the nature of the crime, offer strategies for preventing it, and suggest steps for them to take when they are approached by possible traffickers or they encounter someone who has been victimized.

The Story of Flor

Almost every victim of human trafficking has a previous history of abuse in the family. Flor[3], born in Ciudad Juárez, Chihuahua, came from a middle-class family; her step-father was an alcoholic who constantly abused Flor's mother. As the daughter of a victim of domestic violence, Flor's environment was constantly polluted by emotional, physical and sexual abuse. She was only eight years old when she witnessed for the first time her mother being beaten because her stepfather was "too drunk."

At the age of 15, Flor was a brilliant young straight-A student who dreamed of a successful future. One day on her way home from school, Flor met Carlos, a 17 year-old boy who had just moved into her neighborhood. Carlos came from a dysfunctional family; he was a drug addict and member of a gang, but Flor found him fascinating. They quickly became good friends and lovers, and Flor fell completely and utterly head-over-heels in love with Carlos.

Carlos enrolled in the same school to be closer to Flor. During the next two months they became practically inseparable. One day, Carlos suggested to Flor that once school finished in the summer, they should travel to the United States; since El Paso, Texas, was the closest city, it should be their destination. When school ended, Flor knew her stepfather wouldn't care if she left for a few days, but she was worried about her mother. Since she couldn't come up with a truthful answer for her mother, she lied and said that she was going on a school trip for the weekend.

Friday after their classes were over, Flor and Carlos left for El Paso. As soon as they arrived and got settled in a small motel next to the I-10 highway, Carlos said he had a big surprise for Flor and that she had to wear something special. He gave her a pretty black box tied with a red bow. When she opened it she saw it contained a revealing dress and a set of lingerie such as she had never before encountered except in those magazines her stepfather used to hide in the garage. Flor gave the box back to Carlos and said that she wasn't going to wear these things because they made her uncomfortable. Angry that she didn't like his "surprise," he eventually manipulated her into agreeing to wear the outfit. When night-time came Flor put on the dress and they went out. A few minutes later they arrived at a place with loud music coming from inside.

A big man was standing at the door, and when he saw Carlos he greeted him like an old friend that he hadn't seen in ages. Flor asked Carlos if he had come here before, and he said that he used to come once every couple of months. Downstairs everything was dark except for the spinning neon lights. Flor knew in an instant that this wasn't a good place for her to be. She was afraid and tried to turn around toward the exit. When she asked Carlos to let her leave he just nodded and kept walking by her side. "Do this for me, just this once," said Carlos. "I promise we'll go anywhere you want afterwards." Then he gave her something to drink and Flor passed out.

---

3   Names have been changed to protect the victim's identity.

When she woke up, she was horrified to find herself next to two men, naked, vulnerable, exposed and broken. Flor had been drugged, raped, and abused. She had lost the two things that she valued most in her life: her liberty and her dignity. She experienced her biggest fear—to suffer from the same kind of humiliation her mother had endured for so many years.

On Sunday morning, Carlos was shadowed at all times by a man who seemed to own him. They all got in the car and drove for various hours. Questions filled Flor's mind. Where were they going? What had she done to deserve this? How could Carlos throw away their love so fast? But instead of words only tears came out.

When they reached their destination Flor was locked in a room where she was repeatedly sexually exploited. She was threatened that if she tried to escape they would go back to Cuidad Juárez and would kill her mother. She was forced to service from three to six men every night for almost a year. Back home her mother had done everything possible to find her. She had gone to the police to file a report, and had distributed flyers with a picture of her daughter. Authorities said they were doing everything possible to find her daughter. However as the facts of the case became more obvious, they realized this was a likely case of kidnapping and possibly human trafficking. By then, Flor was already in Odessa, Texas, far from home.

Almost a year and two months later, a man who came into the establishment asked Flor what she was doing there at such a young age. Torn between fear and shame, she stayed silent. To Flor's great fortune, the man was an undercover agent investigating missing people, especially human trafficking victims. The only thing he said to Flor was, "I will come back for you." Later that night, an operation took place with local police in which they arrested seven men and three young ladies who were no older than 17. Flor was very fortunate to have been found by that agent. If it weren't for him, Flor might never have been able to return home and reunite with her mother. Flor and her mother, both certified as victims of human trafficking and domestic violence, were given the opportunity to apply for a U-Visa and now live a happy and quiet life somewhere in the United States.

This case is one among thousands of cases where the exploiter recruits the victim by gaining her trust and then lures her to another place. Cases where the victim knows the exploiter are more common than those in which the victim and perpetrator are strangers to one another. Like Flor's case, most cases are of foreign-born victims who are taken to another country where the language is different, the culture and values are unknown, and they are forced to work under harsh circumstances with the continual threat of punishment by authorities if the case is reported.

Human trafficking is the third-largest global criminal enterprise, surpassed only by weapons distribution and drug trafficking (Tully 2008). It is an industry that is growing worldwide and destroying millions of lives. To protect the victims we must all join our efforts and voices in the movement against one of the world's most heinous crimes. We must believe in the message of the Blue Heart Campaign: A hope for the vulnerable.

Bibliography

Blue Heart Campaign against Human Trafficking. [Online]. Available at: http://www.unodc.org/blueheart/en/about-us.html [accessed: July 15, 2010].

CATWIN. Coalition against trafficking in women and children in Latin American Countries [Online]. Available at: http://www.catwinternational.org/ [accessed: July 15, 2010].

Consulate General of Mexico in El Paso, Texas. Manual for victims of domestic violence.

El Presidente Calderón en la lanzamiento de la campaña Corazon Azul (Video) [Online, April 14]. Available at: http://www.presidencia.gob.mx/2010/04/el-presidente-calderon-en-el-lanzamiento-de-la-campana-corazon-azul/ [accessed: July 15, 2010].

International Organization for Migration. 1999. Counter-Trafficking Database, 78 Countries, 1999–2006, as cited in *UN.GIFT: Human Trafficking: The Facts,* [Online]. Available at: http://www.unglobalcompact.org/docs/issues_doc/labour/Forced_labour/HUMAN_TRAFFICKING_-_THE_FACTS_-_final.pdf [accessed: July 15, 2010].

UNICEF.2003. *UK Trafficking Information Sheet*, as cited in *UN.GIFT: Human Trafficking: The Facts*, [Online]. Available at: http://www.unglobalcompact.org/docs/issues_doc/labour/Forced_labour/HUMAN_TRAFFICKING_-_THE_FACTS_-_final.pdf [accessed: July 15, 2010].

United Nations Convention against Transnational Organized Crime and its Protocols. 2000. [Online]. Available at: http://www.unodc.org/unodc/en/treaties/CTOC/index.html [accessed: July 1, 2010].

USCIS Immigration Remedies for Trafficking Victims Brochure. 2008. [Online]. Available at: http://www.lsnjlaw.org/uploadedfiles/file/167B5EB6-1372-6011-1DF624BB73D38BEB/USCISImmigrationRemedies.pdf [accessed: July 8, 2010]

Tully, A.F. 2008. Experts say human trafficking a major problem in the United States. *Payvand Iran News* [Online, July 13]. Available at: http://www.payvand.com/news/08/jul/1124.html [accessed: July 8, 2010].

Chapter 7

Sex Trafficking in Mexico: The Nexus between Poverty, Violence against Women, and Gender Inequalities

Jenny Clark

In the last 20 years human trafficking has become a global problem of unforeseen proportions. Every year, approximately 800,000 people are trafficked across international borders into forced labor, debt bondage and other forms of servitude for the purpose of labor exploitation and sexual exploitation (The United States Department of State 2008). Human trafficking is the fastest growing, most lucrative source of income for organized crime and is exceeded only by the drug trade in terms of its scope (Kara 2009, Malarek 2009). According to the United Nations, human trafficking generates an estimated \$32 billion in revenue each year (ILO 2005). The commodification of human beings causes intolerable degradation and suffering, yet it is rising dramatically in the current era of globalization.

The United Nations Protocol to Prevent, Suppress and Punish Trafficking in Persons emerged as part of the UN Convention on Transnational Organized Crime adopted in Palermo in 2000. It defines human trafficking as:

> …the recruitment, transportation, transfer, harboring or receipt of persons, by means of the threat or use of force or other forms of coercion, of abduction, of fraud, of deception, of the abuse of power or of a position of vulnerability or of the giving or receiving of payments or benefits to achieve the consent of a person having control over another person, for the purpose of exploitation. (United Nations 2001)

The protocol defines the main forms of exploitation to be sexual servitude, forced labor and the removal of organs (organ trafficking). Trafficking involves deception, coercion, intimidation, threats of violence and actual violence for the purpose of labor or sexual exploitation. Traffickers frequently obtain control of their victims through debt bondage. Human smuggling, in contrast, involves consent and the illegal entry of a person into another country, often a desirable goal for individuals suffering from economic destitution. A common misconception surrounding trafficking in persons is that an individual must cross international borders to be considered a victim of human trafficking. As evidenced by the United Nations' definition, this is not always the case, and much trafficking takes place domestically within the borders of one country.

Investigating human trafficking is impeded by numerous well-known challenges. Trafficking in persons is a sophisticated form of organized crime, which often flows along complex international networks that are obscured and abetted by official corruption. Empirical data are scarce and unreliable, and official statistics likely underestimate its actual incidence. Despite the numerous challenges to examining trafficking in persons, we can form some generalities. For example, trafficking seems to be related to major trends in the global economy. Over the last 30 years we have witnessed the unprecedented spread of economic liberalization. While the global integration that began in the 1990s has encouraged the free flow of goods, services, and capital across national borders and expanded foreign trade and investment, this has come at a cost. The results have been a net transfer of raw materials, commodities, and wealth away from the developing nations towards the richer, more developed countries (Kara 2009, Omar Mahmoud and Trebesch 2009, Bales 2004). Economic globalization has transformed the international division of labor in a way that has led to a deepening of poverty and marginalization for many. Economic globalization provides an ideal climate for the exploitation of vulnerable populations internationally, which is contributing to the trade in human beings. Violence against women and severe gender inequalities also seem to contribute to the increase in human trafficking, particularly when operating in a climate of institutionalized resistance to ending such violations (see Chapter 4 by Kathryn Farr in this volume). These factors are all particularly salient in Mexico.

Trafficking in Mexico

Violence in Mexico is reaching unprecedented levels. Violence against women, a reflection of the patriarchal attitudes and practices embedded in Mexican law and culture, appears to be on the rise as well. Over 40 percent of the Mexican population live in poverty, and 18 percent exist in extreme poverty. Mexico is a country with extreme disparities in wealth—the Gini coefficient for Mexico hovers between .50 and .55 (World Bank 2009).[1] The OECD (Organization for Economic

---

1 The Gini coefficient (developed in 1912 by Corrado Gini) measures the degree of inequality in a distribution of scores along an index or scale ranging from 0 (total equality) to 1 (maximal inequality). When the Gini Index is used to measure inequality in income distribution across the world's nations, those countries with the highest (top 10 percent) of income inequality have Gini coefficient scores of .60 or higher, with the most inegalitarian nation (Namibia) scoring .70. Mexico's Gini coefficient, which ranges between .50 and .55, places it in the third to the highest category in terms of income inequality—only 20 percent of the world's countries have higher economic inequality than Mexico, and 70 percent of them have less. These pronounced economic disparities among its citizens make them vulnerable to economic exploitation.

Co-operation and Development) states that income inequality and poverty levels in Mexico remain the highest of all OECD countries—one and a half times higher than in a typical OECD country and twice as high as in low-inequality countries such as Denmark (OECD 2008). The Organization of American States (OAS) considers Mexico, along with Colombia and Brazil, to be part of the "triangle of extreme poverty" due to its lack of sufficient progress with regard to child mortality rates, levels of unemployment, access to primary education, levels of sanitation, and environmental sustainability. The OAS states that "this intense social polarization brought on by neo-liberal policies has deepened historic inequality and has fostered corruption in the government that maintains oligarchic, patriarchal, authoritarian social structures." (OAS 2005) Mexico's underdevelopment fosters conditions that make poor people, particularly women and children, more susceptible to trafficking. The lack of job opportunities, limited access to education, gender inequalities and violence against women are known to be "push" factors for women to attempt to migrate, which can increase the risk of entrapment in trafficking networks.

The actual extent of human trafficking in Mexico is difficult to ascertain due to the lack of reliable data. There are no official statistics and very few academic studies have been conducted. Most information comes from non-governmental organizations (NGOs) or the media. One recent study estimates that every year approximately 10,000 people are trafficked within Mexico and 5,000 are trafficked out of Mexico to the United States, a considerable increase from 2003–2004, when approximately 6,000 to 8,000 people were trafficked (Acharya 2010). This is likely a vast underestimate. Because trafficking victims are a hidden population threatened by pimps and law enforcement alike, and because most trafficking rings operate in obscurity, most goes unnoticed and underrepresented. The American Bar Association Rule of Law Initiative (ABA ROLI) recently published The Human Trafficking Assessment Tool for Mexico (HTAT), which states that while the phenomenon is believed to be extensive, it has not yet been documented in a systematic manner (ABA ROLI 2009, see Chapter 8 by Brenner Allen in this volume).

In its Trafficking in Persons Report, the U.S. State Department classifies Mexico as a significant source, transit, and destination country for men, women, and children. The groups considered most vulnerable to human trafficking in Mexico are women, children, indigenous persons, and undocumented migrants. Mexican women and children of both genders are particularly apt to be subject to sexual servitude within Mexico and in the United States. The State Department also lists Mexico as a "Tier 2" country, meaning that it does not fully comply with the minimum standards for the elimination of trafficking and has yet to fully implement effective anti-trafficking measures (United States Department of State 2010, 2009).

According to the United Nations Office on Drugs and Crime (UNODC), Mexico ranks "high" as an origin or source country for both labor and sex trafficking (2006). Traffickers employ a variety of strategies to lure their victims, ranging from false promises of employment in the United States to offers of marriage. Others resort to outright kidnapping. Victims can find themselves in sweatshops, brothels or fields in an increasing range of destinations in the United States and Canada. Their vulnerability to trafficking is linked to the circumstances surrounding U.S.–Mexican migration, in which restrictive quotas allow documented entry to only a small fraction of those seeking entrance into the United States.

Mexico is the largest source country for undocumented immigrants to the United States, with estimates of four million crossing the border each year (Protection Project 2008). Migrants employ smugglers to help move them through Mexico and across the border into the United States. Smuggled migrants are not considered to be victims of trafficking if they have entered into the relationship knowingly, and the smugglers keep their end of the bargain to deliver the person to the destination without deception or coercion. However, their undocumented status and reliance on smugglers leaves them particularly vulnerable to exploitation and trafficking if the smuggler reneges on the terms of the agreement and forces the migrant into debt bondage or other forms of slavery or servitude (ABA ROLI 2009, Kara 2009, Protection Project 2008, Acharya 2006). Notorious organized crime gangs such as Los Zetas, known for participating in drug and human trafficking, operate along the migratory routes (McAdams 2009). Smuggling can turn into trafficking if the victim is forced to perform sexual acts for smugglers or sexual favors are coerced by corrupt law enforcement officers.

Reliable statistics on Mexico as a transit country for traffickers are especially hard to come by since many individuals enter Mexico undocumented and pass through the country only briefly. According to the U.S. State Department, "Victims from South America, the Caribbean, Eastern Europe, and Asia are trafficked into Mexico for sexual or labor exploitation, as well as transiting though Mexico on their way to the United States." (U.S. State Department 2008) Central Americans and to a lesser extent South Americans, Eastern Europeans, and Asians are trafficked through Mexico en route to the United States. Women and girls are trafficked along a corridor that runs from the Honduran cities of Tegucigalpa and San Pedro Sula to Guatemala and then to Mexico (Protection Project 2008). The Human Trafficking Assessment Tool estimates that of the roughly 500,000 Central Americans who travel annually through Mexico hoping to reach the United States, between 20,000 and 50,000 fall victim to human traffickers. Many Central American children have fallen prey to traffickers as they have travelled through Mexico to unite with family members residing in the United States (personal communication, A. Salvado, Casa Alianza, 2010; personal communication, M. Ugarte, 2010; U.S. State Department 2008, Protection Project 2008).

Sex trafficking is a crime in which female victims so vastly outnumber males that it is generally considered a form of violence against women, though young males are also vulnerable to sex trafficking and enslavement. This type of trafficking often involves systematic rape, and often results in physical abuse, torture, and death, either directly (through homicide) or indirectly (through suicide, drug abuse, or exposure to sexually transmitted diseases, including HIV/AIDS). Women and children are highly valued commodities for sex traffickers supplying prostitution rings and strip joints in the United States and Canada.

Women and children are also trafficked within Mexico. As the U.S. State Department reports, a "significant" proportion of the women and children who are trafficked within Mexico are forced into the sex industry. Many girls are brought from Mexico's interior to the Cuauhtémoc Zone in Mexico City for the purpose of prostitution. A UNICEF study showed that of all Mexico's children, those in Mexico City and those living along the United States border had the highest risk of sexual exploitation. The conflict between the Mexican Government and the Zapatista National Liberation Army in Chiapas (EZLN) has resulted in approximately 40,000 displaced persons. Trafficking in women from the Chiapas area to Mexico City, Acapulco, and Cancún doubled between 1992 and 2002. Out of every ten women trafficked from the Chiapas area, seven were trafficked inside Mexico and three were trafficked outside the country (Acharya and Stevaneto 2005).

The NGO End Child Prostitution, Child Pornography and Trafficking of Children for Sexual Purposes (ECPAT), reports that Mexico has "long been regarded as a popular sex tourism location," which has made it a focus for trafficking in children. Estimates suggest that more than 16,000 Mexican children are trafficked and forced into sex work in the country's popular tourist destinations, such as Acapulco and Cancún, Guadalajara, Puerto Vallarta, and the border towns of Juárez and Tijuana (UNICEF 2000). These cities have become magnets for sex tourists and especially pedophiles, many of whom prey on minors trafficked to these popular tourism sites (McAdams 2009, Protection Project 2008, ECPAT 2004). In 2003, for example, American investigators uncovered a children's home in Acapulco that supplied foreign pedophiles with children as young as six years old (Bremer 2004, Egerton 2003). With human rights abuses on such a large and growing scale, it is necessary to try to explain the factors that promote sex trafficking in, from and to Mexico.

Causes of Sex Trafficking

The causes of sex trafficking are multifaceted and often overlap with the causes of other kinds of human trafficking. In general, women and children become victims of trafficking because of poverty, unemployment, lack of job opportunities, lack of access to education, and gender inequalities. Poverty seems to be one of the largest contributing factors globally. An International Organization for Migration (IOM) report on 826 victims of trafficking in Southeast European countries showed that more than half the victims claimed to have come from a "poor family" and some 17 percent from "very poor" families (IOM 2002).

Most of the source countries for trafficking in women in children have high rates of poverty. In West and Central Africa and in South Asia, poverty is seen as a key factor promoting trafficking (Kara 2009, Malarek 2008, Bales 2004). Moldova, Bulgaria, Albania and Romania, which experienced serious increases in poverty due to the transition from Soviet-style planned economies to market-driven neo-liberal ones, are all primary source countries for human trafficking (IOM 2005). The same studies also implicated discriminatory hiring practices associated with the transition, and suggested that many women considered migration to be the only way to improve their economic prospects (personal communication, K. Transchel 2010).

Violence against women is another contributing factor. Studies in the Balkan region link increases in women's trafficking to increased levels of domestic violence (personal communication, K. Transchel 2010; Kara 2009). La Strada, a non-governmental organization operating in Moldova, has found that many of the trafficking victims who arrived in shelters cited domestic violence as a key reason they left home, though most also claimed to have been lured by traffickers with false promises of job opportunities elsewhere (La Strada 2008).

Poverty in Mexico

While official sources recognize 40 to 52 percent of Mexicans as poor, some argue that the reality is much worse. Boltvinik and Hernández Laos (2000) maintain that in 2000 more than 75 percent of the population was poor or in extreme poverty. According to a more recent study by the same author, the figure now exceeds 80 per cent (Boltvinik 2005). The United Nations Development Program ranks Mexico among the countries in Latin America with the least improvement in human development in recent years, with barely 1.3 percent growth in per capita income between 1990 and 2003. During the same period real salaries remained stagnant while unemployment increased from 600,000 in 2000 to 1,027,000 in 2005 (UNDOC 2005). Inequality is so extreme and wealth is so concentrated that 5 percent of the income from the richest households would pull 12 million Mexicans out of poverty (González 2003). Inequality and marginalization are especially severe in the southern parts of the country.

The Mexican economy has been plagued with economic crisis after economic crisis, with devastating results for poverty levels and income distribution. In the late 1970s and early 1980s, Mexico embarked on a more market oriented form of capitalism. Declining rates of profit and economic recession in Europe in the 1970s had previously stimulated investment in Mexico. Massive loans were given to Mexico at high interest rates. Mexico's government borrowed huge sums to develop newly discovered petroleum reserves, causing the country's debt to triple in the late 1970s and early 1980s. Its inability to pay its debts and the resulting debt crisis of the 1980s gave the International Monetary Fund (IMF) and the International Bank of Reconstruction and Development (IBRD) greater leverage to impose harsh structural adjustment programs on Mexico. The austerity measures required Mexico to open its markets to foreign investment and integrate its economy into the world economy (Vadi 2001).

The North American Free Trade Agreement (NAFTA), which came into force in 1994, exacerbated poverty and wealth disparities. The financial crisis of 1995–1996 severely limited employment and overall economic growth. Mexico's entrance into NAFTA did not bring the 6.0 percent growth in GDP that had been predicted. Instead, according to the Economic Commission for Latin America and the Caribbean (2006) the Mexican economy grew at a tepid average rate of 2.84 percent from 1994 to 2005. Growth of GDP per capita was even lower, averaging only 1.8 percent during the same time period. Much of this economic growth reflected foreign direct investment, which was, and continues to be, overwhelmingly directed towards the wealthier regions in the north of the country. The poorer southern regions of Chiapas, Yucatán, and Oaxaca saw little or no growth. The concentration of investment in wealthier and predominantly urban regions has intensified regional disparities and has created further marginalization and poverty (INEGI 2006).

Trade in Mexico has followed patterns similar to those of foreign investment. While exports grew from over 60 billion dollars to over 214 billion between 1994 and 2005, and imports grew 200 percent for the same period, trade has been concentrated in wealthier urban regions of the country such as Mexico City, Jalisco, Puebla, and the cities along the U.S.–Mexico border, whereas regions such as Chiapas and Oaxaca have only marginally participated in the country's trade (ECLA 2006).

These regional disparities have been further heightened by inadequate job growth. Trade and investment after NAFTA have been unable to foster sufficient growth to meet the growing demand for stable jobs. Between 1994 and 2002 only 4.4 million jobs were created in Mexico, while 6.5 million people entered the workforce (Zarsky and Gallagher 2004).

The population explosion that has taken place in Mexico has further exacerbated unemployment. Between 1970 and 2000 the Mexican population increased from 53 million to 100 million and the labor force increased from 15 million to 40 million (Alvarado 2008). As economic stagnation has combined with rapid population growth to limit employment opportunities, much of Mexico's employment growth since 1994 has involved informal jobs that pay less than formal ones, and are of poor quality and lacking in legal benefits. Such conditions offer strong incentives for the poor and unemployed to look for work elsewhere, and many migrate to the United States in search of better jobs. Without the legal means to cross the U.S.– Mexico border, migrants become dependent on smugglers, and undocumented people become vulnerable to traffickers.

Poverty and the Geography of Trafficking in Women in Mexico

During the 1980s and 1990s, the widespread poverty resulting from economic liberalization policies forced more women to join the labor force. Women's entrance into the workforce can be a route to empowerment and gender equality, but this has not often been the case in Mexico. Unlike the industrialized countries of France, Germany, and England, where women generally entered the workforce during periods of economic growth and many were protected by strong social movements and labor organizations, in Mexico women have often joined the labor force under conditions of economic contraction in the absence of feminist movements or labor union protections. Often lacking in education and facing gender-based discrimination that limits their employment options, women concentrate in low paid jobs in the service sector or join the informal economy in unstable jobs that lack benefits such as health care, which the Mexican state offers workers in all regular, formal sector jobs. The growth of informal work throughout the economy is more apt to increase women's exploitation than their empowerment. Lack of education goes hand in hand with underemployment and poverty, conditions that can be magnified for rural women and men from indigenous communities.

Women lacking socioeconomic resources are more likely to search elsewhere for alternative means for earning a living—even if potentially fraudulent—because the possible gains are greater. Traffickers target women who are in economic difficulty because they know it is easier to coerce or manipulate women who are desperate. Traffickers use false promises of lucrative employment opportunities as a means to provide for their families or to enjoy an exotic life in Mexican cities or in the United States, to elicit victims' temporary cooperation through fraud and manipulation. In short, a multitude of social and economic factors at both the national and international levels combine to make women in Mexico vulnerable to potential traffickers.

In order to explore further the nexus between trafficking, poverty and gender in Mexico, it is important to know who is being trafficked and the regions to and from which they are being trafficked. In the absence of comprehensive data, information has to be pieced together from trafficking cases that have been prosecuted, victims who have been rescued through NGOs working within the region, and the limited but growing number of studies that have been conducted in Mexico. In a study of trafficked women carried out in Mexico City, the main reasons given for their circumstances were unemployment, poverty, gender-based violence, desertion by spouse, and ethnic conflict. The *machismo* culture and the high incidence of illiteracy among the women were also factors that made them vulnerable to trafficking. In a similar study carried out in Monterrey, the findings mirrored those for Mexico City (Acharya 2008). These findings are consistent with other studies on trafficked women globally (Clark 2010; Mam 2010; personal communication, K. Transchel 2010; Kara 2009; Bales 2004).

Most of the women who are trafficked into border towns or tourist resorts within Mexico or taken from Mexico to the United States are lured from the poorer states of Oaxaca, Guerrero, Chiapas, Michoacán, Zacatecas, Colima, Chihuahua, Yucatán, and Veracruz (ABA ROLI 2009, Acharya 2006). One of first and most infamous cases to emerge in the United States was that of the Cadena-Sosa brothers who, in the mid-1990s, lured women from Santiago Tuxtla with promises of earning $400 a week as waitresses in the Cadena family's restaurants in Florida. After crossing the U.S.–Mexico border, the women realized they had been duped when instead of working as waitresses, they ended up working in brothels servicing up to 30 migrant farm workers a day (De Stefano 2007). In 2002, in one of the largest trafficking operations ever uncovered, the Salazar brothers were discovered to have recruited hundreds of women from Oaxaca, Michoacán, Morales, and Veracruz to work in prostitution camps in San Diego and elsewhere (Protection Project 2008). A similar case in New Jersey uncovered a network of girls and young women recruited from Oaxaca and Hidalgo into forced prostitution and debt bondage in the United States. Typically poverty and marginalization had led the women into prostitution or criminal gangs and then entrapped them in the world of trafficking.

Yet, while poverty appears to be one of the main contributing factors to sex trafficking in Mexico, poverty alone does not make women susceptible to trafficking. In all contexts, including Mexico, the level of discrimination and violence against women in a society plays a key role in influencing women's vulnerability to trafficking.

Violence Against Women and Persistent Gender Inequalities

In order to understand sex trafficking in Mexico, it is necessary to explore the connection that sex trafficking has to patriarchy, gender inequality and violence against women. Patriarchal societies give rise to gender inequality, and the inequitable distribution of resources and power in society is one of the fundamental factors underlying high rates of domestic violence worldwide (Contreras, Barker-Aguilar, and Pick 2006). Sex trafficking needs to be understood in the context of Mexico's high rates of domestic violence and other forms of violence against women.

According to the National Institute of Statistics, Geography and Information (INEGI), forty percent of women in Mexico suffered physical, sexual, and/ or emotional violence in 2006 (INEGI 2007). Every three seconds a woman in Mexico is sexually violated (Acharya 2008). The Inter-American Development Bank estimates that seven out of ten Mexican women have suffered abusive treatment at some point in their lives (Reyes 2006). An extreme example of violence against women in Mexico is the increasing numbers of murders of women throughout the country. The Office of Attorney General's Specialized Unit for Violent Crimes estimates that approximately 6,000 women were murdered in Mexico between 1999 and 2005 (ABA ROLI 2009). This is probably a vast underestimate. According to Congresswoman Marcela Lagarde, more than 5,000 women were murdered in 2002 alone. While violence against women has always existed in Mexico, it appears to be on the rise.

One possible reason for the rising violence against women is the rapid increase in women's labor force participation during the last several decades. While their employment has changed the traditional gender division of labor, it has done so in the absence of changes to the deeply entrenched patriarchal culture and the corresponding male values and attitudes towards women's roles (Oliveria 2006). A United Nations report investigating the murders of women in Ciudad Juárez also stated that the lack of job opportunities for men and changes in their employment patterns have created a conflict towards women, whom they blame for taking jobs which would previously have been reserved for men. The persistence of "traditional patriarchal attitudes and mentalities or the stereotyped vision of the roles of men and women" can cause resentment toward women for stepping out of their traditional gender roles, and physical violence is used as a control strategy to reinforce gender role conformity (CEDAW 2005: 7–11).

Abuse and violence flower in contexts such as Mexico where persistent and deeply entrenched gender inequalities have limited women's opportunities. Out of 109 countries, Mexico ranks 39th on the United Nations Development Program (UNDP) Gender Empowerment Measurement (GEM) index and 73rd on the Gender Related Development Index (GDI). The GDI index assesses the relative well-being of women based on adjusted income, educational attainment and health. The GEM assesses women's empowerment by measuring their share of professional or managerial occupations, their representation in government, and their share of national income (UNDP 2009).

GEM and GDI, however, do not take into consideration regional differences unique to Mexico. A study of regional differences in education and other aspects of gender equality revealed that women in Mexico are far from reaching equality with men and noted that the greatest gender gaps are in the southern states such as Chiapas, Oaxaca, and Guerrero (Frias 2007). These kinds of gender inequalities devalue women socially and promote institutionalized impunity for crimes against women. Many Mexican women's rights advocates claim that rape and other forms of violence against women are not treated as serious crimes and the perpetrators are seldom prosecuted. In indigenous cultures a practice known as *rapto*, where a man kidnaps a woman for the purpose of marriage or just for sex, often goes unpunished; a key state legislator in Oaxaca actually called the practice "romantic." (Protection Project 2008) Institutionalized impunity for crimes against women provides an ideal climate for traffickers to operate.

Corruption and Lack of Rule of Law

Trafficking in persons occurs and often thrives with the assistance of corrupt government officials and the failure to obey the rule of law. Corruption is widespread in Mexico, which weakens the rule of law and the institutions that attempt to enforce it. Human trafficking is a lucrative business, not just for the traffickers, but also for the corrupt officials who receive their bribes and kickbacks. Some Mexican officials are not only on the traffickers' payrolls but are actually key players in the business. A recent study determined that in the state of Sonora, ten high-level officials were receiving a 200,000 U.S. dollar a week pay-off from traffickers at the time of the study (Protection Project 2008). Corruption, especially in the police force, has plagued the criminal justice system and hindered prosecutions and convictions, fuelling the increase in violence across the country and enabling traffickers to operate freely. The low salaries of government employees, particularly law enforcement agents, provide an ideal environment for traffickers to bribe officials to allow them to operate freely. Only 22 percent of Mexicans have confidence in the police, and this distrust also makes people more reluctant to report incidents of trafficking or violence against women to the police. The high level of violence and the Mexican government's inability to curb the violence and protect non-corrupt officials has led to a reluctance to investigate cases that may expose either traffickers or corrupt officials. Before his assassination, an investigator for the Office of Attorney General (OAG) told a journalist that he had information on governors, judges, businessmen, and public officials who were involved in trafficking rings (ABA ROLI 2009). The connection between corruption and trafficking creates parallels between Mexico and the breakaway autonomous region of Eastern Moldova, Transnistria in particular, where organized crime and corruption are rampant and trafficking in arms, drugs, and persons is uncontrollable (personal communication, K. Transchel 2010; Kara 2009).

Mexico has ratified numerous international treaties including the CEDAW and the U.N. Protocol to Prevent Trafficking in Persons. In 2007 Mexico passed the Federal Anti-Trafficking Law, and in 2008 it established FEVIMTRA, which is responsible for investigating and prosecuting federal crimes related to violence against women and trafficking in persons.

Yet corruption and lack of enforcement limit these efforts. According to Transparency International, corruption has been pervasive for many years and remains prevalent despite efforts to combat it. Transparency International ranks Mexico 72 out of 180 countries in its Corruption Perceptions Index, with a 3.5 score (zero being the most corrupt and 10 being the least) (Transparency International 2009). *Transparencia Mexicana* (Transparency Mexico), an independent NGO, noted that just over 2 billion U.S. dollars is spent annually on bribes (Transparency Mexico 2007). The same study showed that in 24 percent of cases a bribe was paid to prevent being detained (ABA ROLI 2009, Global Integrity 2009).

Mexico's inability to maintain the rule of law and the escalating violence that is taking place as the state tries to enforce its laws puts the country on the verge of being classified as a failed state. Cases of sexual violence, disappearances, and killings almost always go unpunished and are particularly prevalent in the regions of Chiapas, Oaxaca, and Guerrero (Acharya 2006, Olivera 2006). Extreme violence and failure to maintain the rule of law provides a breeding ground for criminal enterprises. Increasing militarization to combat the violence has led to reports of abuses by the army, displacement of people, and a climate of fear.

Conclusion

Sex trafficking is a complex phenomenon that cannot be combated unless it is understood and its root causes identified. In this chapter, I have explored the connections between poverty, the violence against women that stems from deep structural inequality, and sex trafficking. Poverty and the lack of opportunity stemming from economic stagnation limit women's economic employment options, making them economically vulnerable to the allure of traffickers who promise them well-paid jobs and other opportunities. But poverty alone cannot be the sole root cause of trafficking. Rather, the confluence of economic stress and prevailing social attitudes that downplay the importance of women's rights creates a fertile ground for the victimization of women.

Fuelled by poor economic conditions, the deeply entrenched gender inequalities that persist in Mexico's traditionally patriarchal society are creating a backlash against women's employment and other aspects of their changing gender roles. This, in turn, is promoting both violence against women and impunity for their male aggressors. Patriarchal norms promote the belief that men are of higher worth than women, making it socially acceptable in Mexico to value men's economic needs over those of women. Patriarchal norms also legitimate men's position of domination over women, thereby allowing women's dehumanization and commodification to become morally acceptable. Violence against women tends to increase in countries with pervasive and systemic gender inequalities, where women are less protected by social norms or legal doctrines. The lack of legal protection coupled with the inability of the Mexican government to enforce its laws, apprehend criminals, and protect people victimized by criminal violations, also allows trafficking networks to flourish and further reinforces the vulnerability of women and children to human trafficking.

In Mexico, as in other nations increasingly troubled by trafficking, until the primary conditions that give rise to sex trafficking—poverty and the deeply embedded structural inequalities that give rise to violence against women—are addressed, human traffickers will continue to victimize the most vulnerable sectors of the population.

Bibliography

Acharya, A. and Stevanato, A. 2005. Violencia y Trafico de Mujeres en Mexico: Una Perspectiva de Genero, (Violence and Trafficking of Women: A Gender Perspective). *Estudios Feministas*, 13(3), 507–24.

Acharya, A. 2006. International migration and trafficking of Mexican women to United States, in *Trafficking and the global sex industry*, edited by K.D. Beeks and D. Amir. Lantham. MD: Lexington Books, 21–32.

Acharya, A. 2008. Sexual violence and proximate risks: A study on trafficked women in Mexico City. *Gender, Technology and Development*, 12(1), 77–99.

Acharya. A and Clark, J. 2010, The health consequences of trafficking in women in Mexico: findings from Monterrey City. *International Review of Sociology*, 20(3), November 2010.

Alvarado, E. 2008. Poverty and Inequality in Mexico after NAFTA: Challenges, Setbacks and Implications. *Estudios Fronterizos*, 9(17), enero—junio, 73–106.

American Bar Association Rule of Law Initiative. 2009. Human Trafficking Assessment Tool for Mexico.

Bales, K. 2004. *Disposable people: New slavery in the global economy.* Berkeley, California: University of California Press.

Boltvinich, J. 2000. Debate, desigualida y pobreza. *La Journada*, April 28, 27.

Boltvinich, J. 2005. Aunento la probreza en la actual administración. *La Journada,* September 18.

Bremer, C. 2004. Child Sex Industry Thrives Despite Acapulco Arrests. *Reuters*, March 19, 2004.

Contreras, C., Barker-Aguilar, A., and Pick, S. 2006. Violence against Women in Mexico Conceptualization and Program Application. *Annals of the New York Academy of Sciences*, 1087(1), 261–278.

DeStefano, A.M. 2007. *The war on human trafficking: U.S. policy assessed.* New Brunswick, N.J: Rutgers University Press.

Egerton, B. and Case, B. 2003. Child Sex Trade Thrives in Some Mexican Towns with U.S. Links. *Dallas Morning News*, November 12, 2003.

Economic Commission for Latin America and the Carribiean (ECLA). 2006. Mexico *Estudio Economico 2005–2006*, Santiago, Chile, Economic Commission for Latin America and the Carribean.

End Child Prostitution, Pornography and Trafficking, (ECPAT) Newsletter. 2004. *Child Sex Tourism in Mexico* [Online]. Available at http://www.ecpat.org.uk [accessed: June 4, 2010].

Frias, S. 2008. Measuring structural gender equality in Mexico: A state level analysis. *Social Indicators Research*, 88(2), 215–246.

Gallagher, K. and Zarsky, L. 2004. *The enclave economy: foreign investment and sustainable development in Mexico.* Massachusetts Institute of Technology.

Global Integrity. 2009. 2006 Country Reports: Mexico [Online]. Available at: http://www.globalintegrity.org [accessed: June 2, 2010].

Gonzalez, R. 2003. *Violencia contra las mujeres deja un millión de víctimas anuales en México.* Cumunicacion e Información de la Mujer (CIMAC), Mexico.

International Labour Organization (ILO). 2005. A global alliance against forced labour. Geneva: International Labor Organization. World of Work: The Magazine of the ILO, 54, August.

Instituto Nacional de Estadística, Geografía e Informática (INEGI). 2006. Estadísticas Económicas Industria Maquiladora de Exportación.

International Organization of Migration (IOM). 2002. Journey of jeopardy: A review of research on trafficking in women and children in Europe. *IOM Migration Research Series*, No. 11.

International Organization of Migration (IOM) 2000. Data and Research on Human Trafficking: A Global Survey [Online]. Available at: http://www.lastradainternational.org/lsidocs/282%20IOM%20survey%20trafficking%20%28Global%29.pdf [accessed: May 10, 2010].

Identification of Trafficked Persons in Moldova. Guidelines for Specialized NGOs acting in the Republic of Moldova. (2008). International Center for Women Rights Protection and Promotion: La Strada. Casa IMAGO

Kara, S. 2009. *Sex trafficking: Inside the business of modern slavery*. New York: Columbia University Press.

La Strada. 2008. Identification of trafficked persons in Moldova. Guidelines for specialized NGOs acting in the Republic of Moldova. Moldova.

Mahmoud, T.O. and Trebesch, C. 2009. The Economic Drivers of Human Trafficking: Micro-Evidence from Five Eastern European Countries.

Malarek, V. 2008. *The Natashas*. New York: Arcade Publishing Inc.

McAdams, M. 2009. Modern Day Slavery in Mexico and the United States. Council on Hemispheric Affairs, Washington DC [Online]. Available at: http://www.coha.org/modern-day-slavery-in-mexico-and-the-united-states/ [accessed: May, 10 2010].

Organization for Economic Cooperation and Development (OECD) 2008. *Growing Unequal? : Distribution and Poverty in OECD Countries,* Country Note: Mexico [Online]. Available at: http://www.oecd.org/els/social/inequality [accessed: June 22, 2010].

Organization of American States (OAS). 2005. *Objetivos del desarrollo del milenio: Una Mirada desde América Latina y el Caribe.* México City: Comisión Económica para América y el Caribe.

Olivera, M. 2006. Violencia femicida: Violence against women and Mexico's structural crisis. *Latin American Perspectives*, 33(2), 104–114.

Polaris Project. *Fact Sheet.* [Online]. Available at: http://www.polarisproject.org [accessed: June 20, 2010].

Protection Project. 2008. *Report on Mexico* [Online]. Available at: http://www. protectionproject.org [accessed: June 4, 2010].

Reyes, A. 2006. Mexico: Gender Violence Continues to Claim Victims. *Inter Press Service* [Online, August 14]. Available at: http://www.ipsnews.net [accessed: May 21, 2010].

The World Bank, 2009. Data [Online]. Available at: http://www.data.worldbank. org/indicator/SI.POV.GINI [accessed: May 10, 2010]

Transparency International. 2009. *Corruption perceptions index* [Online]. Available at: http://www.transparency.org/policy_research/surveys_indices/ cpi/200 [accessed: June 20, 2010].

Transparency Mexico. 2007. *National index on corruption and good government* [Online]. Available at: http://www.transparenciamexicana.org.mx/ENCBG [accessed: June 20, 2010].

United Nations Development Program (UNDP). 2009. Gender empowerment measurement and gender development index [Online]. Available at: http:// transparenciamexicana.org/ms/ENCBG [accessed: May 24, 2010].

Trafficking in persons report. 2008. Washington DC: United States Department of State. United States Department of State.

Trafficking in persons report. 2010. Washington DC: United States Department of State. United States Department of State.

Trafficking in persons: Global patterns. 2006. Vienna: UNDOC. United Nations Office of Drugs and Crime (UNODC).

United Nations. 2000. *Protocol to prevent, suppress, and punish trafficking in persons, especially women and children, supplementing the United Nations convention against transnational organized crime* [Online]. Available at: http://www.unodc.org/documents/treaties/UNTOC/Publications/TOC%20 Convention/TOCebook-e.pdf [accessed: May 23, 2010].

Vadi, J. M. 2001. Economic globalization, class struggle, and the Mexican state. *Latin American Perspectives*, 28(4), 129–147.

Yu, W., and Villarreal, A. 2007. Economic globalization and women's employment: The case of manufacturing in Mexico. *American Sociological Review*, 72(3), 365.

Chapter 8

Assessing Human Trafficking in Mexico: The American Bar Association Rule of Law Initiative's Experience

Brenner Allen[1]

Introduction

Human trafficking is one of the most prevalent and complex crimes in the world. Currently, an estimated 12.3 million adults and children (US DOS 2009) are victims of trafficking either within nations or across international borders. Trafficking does not just deprive these victims of their human rights and freedoms; it also affects a much broader population, fueling organized crime, threatening public health, and impeding economic development and the establishment of the rule of law (US DOS 2009). Governments, organizations, and individuals working to combat human trafficking are faced with complex situations, many-layered causes, and an equally complicated range of solutions. Thus, the American Bar Association Rule of Law Initiative (ABA ROLI) has developed the Human Trafficking Assessment Tool (HTAT) to facilitate the collection and publication of hard-to-find, detailed, and comprehensive information on human trafficking in any given country. The aim of ABA ROLI's HTAT reports is to guide the design of more informed and targeted legislative reforms and programming by governments, local non-governmental organizations (NGOs), and international donors.

In August 2009, ABA ROLI published an HTAT report for Mexico.[2] This report analyzes the codification of Mexico's anti-trafficking efforts as evinced through federal and state anti-trafficking legislation. It also draws conclusions regarding the practical implementation of those laws through data gleaned from freedom of information requests, published statistics, and over 80 interviews with trafficking experts in seven states and Mexico City. These legal (*de jure*) and practical (*de facto*) efforts to combat human trafficking are examined in the context of the HTAT methodology, which in turn is based largely on the Protocol to Prevent, Suppress and Punish Trafficking in Persons, Especially Women and Children,

1   With thanks to Paulina Rudnicka, Gretchen Kuhner, and Simon Conté for their assistance.

2   The publication of the Mexico HTAT report was funded by a grant from the U.S. Department of State's Office to Monitor and Combat Trafficking in Persons.

supplementing the United Nations Convention against Transnational Organized Crime (known as the Trafficking Protocol) (Protocol 55/25 2001).

This chapter is intended to provide the reader with an understanding of the HTAT methodology, legal basis, and goals, and to describe ABA ROLI's experience in implementing the HTAT in Mexico. It summarizes the report's key findings with an eye towards guiding the legislative reforms and programming efforts necessary to combat human trafficking in Mexico.

The Methodology and Purpose of HTAT Assessments

The ABA formed ROLI in 2007 to consolidate its regional international rule of law programs for Africa, Asia, Europe and Eurasia, Latin America and the Caribbean, and the Middle East. Currently, ABA ROLI implements legal reform programs in more than 40 countries, through a staff of over 400 professionals and volunteers.[3] ABA ROLI employs various strategies to combat trafficking in persons. One of the most important is the HTAT, whose methodology and goals are the focus of this section.

ABA ROLI's Efforts to Combat Trafficking in Persons

In the almost 20 years that ABA ROLI has been working to promote the rule of law globally, human trafficking has become one of the organization's main concerns. In addition to developing the HTAT methodology and applying it to complete assessments in Mexico and Moldova (published June 2005), ABA ROLI combats trafficking in persons through a variety of other efforts. ABA ROLI's anti-trafficking activities include raising public awareness, generating funds, and providing expertise for trainings, hosting conferences, and facilitating victim advocacy. Examples of ABA ROLI's successful programmatic efforts include sponsoring a mini-documentary on trafficking in Armenia; training Nigerian immigration officers on victim protection; organizing a regional anti-trafficking conference for East African legal professionals; training personnel and establishing operating procedures for victim shelters in Ecuador; and litigating on behalf of a trafficking victim in Kenya.[4] ABA ROLI has also helped create new anti-trafficking laws and strengthen existing ones, through assistance with legislative drafting in countries such as Armenia, Ecuador, Georgia, and Russia.

The HTAT methodology complements ABA ROLI's technical assistance programs in several ways. While the HTAT methodology does not specifically focus

---

3   More information on ABA ROLI and its reform work can be found on the organization's website, http://www.abanet.org/rol/

4   More information on ABA ROLI's anti-trafficking programming is available at ABA ROLI's Criminal Law and Anti-Human Trafficking Focal Area website, http://www. abanet.org/rol/programs/criminal-law.html.

on determining the success or failure of ABA ROLI's programs, it is instrumental in highlighting the extent to which programmatic efforts have impacted the trafficking problem. In Mexico, where ABA ROLI was not involved in anti-trafficking work and did not have an in-country office prior to the implementation of the HTAT, the report aids ABA ROLI, the Mexican government, and other NGOs in pinpointing future programming opportunities. Perhaps most significantly, HTAT reports are a source of valuable information for reformers seeking to change laws, policies, and programs to obtain increased compliance with the trafficking protocol. The following section provides a more detailed overview of how ABA ROLI developed the HTAT methodology, and how and why assessments are conducted.

The Development of the HTAT Methodology

The HTAT is one of seven different assessment tools that ABA ROLI has created, targeting distinct legal subjects. Four of these assessment tools address aspects of the legal system: judicial reform, prosecutorial reform, legal profession reform, and legal education reform. These four assessments are not based on any particular international treaty; instead, ABA ROLI has drawn on a variety of international and regional standards and best practices as well as the organization's own experience, to develop these four assessment tools. The remaining three tools are each based on the contents of a specific treaty: the International Covenant on Civil and Political Rights Legal Implementation Index (assessing human rights), the Convention on the Elimination of All Forms of Discrimination against Women Assessment Tool (assessing women's rights), and the HTAT.[5] The four non-treaty based assessment tools are divided into between 22 and 30 "factors," with each factor addressing a different facet of legal reform. As will be discussed later in this section, the treaty based assessment tools are divided by treaty article, measuring *de jure* and *de facto* compliance with each substantive treaty article.

Since the HTAT methodology assesses a country's success in implementing the UN Trafficking Protocol, the HTAT Assessor's Manual draws most of its substance from that Protocol. This Protocol entered into force on December 25, 2003, with 132 states having become party to it as of February 9, 2009 (UN 2009). It sets forth a clear definition of human trafficking and enumerates the types of behaviors that fall within the classification of the crime (UN 2009). The Trafficking Protocol calls on states' parties to legally define and criminalize trafficking, and to adopt measures to prevent its occurrence, protect trafficking victims, and prosecute traffickers. At a minimum, states' parties are required to apply this "3 P" approach, and they are encouraged to go beyond this to adopt and enforce laws and apply policies that will further combat trafficking in persons (ABA CEELI 2005).

The HTAT Assessor's Manual contains a wealth of legal commentary that fleshes out the Trafficking Protocol's provisions and offers brief examples

---

5   More information on these assessment tools is available at ABA ROLI's publications and assessments webpage: http://www.abanet.org/rol/publications.shtml.

of compliance and non-compliance with the Protocol. To assess a country's compliance the manual includes questions that focus separately on *de jure* and *de facto* compliance with the Protocol.[6] Interviewees are not asked every single *de facto* question; instead, the assessment team selects questions based on the expertise and focus of the interviewees. The same question may be posed to a large number of interviewees, so as to encompass the full spectrum of opinions on each topic. Additionally, some *de facto* questions form the basis for statistical or informational research efforts, rather than interviewee inquiries. Most *de jure* questions are intended solely to be a guide for legal research, though some *de jure* questions are posed to interviewees who have expertise in the relevant legislation.[7]

As with the rest of ABA ROLI's assessment tools, the HTAT is a legal inquiry, rather than, for example, a statistical survey or a collection of anecdotal case studies. The HTAT draws on international legal standards to examine the specific conditions, legal provisions, and mechanisms that are present in a country. HTAT reports do not assign scores or grades to reflect a country's compliance with international standards. Instead, the reports aim to provide local governments, reformers and international donors with extremely detailed and specific information, which, while not *per se* ranking or grading a country's compliance with the Trafficking Protocol, can be used for an article-by-article determination of the extent to which compliance is occurring.

Each HTAT report consists of a brief introduction to ABA ROLI's assessment methodology; a summary of the findings of the HTAT report; and a discussion of the historical, political, and legal context of the trafficking problem in that country. This is followed by 13 chapters of analysis, each addressing compliance with a different substantive article of the Trafficking Protocol (and any relevant portions of the Convention on Transnational Organized Crime). Following the "3 P" approach, the 13 chapters of analysis focus on the steps that countries take to prevent trafficking, protect trafficking victims, and prosecute traffickers. This includes the examination of issues such as the existence and scope of anti-trafficking legislation (Articles 1, 2, and 4); the legal definition of trafficking in persons (Article 3); criminal procedure issues, such as jurisdiction, extradition, and witness protection (Article 5); the role of corruption and organized crime in

---

6   While the HTAT Assessor's Manual (and thus ABA ROLI's HTAT methodology) is not publicly available, much of the background information and commentary on the Trafficking Protocol that is found in the manual is also included in ABA ROLI's *Introduction to the Human Trafficking Assessment Tool* (Dec. 2005), which is available to the public on ABA ROLI's publications and assessments webpage. This *Introduction* also contains information designed to facilitate enhanced anti-trafficking efforts, such as case studies of successful anti-trafficking efforts by NGOs.

7   Former ABA ROLI Senior Legal Analyst Andreea Vesa spearheaded the development of the HTAT methodology, and led the assessment team during the pilot assessment in Moldova. See Interview with Andreea Vesa, Director of the ABA-United Nations Development Programme International Legal Resource Center (September 25, 2009).

facilitating trafficking; victim identification, assistance, and repatriation (Articles 6–8); preventative measures (Article 9); inter-organizational cooperation (Article 10); and border and immigration security measures (Articles 11–13).

As previously suggested, there are many sources for the in-depth information included in HTAT reports. Each of the 13 chapters of the Mexico HTAT includes a detailed examination of relevant legislation, and assesses the implementation of that legislation in light of statistical data, accounts in newspaper articles, court cases, and information from knowledgeable interviewees. As will be discussed in the following section, the assessment process aims to gather all of this information and use it to produce a thorough examination of the state of anti-trafficking efforts in a given country. Once published, the findings of HTAT reports are intended to catalyze reforms, produce more effective programming and legal enforcement, and support grassroots advocacy.

ABA ROLI's Experience Implementing the HTAT in Mexico

The Mexico HTAT assessment is the largest and most complicated assessment project that ABA ROLI has completed to date. The following is an overview of the trafficking phenomenon in Mexico, and an explanation of how ABA ROLI assessed the Mexican government's and NGOs' response to the crime.

The Scope of the Mexico HTAT Report

Mexico (officially, the United Mexican States) is a democratic, federal state, bordering Guatemala and Belize to the south and the United States to the north. It is large—three times the size of Texas—with a population of over 111 million persons, 40 percent of whom live in poverty. Internal migration and immigration occur on a large scale; as of 2006, 11.5 million persons born in Mexico were living in the United States (Mexico HTAT 2009: 7, 8). Given Mexico's size, and the scale of migration occurring within, to, and from the country, the Mexico HTAT assessment team was faced with a number of challenges to gathering information and developing a clear picture of the trafficking situation. Trafficking in Mexico occurs internally, with victims being transported between cities and states. Also, Mexico is both a source and a transit country for many victims trafficked to the United States, as well as a destination for victims from Central America and elsewhere. Trafficking occurs primarily for the purposes of sexual exploitation, temporary agricultural work, and domestic work (Mexico HTAT 2009: 11, 12). The human trafficking crime is linked to growing concerns over organized crime and drug trafficking; in recent years there has been an escalation in violence linked to these problems (e.g. Beaubien 2009).

The Mexico HTAT's scope includes both federal and state efforts to combat human trafficking. Its focus is on the capital, Mexico City, and seven of Mexico's 31 states—Baja California, Chiapas, Chihuahua, Guerrero, Oaxaca, Tlaxcala, and Quintana Roo— which were selected due to their particular significance to the trafficking issue. Baja California, which borders California, is a portal for northward migration and has been identified as having a high level of human trafficking, particularly for prostitution. Large flows of migrants also pass through Chiapas, which is located on Mexico's border with Guatemala, and is a site where substantial numbers of Central Americans are trafficked for prostitution and forced labor exploitation. Chihuahua, which borders the United States, has high levels of sex tourism as well as large flows of migrants. In Oaxaca, a southern state, trafficking for agricultural labor is pervasive in indigenous communities, as is emigration to the United States. Trafficking for prostitution occurs both to and from Tlaxcala, which is centrally located near Mexico City. Quintana Roo, which is located on the Yucatán peninsula, is the destination point for many victims trafficked for prostitution and forced labor in the tourism industry.

The Assessment Team

Assessment teams for most ABA ROLI reports consist of an outside contractor, assisted primarily by an ABA ROLI legal analyst based in Washington, D.C., and ABA ROLI staff attorneys in the country that is being assessed. As previously mentioned, ABA ROLI does not have a field office in Mexico; so most travel arrangement and interview planning was conducted by the assessment team. Further, given the scale of the Mexico HTAT assessment project, several additional staff and contractors assisted in the assessment process. The Mexico HTAT assessment team was led by Gretchen Kuhner, a U.S.-trained attorney who has practiced law in Mexico City for more than a decade and specializes in women's rights, trafficking, and migration issues. She was assisted by Monica Salazar Salazar, a Mexican attorney with several years of experience in human rights and trafficking issues. Ms. Kuhner and Ms. Salazar were selected and trained by ABA ROLI staff based in Washington, D.C. ABA ROLI Legal Analyst Paulina Rudnicka, with assistance from Legal Analyst Brenner Allen, guided the assessment and editing process, and prepared the Mexico HTAT report for publication.[8] The following is an accounting of the assessment process, including an examination of several of the more significant challenges that the assessment team confronted during their work.

---

8   The assessment team also received strong support from Research and Assessments Office Director Simon Conté, Senior Criminal Law Advisor Mary Greer, Latin America and Caribbean Division Director Michael McCullough and Latin America and Caribbean Division Program Manager Thomas Hare. Additionally, a former FBI Supervisory Special Agent, Paul Vina, participated in the assessment process, accompanying Ms. Kuhner and Ms. Salazar on a number of interviews with law enforcement and border control in Mexico City, Tijuana, and San Diego, California. Mr. Vina then provided written feedback on his findings for incorporation into the final Mexico HTAT report.

The Assessment Process

Following Ms. Kuhner and Ms. Salazar's selection as assessors in November and December 2007 and the completion of their training, they began collecting federal and state anti-trafficking legislation and obtaining relevant statistics from federal government agencies under the Federal Law on Access to Public Information (Official Journal 2002). A group of professors and students from the Public Interest Law Clinic at the *Instituto Tecnológico Autónomo de México* assisted the assessors with legal research and data collection, facilitating a review of the large body of legislation and information that exists regarding human trafficking in Mexico. Following that review, between January and April 2008 Ms. Kuhner and Ms. Salazar completed over 65 interviews with representatives of Mexican federal and state governments, non-governmental organizations, and the U.S. government, as well as lawyers, academics, journalists, and other experts in the field of human trafficking.[9]

Following the completion of these assessment interviews and a review of relevant legislation, the assessment team finalized an initial draft of the Mexico HTAT in June 2008. The report was then translated into Spanish and subjected to ABA ROLI's peer review process. The peer review process is intended to serve two primary functions: first, it contributes to the quality of the final report by verifying its accuracy; and second, it provides advance notice of the content of the report, so that upon publication and dissemination, the report will not contain any unanticipated findings. ABA ROLI's peer review included a number of key interviewees, along with review by the project's funder, the U.S. Department of State's Office to Monitor and Combat Trafficking in Persons. Peer reviewers provided ABA ROLI with suggestions regarding the translation and terminology of the report, along with substantive feedback regarding the accuracy of statements in the report.

During the interview process, and following peer review, several significant legislative developments and resulting programmatic developments occurred. The Federal Law to Prevent and Sanction Trafficking in Persons (Federal Anti-Trafficking Law) was passed in November 2007, just two months prior to the beginning of the assessment team's interviews. In February 2009, Mexican President Felipe Calderón issued Regulations to the Federal Anti-Trafficking Law, to provide guidance on the law's implementation. This development significantly changed the legal landscape in Mexico, necessitating a second round of research and interviews to ensure that the Mexico HTAT report was timely and comprehensive.

The subsequent series of interviews, including follow-up interviews with a number of original interviewees, brought the total number of interviews conducted

---

9 This includes interviews with Mexican federal and state government agencies; intergovernmental organizations; representatives of the U.S. government in Mexico (including USAID and its *Proteja* project, the U.S. Embassy, the U.S. Department of Justice, U.S. Immigration and Customs Enforcement, and the Federal Bureau of Investigation); a Mexican law firm, a Mexican labor union, two Central American Consulates; law students and professors, and several dozen Mexican NGOs.

during the assessment process to roughly 80. The final interviews were completed in February 2009. However, even as the assessment team and ABA ROLI were revising the completed Mexico HTAT report in early 2009, the situation was continuing to evolve. The report was revised in early 2009 to reflect not only the Regulations to the Federal Anti-Trafficking Law, but also the first indictment under the Federal Anti-Trafficking Law, and the first national meeting to discuss assistance models for trafficking victims.

In addition to the difficulty posed by constant legislative and programmatic developments, several other factors complicated the assessment process. For example, to provide readers with a clear picture of the extent of the trafficking problem in Mexico, the assessment team sought to collect reliable data documenting the scale on which it was occurring and the strategies and impacts of attempts to hold perpetrators accountable. The primary means of data collection were freedom of information requests under the Federal Law on Access to Public Information, as well as questionnaires sent to NGOs that work with trafficking victims. The freedom of information requests produced some useful data, as did the questionnaires. But these data sources were insufficient to provide a clear picture of the number of victims of human trafficking in Mexico. The task was beyond our capability because state governments use contrasting definitions of the term and the federal government does not compile data on human trafficking.

Another problem encountered during the interview process was the sensitivity of the trafficking issue. Some key stakeholders were reluctant to meet with the assessment team, and many who did agree to be interviewed declined to answer certain questions. Frequently interviewees were willing to discuss anecdotal information, but would not provide specific data on numerical trends. Some were hesitant to talk to the team at all. On at least one occasion, the Mexican government prohibited a potential interviewee from speaking with the assessment team. Interviewees' reluctance to speak with the assessment team also reflected the fact that some interviewees were subject to threats of violence (Bonello 2009).[10] Such concerns also have a strong effect on the government's response to trafficking. As was revealed in the interviews, prosecutors are often hesitant to prosecute trafficking cases and judges are reluctant to classify crimes as trafficking, due to corruption, impunity for criminal acts, and concerns for their personal safety.

Some interviewees negatively viewed ABA ROLI's planned publication of a report on trafficking, because they had recently completed interviews for other reports on trafficking[11] and did not see the utility of another publication on the

---

10   For example, journalist, Mexico HTAT interviewee, and panelist for the Mexico HTAT roll-out event Lydia Cacho was granted protection from the Inter-American Commission for Human Rights in September 2009. This followed on her efforts to expose a child pornography ring in Cancún, Mexico.

11   Including the U.S. Department of State's Trafficking in Persons Report and a United Nations Office on Drugs and Crime report on human trafficking in Latin America and the Caribbean.

subject. Others assumed that the assessment team members were agents of the U.S. government. Recalling the country's placement on the U.S. Department of State's Trafficking in Persons Report tier two watch list between 2004 and 2007, they feared that the Mexico HTAT report would result in yet another "bad grade" for Mexico. The assessment team addressed these concerns by emphasizing to interviewees ABA ROLI's independence from the U.S. government, and the resulting objectivity of the Mexico HTAT report, as well as the fact that the HTAT does not employ any scoring methodology or assign any grades.

Publication of the 2009 Mexico HTAT Report

The Mexico HTAT report was published on August 27, 2008,[12] and presented to the public during a roll-out event at the *Instituto Tecnológico Autónomo de México*. This event featured a panel of key stakeholders in the fight against human trafficking, including María Guadalupe Morfín Otero, special prosecutor for crimes against women and human trafficking; Carmen A. Rubio López, deputy director for the National Migration Institute; Lydia Cacho, the investigative journalist who received threats stemming from her work exposing trafficking crimes; and Federico Luis Pöhls Fuentevilla, director of the Fray Julian Garcés Center for Human Rights and Local Development.

Approximately 120 persons, including journalists, NGO representatives, academics, and representatives of the governments of Mexico, the United States, and the various Central American countries, attended the roll-out event. A number of news outlets produced stories about the event and the findings of the report (e.g. CENCOS 2009, EFE 2009, Godoy 2009).[13] Section IV of this article delves deeper into the roll-out discussions and the subsequent news stories concerning the findings of the Mexico HTAT report.

The Results and Impact of the Mexico HTAT Report

The Mexico HTAT report assesses the extent to which compliance with the Trafficking Protocol has been achieved, as demonstrated by the analysis of relevant legislation and the examination of hard-to-find statistics and diverse data. While there has been a great deal of progress in the passage of anti-trafficking legislation, especially at the federal level, implementation of new laws is only in the early stages, with mixed results in terms of prosecutions and legislated programs. The following is an overview of the Mexico HTAT's findings regarding *de jure* and

---

12   The report is available for download in English and Spanish on ABA ROLI's Human Trafficking Assessment Tool publication website, http://www.abanet.org/rol/publications/human_trafficking_assessment_tool.shtml.

13   Over twenty news stories about the Mexico HTAT report are available online in English and Spanish.

de facto compliance with the Trafficking Protocol, including implications of the report's findings on future efforts to combat trafficking in persons.

Legal Compliance with the Trafficking Protocol

Mexico's federal laws are largely in agreement with the Trafficking Protocol, though not all states have enacted compliant anti-trafficking provisions in their legislation. Since its passage in November 2007, the Federal Anti-Trafficking Law has provided federal mechanisms for preventing and prosecuting trafficking and protecting trafficking victims, all largely in compliance with the Trafficking Protocol (Mexico HTAT 2009: 1, 22).[14] In cases for which there is no federal jurisdiction, 25 of Mexico's 31 states and its capital, Mexico City, have included the crime of trafficking in persons in their criminal codes, and the six remaining states were developing such legislation as of the drafting of this report. However, in only seven states were the definitions of trafficking in persons in complete compliance with the Trafficking Protocol (Mexico HTAT 2009: 41–42). Further, several aspects of federal and state anti-trafficking laws' provisions were not in accordance with the Trafficking Protocol. In the Regulations to the Federal Anti-Trafficking Law, the definition of "trafficking victim" is so narrow as to potentially limit protection to victims who testify against traffickers or file an official complaint (Mexico HTAT 2009: 59)[15] Additionally, the federal (and many states') definition of trafficking in persons does not mention that a victim's consent to the crime is irrelevant if deception, coercion, abduction, or a similar practice has occurred. This raises the possibility of defendants arguing that the victim consented to the crime, leaving the prosecution responsible for proving that consent had not been given (Mexico HTAT 2009: 44).

The situation is also mixed in terms of the enforcement of these laws through the judicial system. In January 2008, a Specialized Prosecutorial Unit for Violent Crimes against Women and Human Trafficking (FEVIMTRA) was established within the Office of the Attorney General; among other things, FEVIMTRA is charged with investigating and prosecuting federal trafficking crimes (Mexico HTAT 2009: 54). As of the date the Mexico HTAT was drafted, FEVIMTRA had investigated 24 cases and issued 2 indictments, both in regards to the trafficking of eight Chinese victims for exploitation in a factory in the state of Sonora (Mexico HTAT 2009: 55). There had not yet been any federal convictions.

---

14 "Trafficking will be prosecuted as a federal, rather than state crime, if it meets several requirements. This includes crimes that are initiated or prepared abroad; crimes that were committed on federal property; crimes that were aimed at producing an effect abroad; and in some cases, crimes that meet the definition of being 'organized crime'." See also Federal Criminal Code arts. 1–4; Federal Law on Organized Crimes arts. 2, 8; General Law on the Judicial Power of the Federation art. 50(I).

15 See also Regulations to the Federal Anti-Trafficking Law art. 2(XV).

Some prosecutions have occurred at the state level, though the assessment team was unable to obtain accurate data on this subject for most states. In Chihuahua, 15 cases had been investigated between the time of enactment of anti-trafficking legislation in 2007 and the drafting of the Mexico HTAT report. Several cases have been investigated in Tlaxcala, though charges were only filed in regards to pimping, and not trafficking. Several members of an alleged trafficking ring are currently being prosecuted in Michoacán (Mexico HTAT 2009: 55–56). The assessment team received reports that prosecutions were hampered by problems such as corruption and violence within the legal system and a lack of protection for witnesses and victims (Mexico HTAT 2009: 26–28, 33).

The assessment team drew mixed conclusions from its findings on legislative protections against trafficking and prosecutions. According to Ms. Kuhner, the lack of federal convictions "is a very serious problem." However, she acknowledges that "the law against trafficking in Mexico is very new, and more time is needed to evaluate its implementation." Meanwhile government agencies, NGOs, and international donors have been fighting trafficking in persons for a number of years, via preventative measures, victim assistance, and other services. The following section describes these projects, along with growing efforts to coordinate assistance and expand and improve anti-trafficking programs.

Practical Compliance with the Trafficking Protocol

Funding for anti-trafficking programs and assistance has traditionally come mainly from NGOs and international donors. The Federal Anti-Trafficking Law contains a number of provisions for victim protection, assistance, and counseling; but they have yet to be enacted and the law does not consider how their programs are to be funded (Mexico HTAT 2009: 63–64). The Regulations to the Federal Anti-Trafficking Law also specifically call upon certain government agencies to provide services for trafficking victims; again, the source of funding for these agencies is not specified (Mexico HTAT 2009: 64).[16] In terms of government coordination of prevention and protection efforts, the National Migration Institute has formed 32 state-level Inter-Institutional Committees on Trafficking and Smuggling, to direct local anti-trafficking efforts. However, efforts to otherwise coordinate federal government, state government, and non-governmental projects have not yet reached their full potential.[17] The Inter-Secretarial Commission, a high-level body comprised of representatives from a variety of anti-trafficking agencies and organizations, has not yet been assembled (Mexico HTAT 2009: 15).[18] Once created, this Commission is required to develop a comprehensive National Anti-

---

16 See also Regulations to the Federal Anti-Trafficking Law art. 20.

17 See ABA ROLI, Mexico HTAT at 83–84 for several examples of small-scale NGO and government cooperation on anti-trafficking efforts.

18 See also Regulations to the Federal Anti-Trafficking Law art. 2, 4.

Trafficking Program to establish policies and programs. However, this had not yet occurred as of the drafting of this report.

Even without formal coordination of their efforts, NGOs and international donors, as well as the federal and state governments, have made significant efforts to prevent and combat trafficking in persons. With support from the Mexican government, FEVIMTRA has established a shelter for trafficking victims (Mexico HTAT 2009: 64–65). Federal and state governments have also sponsored public service announcements aimed at preventing trafficking and identifying perpetrators and victims (Mexico HTAT 2009: 81). The National Anti-Trafficking Program is expected to increase these activities. Government agencies and NGOs have been active in promoting trainings on victim identification and assistance that are aimed at border control officers and NGOs (Mexico HTAT 2009: 97–98). In terms of victim protection, a small number of NGOs actively seek out and identify trafficking victims, and provide them with shelter, medical assistance, counseling, and legal aid (Mexico HTAT 2009: 58–63). Between 2002 and 2007, these NGOs uncovered 300 cases of trafficking in persons and helped 1,500 Mexican victims in the United States (Mexico HTAT 2009: 7).

Thus, while smaller scale efforts to assist victims and prevent trafficking are succeeding, the government has not yet begun coordinating these efforts, nor has it made funding available to NGOs to assist in research or victim assistance (Mexico HTAT 2009: 3). The 2009 Mexico HTAT report demonstrates that more targeted prevention efforts are needed, as are programs to identify and protect trafficking victims, including witness protection programs.

Conclusion

ABA ROLI's goal in producing the Mexico HTAT report was to demonstrate the full extent of the trafficking problem in Mexico, and to shed light on the nature and success of efforts to combat the crime. Following a thorough and detailed assessment process, the final Mexico HTAT report demonstrates mixed results in the fight against trafficking. Federal anti-trafficking legislation is new and incomplete, yet well-drafted; state laws on the subject are less thorough. While the Mexican government increases its capacity to combat trafficking, a number of privately funded agencies are supplementing its efforts to prevent trafficking and assist trafficking victims.

In the words of Mario Fuentes, director of the Centre for Studies and Research in Social Development and Assistance, and moderator for the Mexico HTAT roll-out expert panel, "As long as political will to combat trafficking is lacking and until further legal changes are adopted, nothing is going to change." It is ABA ROLI's intention that the detailed findings of the Mexico HTAT report will provide leverage for those seeking the passage and strengthening of anti-trafficking legislation, increased levels of prosecution, and a coordinated federal approach to prevention and protection programs. Such developments will need to be accompanied by better and more coordinated efforts to track the trafficking phenomenon and to deliver services to victims. As Mr. Fuentes warns, and as the 2009 Mexico HTAT report demonstrates, without such progress, the crime of trafficking in persons will continue to go largely unpunished, and persons fighting the crime will continue to do so in a vacuum of government leadership and assistance.

Bibliography

ABA ROLI. 2009. Mexico Human Trafficking Assessment Tool. March at page numbers: 7, 8.

ABA ROLI. 2009. Mexico Human Trafficking Assessment Tool March at 11, 12 .

ABA Central European and Eurasian Law Initiative (CEELI). 2005. Assessors' Guide to the Human Trafficking Assessment Tool [Online]. Available at: http://www.abanet.org/rol/publications/human_trafficking_assessment_tool.shtml [accessed: September 3, 2009].

CENCOS. 2009. [Online, August 27]. Available at: http://www.censos.org [accessed: September 2, 2009].

Deborah Bonello. 2009. Mexican Journalist Lydia Cacho seeks protection from new threats. Los Angeles Times [Online, September 17]. Available at: http://www.latimesblogs.latimes.com/laplaza/2009/09/mexican-journalist-cacho-seeks-protection-for-new-threats.html [accessed: September 3, 2009].

Emilio Godoy. 2009. Slow Progress against Human Trafficking. IPS [Online, August 27]. Available at http://www.ipsnews.net [accessed: September 3, 2009].

Federal Law on Access to Public Information. *adopted* June 11, 2002, Official Journal of the Federation (D.O.), *as amended.*

Jason Beaubien. 2009. Violence continues as Drug Wars Rage in Mexico. *National Public Radio* [Online, March 23]. Available at: http://www.npr.org/templates/story/story.php?storyId=102188685 [accessed: September 2, 2009].

Protocol to Prevent, Suppress and Punish Trafficking in Persons, especially Women and Children [Trafficking Protocol; Palermo Protocol]. 2001. U.N. General Assembly, 55th session. (A/Res/55/25).

Sin Sentencias por trata de personas en México desde Nueva Ley de 2007. 2009. EFE [Online, August 27]. Available at: http://www.efe.com/ [accesssed: September 2, 2009].

U.S. Department of State. 2009. Trafficking in Persons Report at 8. citing International Labor Organization data.

U.S. Department of State, Trafficking in Persons Report (June 2009) at 5.

United Nations Treaty Collection. Signature/Ratification Status of the Trafficking Protocol [Online]. Available at: http://www.unodc.org/unodc/en/treaties/CTOC/signatures.html [accessed: Sept. 2, 2009].

PART III
Human Trafficking along the U.S.–Mexico Border

Chapter 9

Human Trafficking and the U.S.–Mexico Border: Reflections on a Complex Issue in a Binational Context

Tony Payan

The U.S.–Mexico border has attracted much attention as a staging area for human smuggling. Considerably less attention has been given to the phenomenon of human trafficking across that same border. Drawing on major debates regarding human trafficking, including its definition and the difficulties of detecting and measuring it within the unique U.S.–Mexico border context, this chapter offers a preliminary glimpse into how the dynamics of the border and the nature of many Mexican and U.S. policies enforced along the border create the conditions for human trafficking to flourish. By allowing human traffickers to hide their activities behind human smuggling and to muddle the ability of law enforcement authorities to separate one phenomenon from the other, the complexities of the border context make it difficult to deal effectively and appropriately with either one of them.

The chapter explores the numerous difficulties in disentangling smuggling from trafficking in the U.S.–Mexico border context. It concludes that human trafficking will not, and cannot, be resolved through its current focus on enforcement of existing laws and regulations and that a more comprehensive set of policies regulating a broader set of border concerns, including migration and trade, is necessary to combat human trafficking. Current policies do little to diminish human trafficking and may actually worsen the pernicious conditions that feed the illicit global human mobility system.

The literature on the U.S–Mexico border features numerous studies on human smuggling from various ideological perspectives and many academic disciplines (Gaynor 2009, Nevins et al. 2008, Segura et al. 2007, Chacón et al. 2006, Maril 2006, Payan 2006, Ellingwood 2005, Dougherty 2004 and others). Over time, this literature has illuminated the issues surrounding human smuggling, particularly undocumented migration and the criminal networks that move people illegally across the border. The complex factors underlying migration have been duly explored, including the "push" and "pull" forces that stimulate migration (Walker 2010, Jenkins 1977) and the migrant network dynamics that channel it in particular ways (Faist et al. 2004, Kuznetsov 2003). The same is true for many other aspects of the U.S.–Mexico border, from its culture, demography, infrastructure, and trade, to its environmental and resource issues, congestion, and pollution. In short, the U.S.–Mexico border is one of the most thoroughly studied borders in the world.

Despite the extensive scholarship on the U.S.–Mexico border, little attention has been directed to human trafficking. A literature search on human trafficking on the U.S.–Mexico border yields very few results, suggesting that we still understand relatively little about its nature, frequency, and the ways it manifests in the U.S.–Mexican borderlands. U.S.–Mexico border scholars confront many of the same challenges as those who study the phenomenon worldwide: how to define human trafficking, how to distinguish it from human smuggling, and how to train border agents to identify and to be sensitive to the differences between trafficking victims and other types of undocumented border crossers. Intuitively we may know that the border itself contributes to human trafficking but since research is scant, we understand little about how and why human trafficking occurs in the region—at least when compared to human smuggling, whose dynamics are better understood.

The questions that frame this chapter are broadly based. Why it is difficult to identify and deal with human trafficking on the U.S.–Mexico border? How does our current focus on illegal drugs, undocumented migration, and human smuggling distract our attention away from this serious problem? How does our preoccupation with human smuggling to the neglect of human trafficking lead us to conflate the two issues? And how does this influence our ability to create effective policies to fight human trafficking in the borderlands?

I shed light on these questions by addressing how and why the United States' and Mexico's border management systems, particularly their immigration policies, set up and magnify the borderlands as a staging area for human trafficking, while at the same time making it easier for it to operate in the guise of human smuggling or other types of illicit migration. I argue that the relative lack of attention to human trafficking is one of the reasons why criminal networks are able to carry out their human trafficking activities largely undetected and unpunished. The chapter concludes with some relevant suggestions for revising our border management system, retraining our agents, and implementing strategies to diminish the problem on the border. In general, the analysis emphasizes the need for future research to explore how the complexities of the border context shape the nature of human trafficking in the U.S.–Mexico borderlands.

Defining Human Trafficking

One cannot speak of human trafficking on this or any binational border without making a clear distinction between human smuggling and human trafficking. The United Nations Protocol against the Smuggling of Migrants by Land, Sea and Air (2000) defines smuggling as the "procurement for financial or other material benefit of illegal entry of a person into a State of which that person is not a national or resident." Human smuggling is characterized similarly by the U.S. Department of State (2010) as "The facilitation, transportation, attempted transportation or illegal entry of a person or persons across an international border, in violation of one or more countries' laws, either clandestinely or through deception, such as the use of fraudulent documents." By contrast, The United Nations Protocol to Prevent, Suppress and Punish Trafficking in Persons defines human trafficking as "the recruitment, transportation, transfer, harboring or receipt of persons, by means of the threat or use of force or other forms of coercion, of abduction, of fraud, of deception, of the abuse of power or of a position of vulnerability or of the giving or receiving of payments or benefits to achieve the consent of a person having control over another person, for the purpose of exploitation." (UNODC 2009)

Human smuggling is an activity in which the victims have consented to participate—in fact they pay for assistance in the (illegal) act of crossing the border without papers or inspection—even through the smuggling often involves degrading or dangerous conditions, such as those present in the hot Arizona desert. The element of consent distinguishes immigrant smuggling from human trafficking even though smugglers, like traffickers, may also abuse, deceive, or coerce the immigrant. A key difference is that human smuggling appears to end once the migrant reaches his or her destination, whereas a human trafficker "captures" his (or much less frequently her) victims and keeps them in confinement in order to exploit them in various activities to produce a profit or derive other benefits for their captors. Human trafficking is, in effect, a kind of modern slavery.

These distinctions would seem to settle the issue, enabling us to distinguish one from the other and to give each the proper attention. But the picture is never that clear, particularly in a border region as complex as that between Mexico and the United States. Human smuggling can turn into human trafficking if the person being smuggled decides to withdraw his or her consent to the arrangement or to end the relationship with the coyote[1] who is acting as a paid "guide," and the latter in response utilizes coercive, deceptive, or abusive tactics to exploit the vulnerability of the smuggled individual for the coyote's financial gain. Sometimes, a human smuggler decides to hold the smuggled person for ransom, while in other instances the person is subjected to labor or sexual exploitation. Identified cases involving kidnapping for ransom, debt bondage, forced labor, extortion, or other forms of criminal victimization by traffickers are not uncommon on the U.S.–Mexico border. Recently, Phoenix, Arizona, acquired the unenviable title of "the kidnapping capital" of the United States (Eslocker, Esposito, and Ross 2009), because so many undocumented migrants were being held in captivity for ransom or debt bondage (Associated Press 2008).

Under these circumstances, it is hard to disentangle smuggling from trafficking. Often we find ourselves having to sort out whether a person actually hired a smuggler or was instead a victim of human trafficking. Someone may have initially consented more or less voluntarily to an illegal activity (e.g. prostitution) only to end up being forced through physical and emotional abuse, confinement,

---

1   "Coyote" is the term used for paid guides who help people cross the international border.

manipulation, or other trauma to submit to exploitation and enslavement. Manipulation may be subtle or achieved by creating emotional attachments between trafficker and victim that create the appearance of voluntary consent.

Threats against the families of the victims are not uncommon. Many cases have come to light of persons held in debt bondage in the United States under the threat of harm to their families back home. Such was the experience of 55 Central American hostages who were held against their will just a few blocks from the international bridge in Tamaulipas, Reynosa, pending payment of ransoms demanded from their families back home (Roebuck 2010). In such situations it can be difficult to identify and prosecute traffickers, particularly because many victims do not want to reveal the circumstances of their confinement or the names of their captors for fear of retaliation against them or their families. And because they are often enticed into the trafficker's hands by promises of jobs in "El Norte" they are difficult to distinguish from more stereotypical smuggled migrants. Defining and detecting human trafficking is very difficult anywhere, but the complexities of the border context compound the challenge, to the detriment of accurate research and effective policy making.

Measuring Human Trafficking

If human trafficking is difficult to define in a way that neatly distinguishes it from human smuggling, there are even more problems when it comes to measuring it. Savona, Stevanizzi, and Stefanizzi (2007) discuss several methodological obstacles to researching human trafficking. These authors emphasize the typical conflation of human trafficking and smuggling and the resulting difficulties for arriving at a uniform definition of the former. Without a reliable method for identifying the two phenomena, we will hardly be able to measure their extent. Moreover, because it is largely a hidden problem and data collection and analysis are notoriously inconclusive, much of what we know about human trafficking is case-specific and anecdotal. This makes it difficult to estimate its size and scope.

The U.S. Congress recently recognized that official estimates of human trafficking are questionable and that data gathering on the subject is terribly fragmented (Government Accountability Office 2007). This could lead either to an underestimation of the problem because much of it goes undetected or to an overestimation of its incidence caused by over-correcting for this fact or mistaking smuggled migrants for trafficking victims. The very nature of trafficking as an "underground" activity makes it difficult or impossible to know its dimensions. Although the State Department's annual report suggests that Mexico is a source, transit and destination place for human trafficking, it does not appear to have reliable data on the incidence or scope of the problem, beyond the limited evidence gathered from a few prosecuted cases or a few individuals rescued from their exploiters (United States Department of State 2007: 148).

The U.S.–Mexico border showcases the methodological problems pointed out by Savona, Stevanizzi and Stefanizzi. Measuring human trafficking is complicated by a variety of factors, including the increasingly clandestine nature of the region and the heavy volume of human smuggling it receives. The likelihood that human trafficking cases will go undetected is magnified because the focus of both law enforcement and the media is almost exclusively on human smuggling. Law enforcement authorities are often reluctant to believe that victims of human trafficking are actually non-consensual victims rather than accomplices to the illegal activity of having hired a coyote to bring them across the border. Thus many victims are "lumped together" with undocumented workers as people who have violated U.S. law by entering the county without official permission. It may be understandable for law enforcement officials to become jaded by their experiences with people lying and to begin to see all law-violators as uni-dimensional. Yet when this happens, these officials are unable to distinguish between trafficking and smuggling and thus are unable to apprehend the traffickers and protect and rescue the victims. Some officials may be inclined to take the easy route and label the case a human smuggling case rather than dig around enough to figure out if the person is a victim of human trafficking. A precise line between consent and coercion is often hard to draw, and depends on the perceptions of the smugglers or the victims as well as the police, which may not always be consistent. Such factors combine to make it particularly difficult to know the extent of human trafficking on the border.

The sheer numbers of people handled as suspects of human smuggling—both victims and perpetrators—are also quite large. Although no one really knows how many people are smuggled across the U.S.–Mexico border every year, the number probably ranges in the hundreds of thousands[2] and law enforcement agencies are overwhelmed by the sheer scope of the activity. I have noticed that most law enforcement officers would rather treat every case as a case of human smuggling and process it as such rather than expend the effort to separate undocumented workers from human trafficking victims. The only distinctions that law enforcement officers seem to try to make, and where they focus their attention and resources, is in trying to find out who is the coyote and who are the undocumented crossers. My impression is that law enforcement officials never really ask whether someone is a human trafficker or a victim of trafficking, an undocumented worker or a smuggler. Skipping these distinctions makes their work considerably easier. Thinking about these differences would only complicate their job and their agency's work load and responsibilities.

Law enforcement agencies in the United States are also somewhat reluctant to ask questions about human trafficking. If any given case makes it to the

---

2 The numbers vary widely and I am becoming increasingly convinced that no one really knows how many there are, how many attempt to cross the border, how many make it, how many are caught, how many are caught only once and how many are caught several times. Moreover, both academics and the media often end up citing a number simply because we heard it from someone else and not because we really know what is going on.

investigation docket for any number of possible reasons, it is not likely to be thought of as a case of human trafficking or to be dealt with as such. Worse, once under investigation a lot of cases are difficult to categorize because the facts are so complex or the parties involved lie to protect themselves (Bhabha 2005). The same thing can happen if the case makes it to court—the evidence is often scarce and distorted, and victims of human trafficking may view themselves as victims of human smuggling or vice versa, thereby confusing rather than clarifying the facts through their testimony. Victims may be intimidated into lying about who they are or giving false testimony. Others may simply not have a clear concept of what has happened to them, or they may be unsure about who their victimizers are. They may have little understanding of human trafficking because they lack access to legal counsel and are unable to learn about U.S. law.

It is not necessarily the case that trafficking is confined to large criminal organizations. Along the U.S.–Mexico border much human trafficking occurs through smaller-scale, more independent entrepreneurs. We know that human smuggling on the border is often the work of smaller groups, often formed of very tight-knit family networks, which prefer not to belong to large organizations so as to remain undetected. It is likely that many trafficking organizations operate similarly, and if apprehended would be confused with smugglers. Even though human trafficking may often be the work of smaller groups, the stereotype that traffickers are always large criminal organizations could allow much of it to go undetected.

If we are to sort out what is happening on the U.S.–Mexico border in regard to human trafficking, it is essential that we conceptualize and define human smuggling and human trafficking as two distinct phenomena and that we measure each one accurately. Strategies for differentiating undocumented workers from victims of human trafficking are critical to this endeavor. This may mean retraining and sensitizing Customs, Border Patrol, U.S. Citizenship and Immigration Services (USCIS) and U.S. Immigration and Customs Enforcement (ICE) agents to enable them to sort out the cases. A sound definition and set of criteria for distinguishing human trafficking should constitute the beginning of a solid methodology for understanding the causes, conditions, and patterns of human trafficking in the borderlands. As we become better able to estimate the dimensions of the problem on the border, our ability to refine our strategies for dealing with the problem will follow suit.

Ultimately, accurate assessment of human trafficking depends on understanding the broader structural context of immigration policy and border mismanagement that contributes to the lack of clarity around the issue of human trafficking on the U.S.–Mexico border. Prior to this discussion, several additional dynamics that deflect attention from this phenomenon must be explored.

The Confusion of Numbers and a Number of Confusions

From time to time a gruesome account of human trafficking may hit the news, but the stories that capture the attention of the public, the media, the law enforcement community, and policymaking leaders on both sides of the border are mostly human smuggling-related tragedies, such as the undocumented workers who perish in the Sonoran desert of Arizona, or the disruption of lives as a result of ICE's pursuit of undocumented workers in workplace sweeps. This may, unwittingly, enable human trafficking to thrive in the guise of human smuggling.

The relative inattention to human trafficking by law enforcement officials and the media as well as the general public is related to the numbers themselves. Documented cases of human smuggling over the decades range in the millions of undocumented persons and in the thousands of human smugglers. The number of individuals serving jail time for human smuggling, including both the smugglers and increasingly under more punitive immigration laws the smuggled themselves, is now in the hundreds of thousands. The numbers in regard to human trafficking on the U.S.–Mexico border are considerably more confusing and imprecise; official estimates range from a few hundred to a few thousand. This is a small amount relative to worldwide trends, where they may number in the thousands and even millions, a discrepancy that highlights the definitional issues surrounding human trafficking.

Between 2001 and 2005, the U.S. Justice Department reported that across the entire United States only 110 human traffickers were prosecuted and just 77 were convicted or pled guilty (United States Department of Justice 2006). In the same period, the quantity of individuals smuggled across the border from Mexico may have been as high as 400,000 a year (Department of Homeland Security 2010). The sheer magnitude of human smuggling, the disproportionate ratio of smuggled persons to trafficked ones among apprehended cases, and the relatively better research data on the quantity of smuggled persons combine to draw our attention away from the problem of human trafficking. Trafficking victims can easily get lost in the flood of numbers that human smuggling overwhelmingly generates. In this sense, rather than clarifying and explaining, the numerical data can instead muddle and confuse.

Conflating the Problem

Complicating our ability to distinguish human trafficking from human smuggling on the U.S.–Mexico border is the increasingly hostile discourse that considers all undocumented migrants to be "guilty" of breaking the law, regardless of how, where, and why they crossed the border. The rhetoric and politics behind U.S. migration policy can lead to stereotypical generalizations that view all "undocumented" people as being alike. This "selective perception" may prevent us from detecting human trafficking unless it is so patently obvious that we cannot ignore it. Anti-immigrant sentiments and stereotypes make it likely that human trafficking victims will be seen simply as undocumented workers who have violated U.S. law and are therefore criminals. The criminalization of undocumented workers may thus doubly victimize those who may have been exploited by human traffickers. And since undocumented workers are often not listened to because

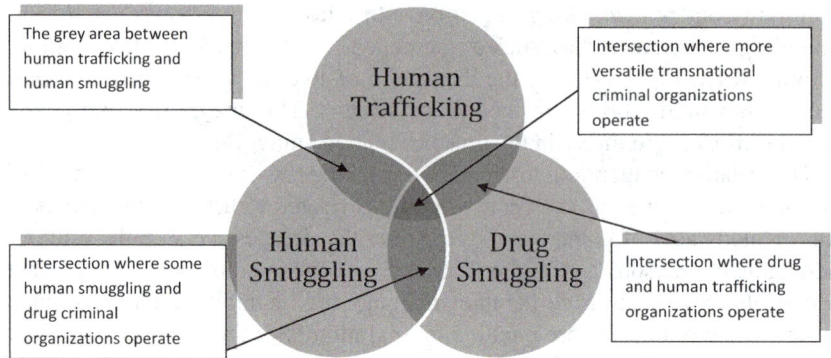

Figure 9.1   Human Trafficking and Human Drug Smuggling: Separate but Intersecting Spheres of Activity

Source: Tony Payan 2011

"criminals" are not seen as being credible witnesses, trafficking victims may never have the opportunity to report their experiences or testify against their captors.

This conflation creates a vicious circle. When there is no way to disentangle human trafficking from human smuggling, it is impossible to detect it. This further reinforces the tendency to focus institutional, political, and legal resources on human smuggling to the neglect of human trafficking, which in turn makes it less likely that trafficking cases will be detected and defined as such.

The law enforcement emphasis on drug smuggling to the neglect of both human smuggling and trafficking further compounds the problem. As Figure 9.1 suggests, these three different "businesses" are still largely separate but they are increasingly intersecting and there is a small area where these criminal organizations may be cooperating across trades. Better training of law enforcement agents and the public at large is essential to enable them to distinguish among the three types of crime. Through education, politicians, immigration officials, and society-at-large may begin to make the necessary categorical distinctions between drug smuggling, human smuggling, and human trafficking (Jordan 2002).[3]

The Transnational Clients of Non-Transnational Human Trafficking Victims

Unlike human smuggling, which by definition has to do with the transnational or transborder movement of people, human trafficking can occur within the boundaries

---

3   This conflation has been expounded in a different context by Ann D. Jordan in Human Rights or Wrongs? The Struggle for a Rights-Based Response to Trafficking in Human Beings (2002), in *Gender and Development*, 10(1), 28–37.

of a country and need not involve cross-border activities. This does not imply that the victims of human trafficking are not made to serve a cross-border clientele. The numerous bordellos, bars, clubs, and other "service" establishments that exist in Mexican border cities and towns are often staffed with persons who have been recruited, coerced, or threatened to offer their "services" to the clients—who may be locals, but frequently are transnational tourists who come to town "to party" and then go back home. This is not a new phenomenon along the U.S.–Mexico border. Movies from the 1950s and 1960s, among them the well-known film *Aventurera*, portray the conditions under which many women were forced into prostitution and exploited in border towns while being made to serve a transnational clientele. In *Aventurera*, a young woman (Mexican actress Elena Tejero) comes from southern Mexico to try to find a job in Ciudad Juárez, Chihuahua, and is seduced and then forced by one of her admirers to provide sexual services in a brothel. She consents to doing so because she feels that she has "no choice." This movie shows how the border has always been dotted with "sin cities" such as Tijuana and Ciudad Juárez, where women and children are forced into prostitution and sexual services in brothels and clubs that mainly exist to serve international clients.

Human trafficking has fed the sex industry that has emerged along the border in a way that reflects the transnational forces that make the border unique—and uniquely susceptible to human trafficking. Yet the transnational aspects of human trafficking should not obscure the fact that much of it goes on domestically and does not cross national borders. This is important because an overemphasis on the transborder component can make it difficult to detect the trafficking and exploitation that stays on one side of the border. U.S. law enforcement agencies along the border may be less inclined to pay attention to it if they see it as out of their jurisdiction because it "does not cross" the border. If it is simply a domestic case, it may get lost in the possible corruption of the Mexican law enforcement authorities. It is hard to believe that the bulk of the trafficking and victim exploitation occurs without the knowledge or even the consent of at least some Mexican law enforcement authorities. Mexican law enforcement officials have been known to look the other way when they detect human trafficking on their side of the border or even to be paid to refrain from looking into it. The corruption of Mexican police forces along the border is well corroborated and nothing new. It is not difficult to formulate hypotheses regarding their neglect of, or outright participation in, these kinds of activities. The ambiguity of the border context makes it easier for such collusion to occur.

Where Human Trafficking and Human Smuggling Intersect

Human smuggling and human trafficking appear to blend together on the U.S.–Mexico border, in part because the multi-layered complexity of the borderlands muddles and confuses the issues surrounding human trafficking and human smuggling. In both situations human beings are turned into valuable "cargo," whether to make money by smuggling them across the border, keeping them hostage to exploit them over a longer period of time, or kidnapping them to demand a ransom from their relatives back home. To understand the fine line between smuggling and trafficking, we must look at the actors, both victims and perpetrators, and the role that each plays in creating, recreating and perpetuating these problems on the border.

On the U.S.–Mexico border, human smuggling and human trafficking are increasingly conducted by the same criminal organizations. This should not be surprising; what motivates these organizations is money, so smugglers are often willing to cross the line in order to enhance their profits. Just as undocumented border crossers are often used as "mules"—drug carriers—human smuggling networks may hold people for ransom or even exploit them, as is shown by, among others, the cases of the Central Americans held in Reynosa, Tamaulipas, and the Mexican undocumented workers held in Phoenix, Arizona. Profit is in fact the reason why human smugglers might cross the line into becoming human traffickers, sometimes without even being aware that they have done so, though this makes them no less culpable. As evidence emerges it becomes clear that it is often done knowingly and deliberately. For example, *The New Yorker* reported on a case where three Mexicans were forced to labor in agriculture, under threats and constant surveillance, for up to twelve hours a day and seven days a week, for almost no pay (Bowe 2003). For them, smuggling was the pretense through which their trafficking and enslavement could occur. The Phoenix kidnapping cases, in which smuggled migrants were held for ransom extorted from frantic family members, also reveal a clear intersection between human smuggling, human trafficking and other crimes such as kidnapping, even though all these phenomena are generally considered to be largely separate business enterprises.

The successes in U.S. immigration law enforcement and the shifts at the policy level, however partial, have compounded the problem by decreasing the mobility of the undocumented population within the United States, and between the United States and Mexico. Undocumented people are now effectively trapped by the specter of being detected, reported and deported by immigration enforcement authorities. This makes them vulnerable to abuse and exploitation because fear of arrest and deportation makes them less willing to report abuses to the police. The Southern Poverty Law Center reports that only about 46 percent of undocumented workers have confidence in local police forces because they know, or at least suspect, that local enforcement officials may cooperate with immigration law enforcement authorities. We recognize these agreements as 287(g) agreements (Southern Poverty Law Center 2009). That same Center has reported that guest worker programs in the United States are also a form of modern slavery because H-2 visa holders are bound to serve a single employer and have no access to legal recourse. The Center describes their circumstances as deplorable. Their jobs are insecure and poorly paid. As "guest workers," they are routinely cheated out of their wages, forced to live in squalid conditions, and denied medical treatment; but their documents are often held by their employers to prevent them from leaving.

Both situations demonstrate that success in immigration law enforcement has come at the expense of worker safety, whether documented or undocumented (Southern Poverty Law Center 2007).

The Roles that the U.S. and Mexico Play in Human Trafficking on the Border

The U.S. State Department's report, *Trafficking in Persons 2007*, classifies countries into three groups: origin countries, transit countries, and destination countries (United States Department of State 2007). It is only natural that if the United States is classified as a "destination" country, the U.S.–Mexico border would be a transit area and a site of considerable human trafficking activity. This is particularly true given the voracious demand for cheap labor in destinations such as California and Texas, though individuals are also trafficked to other locations throughout the United States (California Alliance to Combat Trafficking and Slavery Task Force 2007). The State Department report estimates that between 14,500 and 17,500 human beings are trafficked into the United States every year for exploitation purposes, but few are apprehended. Among apprehensions, Asians and Africans greatly outnumber people from Mexico and elsewhere in Latin America. One possible reason why officials might underestimate Mexican trafficking victims is that the obsession with human smuggling and undocumented labor among Mexican and other Latin American migrants obscures the very real issue of their vulnerability to human trafficking.

Unaccompanied Minors

An important question along the U.S.–Mexico border is whether the issue of unaccompanied minors is more like human trafficking or more like human smuggling. This problem has been growing, given that undocumented workers from Mexico are increasingly unable to move across the border freely and many of them are resorting to having their children brought to the United States by third parties, more and more frequently by organized criminal groups. Often, migrants already living in the United States send money home to have their children sent or brought to the United States, which frequently means that a human smuggler is hired to bring a child across the border (Farmer 2009). If the arrangement ends with the child getting to his or her destination, then the process can be simply classified as human smuggling—even if the child is essentially treated as merchandise "for delivery."

The situation of unaccompanied minors blurs the lines between smuggling and trafficking because there is a vast difference between smuggling an adult—a willing worker—and smuggling a child who may not know what is happening to him or her. A child may be entrusted to a smuggler for transportation (and safe keeping) only to end up being held for ransom or falling prey to illicit labor contractors. Anecdotal evidence suggests that the two may coincide because children are often forced to work while they wait for their relatives to pay the ransom. It is also important to make a distinction between children migrating of their own volition and those who are smuggled by their relatives or even by those who would exploit them—for prostitution, forced labor or services, slavery, or even removal of organs. The border provides opportunities for all these scenarios to occur, but research on these unaccompanied minors is still in its early stages.

Better Enforcement Makes for Better Criminal Networks

When compared with more "respectable" cities in the U.S. and Mexican interiors, Mexican border towns have always had an image of moral corruption as "dirty" places where many Americans go to satisfy questionable habits. Moral corruption shades into political corruption with the participation of the local and state police forces along the border not only in drug trafficking, but also in providing information, protection, and other services to both human smugglers and human traffickers. This official complicity further complicates our ability to sort out the problem of human trafficking on the border.

A large part of the problem is that the U.S. and Mexican governments have been unable to establish appropriate institutions to manage the flow of persons and objects between the two countries. The economic and political asymmetries between the two nations and the relative neglect of border institutions by federal governments in both countries have created a zone along the border where criminal organizations have increasingly honed their skills to transport anything from drugs to weapons to money to human beings. The low institutionalization has created grey areas where these organizations can exist, move and operate freely. Criminal networks exploit the low levels of coordination between law enforcement agencies, including the fact that the authorities do not seem to share databases to detect human traffickers and their victims or even other criminals beyond the drug trafficking business. Moreover, as law enforcement continues to be largely fragmented, ad hoc, unilateral, and top-down, criminal networks have learned the modus operandi of the different law enforcement agencies and have become better at circumventing their activities in order to continue their illicit behavior. The only place where the real effect of law enforcement is felt appears to be the increasing premiums that have to be paid for the goods or services that criminal networks provide, though they appear to do little to impede the trade. Tougher U.S. policies have in fact had the opposite effect. The networks are becoming more adept at their illegal work, joining efforts to perform it and passing information to each other about the best ways to skirt law enforcement. In an ironic sense, better law enforcement has created better transnational criminal networks, including those who would traffic in human beings.

Border Civil Society and Human Trafficking

The confusion surrounding human smuggling and human trafficking that confounds law enforcement, politicians and the media is shared by the people and organizations that constitute civil society in border communities. The preoccupation with human smuggling and the general misinformation about human trafficking may be even more prevalent on the U.S. side of the border than in Mexico. An oral survey among University of Texas at El Paso (UTEP) students showed that the students generally did not distinguish between human smuggling and human trafficking and used the terms interchangeably. In comparison, students at the *Universidad Autónoma de Ciudad Juárez* (UACJ) in Ciudad Juárez were better able to distinguish between the two. This may be because in Mexico the word "*trata*" (trafficking) is never used in the context of human smuggling, while in common U.S. terminology, the terms "trafficking" and "smuggling" are used interchangeably. Juárez students were not well-informed about human trafficking, however, as they often mentioned that trafficking was confined to women and was for the purposes of prostitution. They were somewhat shocked when informed that "*trata*" could also refer to children, workers, and other such victims and was not exclusively a problem faced by women who were forced into sex work. It would seem that on both sides, human smuggling draws the attention of the public and the media while human trafficking is seldom thought about or looked into.

This myopia also affects the non-profit organizations that provide services to victims. There are, for example, numerous activists and organizations that cater to undocumented migrants in practically every city along the border. Many provide services to migrants on their way to the United States, while others serve migrants after being deported, such as the *Casa del Migrante* and other organizations in Mexican border towns that receive the migrants and give them food, clothes, and money to return home. But there are few specialized organizations or safe houses on the border that are dedicated to the victims of human trafficking. This is not only because many of the victims are confused with undocumented workers and their experiences confounded with those of abuse by coyotes or human smugglers, but also because human trafficking is seen as a global problem and not necessarily one specific to the U.S.–Mexico border region.[4]

Structural and "Acceptable" Human Semi-Bondage

A phenomenon known as "structural" exploitation, which denotes a pattern of exploitation that is built into a system of social and economic relations, is well studied in many places but has yet to be applied to the U.S.–Mexico border context particularly in relation to human trafficking. Structural exploitation aptly describes

---

4   See for example, the global focus on the problem by a prominent organization against human trafficking: www.humantrafficking.org.

the daily legal crossers who traverse the border to work, receive low wages and few or no benefits, and then go home at the end of the day with little money in their hands. These legal crossers include the maids, day laborers, nannies, gardeners, and many others who cross to work in U.S. border towns and cities and go home with a mere $20 or $30 dollars in hand after working for eight, ten, or more hours. Researchers (Pisani and Yoskowitz 2002, Ruiz 1987) have studied the U.S.–Mexico border phenomenon of what Pisano and Yoskowitz call the "maid trade." Tens of thousands of women cross the border to work in domestic settings in the United States, typically in poorly paid jobs (even though they are paid a little better than they would be in Mexico) and many of them end up living in American homes, cooking, cleaning, and taking care of children or the elderly with meager pay and no benefits.

These hard-working women, though seemingly free to go, may in fact be the victims of "structural exploitation" because, though they may have the theoretical "choice" to leave at any time, their actual economic circumstances and lack of alternatives may force them to stay in situations of exploitation or victimization (Pisani and Yoskowitz 2002). This is precisely where the border context presents challenges for the study of human trafficking. Although these workers may not technically be victims of human trafficking, their exploitation is no less real and their lack of choice may imply an indirect type of coercion, in that they may end up staying in conditions of exploitation due to forces beyond their control. Structural exploitation may, in fact, be equivalent to human trafficking in many key aspects, though its coercion is more subtle, and its stories unfold in quiet desperation rather than in the flashy headlines of the newspapers and TV news programs that occasionally dramatize trafficking cases. Whether structural poverty is an expression or a cause of human trafficking, if it is not addressed, human trafficking and its quieter varieties such as the maid trade are likely to continue.

The Immigration System and Human Trafficking

The history of the border and the immigration system sheds light on the conditions that can encourage human trafficking. Similarly, current immigration policy leads many cases to go from human smuggling to human trafficking. It is well known that after the *Bracero* or guest worker program ended in 1964, undocumented migration started rising as the difficult economic conditions in Mexico "pushed" people out of the country and the insatiable U.S. labor market "pulled" people from Mexico into the United States. In those days the border was so porous that people were able to come and go on their own. Until the 1980s, hardly anyone needed to rely on a "coyote" to cross the border. Many daily commuters used the areas between ports of entry to come and go every day without documents. Many of us recall standing on the bridge and seeing people wading through the river with their shoes in their hands and then making the run to get lost in the streets of downtown El Paso. After 1994, when Operation Gatekeeper and other similar operations were implemented along the border to impede undocumented crossers, many began to rely on coyotes (called "*polleros*" in Mexico) to cross the border.

As fences went up and the number of Border Patrol agents increased in the larger cities and towns, it became harder to cross in or near urban areas. Undocumented border crossers had to rely on even more "skillful" guides who would lead them through the wilderness for a price that often reached hundreds of dollars. As the situation worsened and more fences and walls were erected, undocumented crossers had to make their way across the border at points farther from urban centers and in more hostile terrain where they were considerably more vulnerable to the exploitative intentions of human smugglers. The price charged by the coyotes increased to stabilize finally in the thousands of dollars per person, which presumably compensated the coyotes for their higher risks. This, of course, provided human smugglers with greater resources that increased the incentives for organized crime networks to enter the business of human smuggling.

As a result, undocumented border crossers have become more vulnerable to exploitation by savvier and more professional criminals who are more likely to victimize them through forced labor, sexual exploitation, or extorting money from them or their families by holding them for ransom. Moreover, as the U.S. environment has become more hostile to undocumented workers, a condition of "entrapment" has ensued wherein undocumented workers have limited mobility and are afraid to call the police if they are not paid for their services or are exploited, because they fear they will be deported. These hostile conditions are ideal for making migrants vulnerable to exploitation yet afraid to complain about it. It may legitimately be argued that when it comes to human rights violations, the effects of these policies may compare with the abuses of human trafficking because they create the ideal conditions for captivity, exploitation, mistreatment, and abuse. American immigration laws and law enforcement agencies and their penchant for punishment and deportation of undocumented persons are creating the exact conditions for greater human entrapment, a quintessential characteristic for exploitation and modern human slavery.

Binational Problems Require Binational Solutions

Texas Attorney General Greg Abbot believes that at least one quarter of the people trafficked into the United States (200,000 out of 800,000) go through Texas. He has identified El Paso and Houston as two major human trafficking staging areas for both forced labor and prostitution (HumanTrafficking.org 2010). Yet, although Attorney General Abbot created a special task force to deal with the problem, coordination with Mexican authorities remains weak. Criminal organizations are thriving in the "gap" in cross-border cooperation—in the "grey area" that exists due to the lack of trust and cooperation between law enforcement in Mexico and the United States, particularly at the local and state levels. Of course, both countries' worries over international drug trafficking—which keeps consuming vast resources and attention on both sides of the border—does not help to keep the focus on human trafficking. But even when governments try to tackle the problem head on, their efforts are confounded by jurisdictional differences and lack of coordination across national borders. While many acknowledge the need and have made some advances in this direction, effective coordination has proven elusive.

A binational approach is essential for confronting the problem. Combating human trafficking must be seen as a common challenge because it begins on one side of the border and ends on the other. The two countries must recognize their interdependence in ways that go deeper than mere rhetoric, and acknowledge that factors such as globalization, economic interdependence and migration patterns are as responsible for human trafficking as the more conventional explanations of organized crime or inadequate law enforcement. Enforcement, particularly unilateral enforcement, is not likely to end the problem. Instead, these root causes must be addressed comprehensively in a much more effective binational (not bilateral) border management system, involving not simply deeper enforcement cooperation, but also investment in education, health care, and other aspects of human and social development.

Without a binational approach that considers how each country's immigration policies impact the other's, human trafficking across the Mexico–U.S. border is not likely to stop. Indeed, it has become clear that one of the major advantages for human traffickers—like all transnational criminal networks—is that they live, move and sustain themselves in that grey area that governments allow to exist by failing to create effective border management systems. Traffickers are well aware of the legal and law enforcement gaps, and they use them to accomplish their objectives by pitting one side against the other. Unilateral enforcement has proven to be ineffective in the context of the U.S.–Mexico border. The United States and Mexico have to collaborate to distinguish between human smuggling and human trafficking and to address each with its own specific set of strategies. Moreover, for both human smuggling and human tracking, governments need to implement measures to address not only the effects of the problem, but also its root causes. An essential first step is to synchronize policies, create binational enforcement teams, and take the aforementioned root causes much more seriously.

There should be little or no disagreement between the two countries that human trafficking is pernicious and that it hurts thousands of people every year, robbing them of all dignity and self-respect. There should be uniform agreement in civil society on both sides of the border that this is a serious problem and that prevention should take priority over punishment. There should be little disagreement among government agencies, branches and levels on both sides of the border that the governments need to close jurisdictional ranks to fight this scourge more efficiently. There may be profound disagreements between the U.S. and Mexican governments regarding many other issues, from immigration to drugs, but in regard to human trafficking there is widespread agreement that should enable cooperation across borders, among branches of governments, and throughout government levels. This consensus should serve to reframe all approaches to combating human trafficking. If we are to create a twenty-first century border, one that is better managed, we need binational structures that have been cooperatively negotiated by both sides so that human trafficking is a point of agreement, not disagreement. In formulating the new agenda, reason would dictate that cooperation should begin with the greatest point of agreement and expand from there. The issues surrounding human trafficking offer many such points of consensus and foci for binational cooperation, and upon this foundation a beneficial relationship could continue to develop and prosper.

Final Recommendations

David Feingold (2005) offers an enormously useful insight into the U.S.–Mexico border and the state of human trafficking along it. Applying Feingold's myth-dispelling insights, we can clarify a number of issues regarding human trafficking in the region, and derive a set of final recommendations for addressing it (Feingold 2005).[5]

Although it is well known that many women and children are trafficked for sexual slavery, Feingold argues that most human trafficking is done for labor exploitation purposes. Following this train of thought, the reality of the U.S.–Mexico border may be that humans are more apt to be trafficked into forced labor in manufacturing, agriculture, and commerce, than into the sex industry. Similarly, evidence is beginning to show that undocumented migrants are often kept in bondage, under various threats, until they pay their smuggling fee or other imposed costs. In both situations, the emphasis on sex trafficking obscures the complex face of human trafficking in the borderlands.

Continuing Feingold's line of argument, it is possible to say that immigration policy on the U.S.–Mexico border has been an abysmal policy failure, but it is often a political success. Tightening the border has proven fruitless in terms of stopping undocumented immigration but it has helped quell the U.S. public outcry that "something be done" to control immigration. Yet it has serious repercussions for migrants in that it exposes them to greater risk of exploitation and captivity because they have to rely increasingly on criminals to make it across the border. And they have nowhere to turn if their smugglers deliver them into trafficking rings or become traffickers themselves when they steal their documents or manipulate, deceive or entrap them in other ways. Tightening the border likely increases the number of individuals who are held for ransom or exploited sexually because desperate people often feel they have no choice but to turn to criminals who are more likely to victimize them.

---

5 Feingold's work is not about the U.S.–Mexico border but, putting together his insights and our knowledge of the U.S.–Mexico border, interesting conclusions and recommendations can be drawn.

In spite of the 2000 Trafficking Victims Protection Act that aimed at prosecuting human traffickers and assisting victims, only a few hundred people have received a T-Visa, which would enable a victim to stay in the United States as a resident after cooperating with the authorities. Until the push and the pull factors that promote undocumented migration are transformed, people will continue to put themselves in the hands of criminals who may exploit them. A few prosecutions and a few hundred T-Visas are not likely to make much of a difference. Addressing the problem of human trafficking in isolation from its root causes is unlikely to bring success. As Feingold argues, trafficking is driven by a host of factors that have to do with economic opportunity, political instability and violence, all of which may propel migrants across the border in search of a better way of life. The reality of the U.S.–Mexico border is that it links two hemispheres with widely different political and economic systems, and the contrast between them continues to spur migration, human smuggling and human trafficking.

Conclusion

Just as it is easy for anyone to believe that human smuggling goes on at the U.S.–Mexico border (the evidence is simply overwhelming), it is very hard for anyone to imagine that in the 21st century slavery and human trafficking would occur as well. There is a systemic, though not necessarily culpable, inclination to deny that human trafficking is a reality on the border. The fact that it masquerades as human smuggling makes it especially hard to detect. And many law enforcement agents, politicians, and policy makers on both sides of the border would prefer to avoid the issue. They want to simplify their work, not compound it. It is already a complicated border where agents must deal with human smuggling, gun-running, drug dealing, money laundering, violence, and femicide, in addition to pollution, water and environmental issues, trade infrastructures and other challenges. It is asking a lot of them to add one more sordid item to the already convoluted binational agenda. It is much easier to ignore the issue or lump it together with human smuggling, or even to claim that it happens much less frequently than victims' advocates suggest, than to invest the time to define it, measure it, disentangle it from other crimes, and create and implement effective policies against it.

But deal with this important problem we must. It would be a mistake for the two nations to allow the human trade to continue to flourish on the border because this would further complicate their binational relationship. Human trafficking on the U.S.–Mexico border symbolizes the failure of the two nations to create and implement an effective border management system. Yet it may be the ideal issue on which the two nations could cooperate because if the facts of its nature and magnitude were confronted head on, neither nation could fail to admit that something must be done. It is around pressing issues like human trafficking that both countries could find it imperative to cooperate and once this cooperation began, it could eventually spread to other border problems. In cooperating to address border trafficking, the two nations could forge a model of binational collaboration that could make it easier for both countries, individually and collaboratively, to address the challenges of the 21st century.

Bibliography

Anderson, B. and O'Connell-Davidson, J. 2002. *Trafficking — a demand led problem? : A multi-country pilot study.* Stockholm, Sweden: Save the Children Sweden.

Anderson, B. and O'Connell-Davidson, J. 2003. *Is Trafficking in Human Beings Demand Driven? A Multi-Country Pilot Study.* Migration Research Series No. 15. Geneva: International Organization for Migration.

Associated Press. 2008. Kidnappings Cross Border into U.S. Cities. *MSNBC News* [Online, January 11]. Available at: http://www.msnbc.msn.com/id/22614102/page/2/ [accessed: November 15, 2009].

Bhabha, J. 2005. Migration Fundamentals: Trafficking, Smuggling, and Human Rights [Online]. Available at: http://www.migrationinformation.org/Feature/display.cfm?ID=294 [accessed: November 16, 2009].

Bowe, J. 2003. Nobodies: Does slavery exist in America? *The New Yorker,* 21, April 28, 106.

California Alliance to Combat Trafficking and Slavery Task Force. 2007. *Human Trafficking in California: Final Report* [Online]. Available at: http://www.humantrafficking.org/publications/613 [accessed: November 18, 2009].

Chacon, J.M. 2006. Misery and Myopia: Understanding the Failures of US Efforts to Stop Human Trafficking. *Fordham Law Review*, 74(6), 2977–3040.

Department of Homeland Security. 2010. [Online]. Available at: http://www.dhs.gov [accessed: May 20, 2010].

Ellingwood, K. 2004. *Hard line: life and death on the U.S.–Mexico border.* New York: Pantheon; reprinted, 2005, New York: Vintage Books.

Eslocker, A., Esposito, R., and Ross, B. 2009. Kidnapping Capital of the U.S.A. *ABC News* [Online, February 11]. Available at: http://www.abcnews.go.com/Blotter/story?id=6848672&page=1 [accessed: April 30].

Faist, T. 2004. *Transnational Social Spaces: Agents, Networks and Institutions, Research in Migration and Ethnic Relations.* United Kingdom: Ashgate Publishing.

Farmer, A. 2009. The New York Times Under Age and Alone, Immigrants See a Softer Side of Detention. *The New York Times* [Online, July 14]. Available at: http://www.nytimes.com/2009/07/15/nyregion/15minors.html [accessed: November 20, 2009].

Feingold, D. 2005. Human Trafficking. *Foreign Policy*, September/October, 26–32.

Gaynor, T. 2009. *Midnight on the Line: The Secret Life of the U.S.–Mexico Border* New York: Thomas Dunne Books.

General Accountability Office. 2006. *Illegal Immigration: Border-Crossing Deaths Have Doubled Since 1995; Border Patrol's Efforts to Prevent Deaths Have Not Been Fully Evaluated.* Report GAO-06-770 to Bill Frist, U.S. Senate [Online]. Available at: http://www.gao.gov/new.items/d06770.pdf [May 20, 2010].

Government Accountability Office. 2007. Human Trafficking: Better Data, Strategy Reporting Needed to Enhance U.S. Antitrafficking Efforts Abroad. Report GAO-06-825 to Chairman, Committee on the Judiciary and the Chairman, Committee on International Relations, House of Representatives [Online]. Available at: http://www.gao.gov/new.items/d06825.pdf [accessed: November 15, 2009].

HumanTrafficking.org. 2010. *New Task Force Aims to Fight Human Trafficking in Texas* [Online, April 5]. Available at: http://www.humantrafficking.org [accessed: May 30, 2010].

Jenkins, C. 1977. *Push/Pull in Recent Mexican Migration to the U.S.* New York, NY: Center for Migration Studies.

Jordan, A. 2002. Human Rights or Wrongs? The Struggle for a Rights-Based Response to Trafficking in Human Beings. *Gender and Development*, 10(1), 28–37.

Kuznetsov, Y. 2006. *Diaspora Networks and the International Migration of Skills: How Countries Can Draw on Their Talent Abroad.* Washington, DC: World Bank Publications.

Maril, R. 2006. *Patrolling Chaos: The U.S. Border Patrol in Deep South Texas* Lubbock: Texas Tech University Press.

Nevins, J. 2008. *Dying to Live: A Story of U.S. Immigration in an Age of Global Apartheid.* San Francisco: City Lights Publishers.

Payan, T. 2006. *The Three U.S.–Mexico Border Wars: Drugs, Immigration, and Homeland Security.* Lanham, MD: Lexington Books.

Pisani, M. and Yoskowit, D. 2007. The Maid Trade: Cross-Border Work. Social Science Quarterly, 83(2), 568–579.

Roebuck, J. 2010. Held for ransom, 55 migrants rescued from Reynosa stash house. *The Monitor* [Online, May 21]. Available at: http://www.themonitor.com/articles/migrants-38916-house-stash.html [accessed: June 10, 2010].

Savona, E. U., Stevanizzi, S. and Stefanizzi, S. (eds).2007. *Measuring Human Trafficking: Complexities and Pitfalls.* USA and Germany: Springer.

Southern Poverty Law Center. 2009. Reporting Crime [Online]. Available at: http://www.splcenter.org/publications/under-siege-life-low-income-latinos-south/reporting-crime [accessed: June 3, 2010].

Southern Poverty Law Center. (2007). *Close to Slavery: Guestworker Programs in the United States* [Online]. Available at: http://www.splcenter.org/sites/default/files/downloads/Close_to_Slavery.pdf [accessed: June 7, 2010].

UNDOC.2009. *Human Trafficking* [Online, United Nations Office on Drugs and Crime]. Available at http://www.unodc.org/unodc/en/human-trafficking/what-is-human-trafficking.html?ref=menuside [accessed: November 16, 2010].

UNODC. 2010. *Migrant Smuggling FAQs* [Online, United Nations Office on Drugs and Crime]. Available at http://www.unodc.org/unodc/en/human-trafficking/faqs-migrant-smuggling.html [accessed: May 19, 2010].

United States Department of State. 2007. *Trafficking in Persons Report* [Online]. Available at: http://www.humantrafficking.org/uploads/publications/2007_TIP_Report.pdf [accessed: November 21, 2009].

United States Department of State. 2010. *Distinctions between human smuggling and human trafficking* [Online]. Available at: http://www.state.gov/m/ds/hstcenter/90434.htm [accessed: May 19, 2010].

United States Department of Justice. 2006. *Report on Activities to Combat Human Trafficking* [Online]. Available at: http://www.justice.gov/crt/crim/trafficking_report_2006.pdf [accessed: May 25, 2010].

United States Department of Justice. 2010. [Online]. Available at: http://www.justice.gov/olp/human_trafficking.htm [accessed: May 20, 2010].

Walker, R. 2010. *Pushes & Pulls: Why do People Migrate? Investigating Human Migration & Settlement.* New York: Crabtree Publishing Company.

Chapter 10

The Best Smugglers in El Paso

David B. Ham

The information in this chapter is based on my 31-year career as a Border Patrol agent along the U.S.–Mexico border. During that time, I spent about 15 years working in the field in duties related to human smuggling. This chapter, based on that field experience, has three main objectives: first, to use the narrative of a case that I worked in the early 1990s to illustrate the strategies used by smugglers to turn their clientele—who paid money and gave their consent to be smuggled across an international border—into human trafficking victims; second, to highlight the complicated transnational networks involved in smuggling and trafficking rings that make the dismantling of such mafias difficult; and third, to explain some of the methods that law enforcement agencies implement to confront the smugglers and traffickers. To avoid compromising any current investigations, the case selected for inclusion is long-past and the names of most of the individuals mentioned in this chapter have been changed.

In the early 1990s, the El Paso Border Patrol's Anti-Smuggling Unit (ASU)[1] worked on two cases in which smuggled immigrants confronted a reality in the United States far different than the one they imagined when they agreed to be smuggled into the country. In both cases, though the undocumented individuals in the cases originally agreed to be transported into the United States with the promise of work, they did so with the understanding that they were going to be working in decent, relatively well-paying jobs. In the case included in this chapter, a group of Costa Rican women agreed to be smuggled into the United States. They did not pay a fee to be taken to the United States like most smuggled individuals, but rather were told they could make big money by entertaining rich gentlemen at a private club. However, when they arrived in the country they were forced into prostitution.

In 1978, with Immigration and Naturalization Services (INS) approval, the United States Border Patrol started an investigative program that targeted human smugglers. Eventually, all 21 Border Patrol Sectors had an ASU working on human smuggling cases. In 2003, with the formation of the Department of Homeland Security, the Border Patrol was put in the Bureau of Customs and Border Protection (CBP). INS investigations and Border Patrol ASU agents were placed in the Immigration and Customs Enforcement Bureau (ICE). The Border Patrol currently has no investigative unit. ICE is generally the lead agency in alien

---

1   Throughout this chapter, the abbreviation ASU is used for "Anti-Smuggling Unit."

smuggling and trafficking cases, although the FBI may also investigate egregious trafficking cases, especially when kidnapping or hostage for ransom are concerned.

It was the mission of the El Paso Border Patrol's ASU in the early 1990s to go after everyone in the smuggling organization being investigated. However, because of legal restrictions, agents could not bring anyone into the United States, or have one of our informants transport human cargo into the country. We could, at the direction of the targeted principal in the case, transport individuals after they were in the United States. This allowed us to identify other principals in the organization, locate drop houses, and develop all the intelligence we could about the organization. Once enough evidence was gathered, and upon approval of an Assistant U.S. Attorney, agents could begin arresting those involved in the investigation.

Smuggling and trafficking organizations often have similar structural features. Although the actual make-up of an organization that transports human cargo may vary from one group to another, there are generally three distinct components: the recruiters, the transporters, and the facilitators or gatekeepers. In the larger organizations, there is usually someone in charge of making the decisions about who gets the lion's share of the money. It is because of their structure that smuggling organizations can quite easily turn their clients (who originally gave their consent to be transported) into trafficking victims through inhumane conditions, bribery, extortion, confiscation of documents, physical confinement and psychological manipulation. The far-reaching influence of international criminal organizations leaves their victims virtually helpless in the new country to which they have been transported.

This chapter describes a case that was worked by the El Paso Sector ASU that involved individuals who were smuggled into the United States and became victims of human traffickers. The experience of the individuals in this case provides insights into the relationship between smuggling and trafficking, the transnational reaches of criminal organizations, and the opportunities and limitations of law enforcement when trying to deal with smuggled or trafficked human beings.

From Hostesses to Sex Workers

One day in the late spring of 1992, Border Patrol Agents in El Paso, Texas, were doing transportation checks at the Amtrak train station just across the border with Mexico. The agents were looking for undocumented immigrants attempting to board the train to travel into the interior of the United States. In the parking lot of the train depot they observed a young man leading two young females toward the station. The young man appeared nervous and continually looked around as if he were trying to spot Border Patrol agents who might be searching for him.

The plain-clothes agents closed in on the group and, as they did, they recognized the guide and he recognized them. The chase was on! The guide was quicker than the agents and soon escaped to the south, outrunning the agents to the border. The young women appeared confused and simply squatted down, trying to hide between some cars. Another agent walked up to the crouching females, identified himself, and soon found out that they were from Costa Rica and were in the country illegally.

The agent began talking to the women. They readily admitted that they were headed to Los Angeles, California, where they had been promised jobs as hostesses. They were reluctant to reveal any details about how they got to El Paso, but they acknowledged that someone was waiting for them in Los Angeles. Upon the return of the other agents, the women were put in an unmarked patrol vehicle and the decision was made to contact agents from the ASU to see if they wanted to interview the women.

Special Agents George Garcia and Rudy Valdez met the agents at a location away from the train depot and began talking to the women. The agents soon determined that they had been smuggled from Costa Rica to Mexico City, and then flown from Mexico City to Cd. Juárez. In Cd. Juárez they stayed in a hotel near the border while waiting for a guide who was to cross them into the United States and take them to the Amtrak station in El Paso, Texas, the U.S. city just across the international border from Cd. Juárez. The women had been accompanied on their trip by a man they identified as "Tino;" it was he who had contacted the guide in Cd. Juárez and paid the fee to the guide to lead the women illegally into the United States. The women stated that "Tino" had told them not to talk to anyone and that they could not leave their room. In addition, he told them that if questioned by anyone, they were to state that they were from Mexico City. One of the women, Blanca, pulled a piece of paper from underneath her shirt and gave it to the agents. On the paper were a name and a phone number that the women had been instructed to call if they ran into any problems. The women said that they didn't know this person, but "Tino" had told them that the person whose name and number were on the paper was a "Chino"[2] and he was very important.

Agents found a card from the All Star Motel on Montana Avenue in El Paso in one of the women's purses. When shown this, the women admitted that they had stayed at the motel for a few days, waiting for tickets to travel to Los Angeles. Iselda, the other woman who had been found with Blanca, then produced a key from the motel. Thinking that there might be other people still in the room at the motel, the group traveled to the motel and entered the room indicated by the Iselda's key, but the room was empty.

Special Agent Garcia then asked the women if they would be willing to help the agents catch the "Chino" in Los Angeles. When the women agreed, I was called by Agent Garcia and asked to meet them at the motel. On my way to the motel, Agent Garcia again called me and said that it appeared that the women's room was being watched by someone in a pickup truck parked across the street, and that I needed to be careful entering the room. Upon arriving at the motel, I

---

2   "Chino" is a general term used in Spanish to indicate an individual who is from one of the many Asian countries, including China, or who has physical features generally considered characteristic of people from Asia.

observed a gold Ford pickup leaving the parking lot of the shops across the street from the motel. When I verified that it was traveling east on Montana Avenue away from the motel, I drove into the parking lot and quickly entered the room.

We began to question the women in greater detail and found that they had been recruited in Costa Rica by an older lady named "La Vieja,"[3] who said she would take them to Los Angeles where they would be employed as hostesses at a private club. When I asked if they meant that they would be working as prostitutes, they became indignant and stated that they were not prostitutes and that "La Vieja" told them that they would just welcome members of the club and let the men buy them drinks.

I then asked them if they would be willing to call the phone number in Los Angeles and tell their contact that they had been chased by Immigration in El Paso and had gotten away. I explained that we would record the call, if they agreed. They were a little reluctant initially, but agreed to make the call after Agent Garcia assured them there would be no problem and that we would tell them what to say before making the call. The women, who had developed a liking for Agent Garcia, agreed. It was decided not to make the call until the evening, allowing us time to coordinate the investigation with the Los Angeles Immigration and Naturalization Service ASU. A lot of paperwork had to be done before proceeding with our plan.

In federal investigations, consensually monitored calls can be made if one of the parties involved agrees to have the conversation recorded. The State of Texas only requires one of the parties to agree to have the conversation recorded. Federal law generally mimics the law in effect in the state where the call is generated—especially if it crosses state lines. Initial calls and several more exploratory calls may be made. If the conversations are expected to continue, then a Request for Consensual Monitoring must be submitted and approved before additional recordings can be made. Since this was our initial call and I didn't anticipate many more, the Request for Consensual Monitoring was not prepared. I did prepare an emergency request for an Undercover Operation, and had it approved by the El Paso Sector's Chief Patrol Agent. If the case developed further, then the paperwork required to work the case would take several days to complete and get approved. Our hope was that the Los Angeles ASU Office had an open case onto which we could piggy-back our case.

A call to the Supervisory Special Agent (SSA) in Los Angeles confirmed that they had an open case on several organizations smuggling undocumented females into the United States to work as prostitutes. It was agreed that if our call to the phone number in Los Angeles worked out, our agents would accompany the women to Los Angeles and the agents under the SSA in Los Angeles would arrest the people who picked up the women after their arrival in Los Angeles.

Returning to the motel later in the evening, I informed the agents of the developments and the plan worked out with the Los Angeles ASU. Blanca then

---

3   "La Vieja" means, literally, "the old lady." It is common in Spanish to refer to people by their physical characteristics or their ages. "La Vieja" can also be a term used for one to refer to his/her mother or his wife.

made the call to the number in Los Angeles. She was very convincing in her story of nearly being caught by Immigration at the train station, about the guide disappearing, and about her (and Iselda's) uncertainty as to whether the guide had been caught by Immigration. She said that they hadn't gotten their tickets and asked for instructions on what to do next. After some hesitation, the voice on the other end asked if they were alone. Looking somewhat surprised, but responding calmly, Blanca responded that no, they were not alone, as they had gotten a ride back to the motel from a woman who had seen them running down the sidewalk. The voice on the other end seemed convinced and told Blanca that someone would deliver the tickets to them at the motel in the morning, and that she and Iselda were to catch the train to Los Angeles later in the day after getting the tickets. When Blanca asked who was to meet her, she was told not to worry about that, that they knew who they were, and instructed her and Iselda to walk to the entrance to the train station in Los Angeles. The person on the other end of the phone then terminated the call.

After replaying the call, we concluded that we had several problems to deal with if we were to accompany Blanca and Iselda to Los Angeles. First, there was the distinct possibility that someone from the organization might be on the train watching the women. Second, it was obvious that the organization knew the women had returned to the motel and that someone would visit them and give them their tickets. We had to make sure that we identified this person, and that we left the women in the room by themselves in case this person showed up unexpectedly.

To solve the first problem, we decided that Agents Garcia and Valdez would accompany the women to Los Angeles but that they would arrive at the train depot in El Paso at separate times. Because of the distinct possibility of someone from the organization being on the train, any contact with the women would have to appear accidental. Both the agents and the women were to refrain from contacting each other unless absolutely necessary.

To solve the second problem, we rented several rooms in the motel where we could observe the women's room, and we had some plain-clothes Border Patrol Agents conduct a mobile surveillance of the area during the night. After making these arrangements, I returned to the El Paso Sector Headquarters to inform my boss of the latest developments. Since the westbound Amtrak train left El Paso in the afternoon and arrived in Los Angeles the following morning, it was decided I would fly to Los Angeles the next day and coordinate the arrests with the Los Angeles ASU. Everything seemed to be going well.

The following morning I was called by surveillance units who reported that a young Mexican male had walked up to the women's room at the motel. After knocking on the door, he entered the room, then about five minutes later he left, walking west for several blocks where he was picked up by a gold Ford pickup with Chihuahua plates. The agents had gotten the plate numbers, but allowed the pickup to return to Mexico through the Santa Fe Bridge.[4]

---

4   The Santa Fe Bridge is an international bridge that connects El Paso and Cd. Juárez.

The women soon made contact with Agent Garcia and told him that they had their tickets and would be leaving that afternoon for Los Angeles. They had been told to be ready for the arrival of a taxi that would take them to the train depot. As I boarded the plane for Los Angeles, the agents were at the train depot waiting to board the Amtrak train to Los Angeles. Our plan was starting to come together.

I was met at the Los Angeles International Airport by the SSA of the Los Angeles INS ASU. He took me to a hotel located near his office in downtown Los Angeles. It was to be my home for the next week. During our ride to the hotel he told me that the Amtrak train arrived around 8:30 a.m. and the depot was fairly close to the ASU office. He said he would pick me up for breakfast around 7:00 a.m. and we would then proceed to the Amtrak Station from there. He also said they would have three or four more agents to help with the arrests.

The following morning SSA Smith arrived at the hotel about 30 minutes late. He said traffic had been bad, but we still had plenty of time for breakfast. I asked how far the Amtrak station was from the restaurant. He said it was pretty close and we would go directly to the station after a quick breakfast. After eating an unsettled breakfast, we left, I thought, for the train depot. SSA Smith then told me he was going to drop by his office to take care of some paperwork and meet with his agents. I reluctantly agreed, but told him we could not be late. Again, he reassured me we had plenty of time and told me that Amtrak was seldom on time.

Arriving at his headquarters, he introduced me to the other agents, then went into his office and started talking on his phone. I asked the other agents if we were very far from the train depot. They replied that we were pretty close and asked what time the train was supposed to arrive. This surprised me, because I thought surely they would have been briefed on the situation. When I told them 8:30, they glanced at the wall clock which said 8:10. The agents informed me that we should probably get going even though the Amtrak train was seldom on time. I had no sooner sat down in a chair when my cell phone rang. It was Agent Garcia saying that they were arriving in Los Angeles and should be at the station on time, maybe even a little early. I panicked.

Agents began running for their cars as SSA Smith hung up his phone and we ran out to his car. I didn't say a word as we began the torturous ride to the train depot. We arrived at the train depot at 8:40. As the agents pulled off of the highway and down into the parking lot, I received another phone call from Agent Garcia, wanting to know where we were. He wanted to know if we had arrested anyone. I told him we had just arrived and were trying to find parking spaces. He uttered a profanity and hung up the phone. I then told SSA Smith to drive to the front of the train station. As we drove up I saw Agents Garcia and Valdez walking out of the station. I jumped out of the car and ran up to them asking about the location of Blanca and Iselda. Agent Garcia pointed to an empty parking space directly in front of the station and said, "They were there, right there. How could you miss them?" Agent Valdez said the car that had picked up the women was a dark colored Lincoln or similar car. He and Agent Garcia had been hanging back, he explained, expecting us to arrest the crooks. He also told us that the men who had picked up Blanca and Iselda were Chinese. At least that gave us a place to start looking—Chinatown.

My agents accompanied the Los Angeles agents as they took off to look for the car with the women in it. It was hoped that they could catch up to them in the morning traffic. Agent Valdez had the best description of the car, but they hadn't been able to get the license plate numbers. SSA Smith had started making calls to the Los Angeles Police Department and the Los Angeles Sheriff's Department. I called my supervisor in El Paso with the bad news that we had lost the women. He was not happy.

After several hours, the agents returned to their office without having located Blanca and Iselda. In the meantime, SSA Smith had set up a meeting with local law enforcement intelligence and gang units for the purpose of getting help in locating the women. It was agreed to establish a task force to begin looking for them and each agent was assigned with a local officer to begin the search.

For two weeks this task force searched the seamy side of Los Angeles, looking for the missing women. I had to return to El Paso after the first week to brief my boss and the Chief Patrol Agent. Technically, the fault in losing the women rested with the Los Angeles Unit, because it was going to be their arrest and to be tied to an open case they had on Chinese gangs and undocumented immigrant prostitutes. I had relied on their expertise and knowledge in making the arrests, yet now had to confront the reality that I was wrong in letting them take the lead in the case when our undercover agents were involved. It was not a mistake I would ever make again.

In Los Angeles, the agents searched furiously for the women, finding and arresting several groups of undocumented female immigrants working as prostitutes for a variety of criminal gangs. But Blanca and Iselda were not found, and the decision was made to terminate our agents' involvement in the search and have them return to El Paso. Agents Garcia and Valdez were angry and sad. Having seen the ugly side of the sex trade during the search for the women, they could only hope that Blanca and Iselda had somehow escaped that fate.

Six months later, Agent Garcia received a phone call from a Los Angeles ASU agent asking him for the number of our undercover phone. Apparently, a Los Angeles Sheriff's deputy had found a young female from Costa Rica and she had given him the phone number and asked him to call the number and ask for Tony, who was an agent. Blanca and Iselda had been found!

According to the Los Angeles agent, a Los Angeles County Sheriff's deputy was driving down a street when he noticed a young woman run into the street and begin waving her hands to get his attention. She was naked. Taking her into custody, she soon led him to a nearby motel and to a room where he located 15 other females in various stages of undress. Other officers were called in to assist and, on the suspicion that the group was in the country illegally, INS investigators were called. Agents soon determined that the whole group was in the country illegally. Located in this group were Blanca and Iselda.

An interrogation of the group determined that all of them had been forced into working as prostitutes, servicing primarily Asian clients. Those who resisted were beaten or threatened with extreme violence by people they identified as Chinese gangsters. They were expected to work seven days a week and to work as long as there were clients. About once a week they were moved to a different motel and were kept in skimpy clothing as a method of ensuring that they wouldn't escape. During the interrogations, Blanca produced the piece of paper with Agent Garcia's undercover name and phone number, and the connection was made with the El Paso office. Several members of the Chinese criminal gang were located and arrested at the motel and, with information from the victims several others were eventually arrested in other locations.

Blanca and Iselda and another female from El Salvador agreed to testify against the Chinese gangsters. They were placed in a safe house in Los Angeles and were guarded sporadically by members of the Los Angeles ASU. Sometime during the months that they stayed at the safe house, one of the women, missing her homeland, called Costa Rica to talk to "La Vieja" and asked for news and for some new clothes. "La Vieja" asked for her address and phone number and said she would send something.

About two months after being rescued, the women were kidnapped from the safe house by members of the Chinese gang and taken to New York by car. We all suspected that "La Vieja" had informed the gang about the women's whereabouts. To keep them from escaping during their trip from Los Angeles to New York, the women were kept in their underwear even though it was now winter time. Arriving in New York, the car stopped at a convenience store and the two gang members left the car to get coffee. Seeing their chance, the women jumped out of the car and began running. Rounding a corner, they ran right into a New York Police car parked on the side of the road. They quickly surrendered to the officers, and led them to the convenience store where the officers arrested the two gangsters.

The women were returned to Los Angeles where they were placed in a motel and guarded 24 hours a day by Special Agents of the Los Angeles and El Paso Sector ASU while waiting for the case to go through the judicial system. All of the defendants in the case were eventually convicted on a variety of federal charges. The women were offered permanent residence in the United States but declined, saying they wanted to return to Costa Rica. They had had enough of life in the United States.

It was later learned that these women and others like them had been smuggled into the United States by the Gloria Canales smuggling organization based in San Juan, Costa Rica. Ms. Canales was a notorious human smuggler, dealing primarily in Central Americans but also suspected of smuggling thousands of Indians and Chinese into the United States, for a price of $6,000 a head. Her organization reportedly smuggled 10,000 people a year into the United States. It was also learned that she had begun supplying female victims to Chinese gangs ("snakeheads") working in Los Angeles and New York. These gangs ran brothels and provided protection for the brothels. She was eventually arrested in Ecuador and deported to Honduras in 1995, where she was charged with a variety of smuggling offenses. INS intelligence eventually identified over 100 individuals who worked for her organization.

Conclusion

The line between smuggling and trafficking in human beings is a fine one that often gets crossed. In the case outlined in this chapter, the individuals who ended up as trafficking victims initiated their journeys with a smuggler. The eventual victims consented to be transported to the United States and knew that once they arrived they would be undocumented. However, though promised or led to believe that the employment they secured in the United States would enable them to earn a decent wage, the victims instead found themselves, whether through coercion or resignation, in an exploitative, slave-like employment relationship. This case illustrates how, once in the hands of people who transport others for profit, unsuspecting individuals can get trapped in debt bondage or other forms of coerced labor, with no way out. For every case such as this one that law enforcement manages to solve, there are hundreds of others that are never discovered.

Human smuggling and trafficking organizations—often one and the same as the case of the Costa Rican women attests—span several countries and continents. Though all of the individuals involved in the case described in this chapter crossed the U.S.–Mexico border from Cd. Juárez into El Paso and beyond, smuggled and trafficked people are transported through various entry points using various means of transportation. They are typically and often forcibly moved long distances with stops in several countries. Smuggling and trafficking organizations are complex, well-organized and transnational; they deal in globalized human misery. U.S. law enforcement officials' dedication to catching smugglers and traffickers once on United States' soil may be the only thing keeping them from enriching themselves at the expense of enslaved and exploited victims.

Chapter 11

Human Trafficking Through Mexico and the Southwest Border: Accounts from Hidalgo and Cochise Counties

Richard J. Schaefer and Carolyn Gonzales

This story is a 21st century human rights tragedy—one that is seemingly preventable, but politically expedient. It tells how employment-seeking migrants and border residents have been harmed by a political rhetoric that conflates citizens' fears of crime, terrorism, unemployment and the costs of providing education and health services to the foreign-born and their offspring. The tale relates how a once porous and safer border that permitted a migratory ebb and flow of people across it has been progressively closed, particularly in the wake of 9/11 when the newly formed Department of Homeland Security (DHS) started to make it more difficult for Latin American family members and migratory laborers to obtain U.S. entry visas, thereby funneling undocumented immigrants into clandestine crossing routes along the U.S.–Mexico border.

Tighter border enforcement efforts have squeezed off the most common legal and illicit migratory pathways into the United States and delivered a new, increasingly lucrative human contraband to transnational drug smuggling organizations that have expanded people-smuggling and human trafficking operations by seizing control of old human migratory pathways and developing new routes through urban barriers and across the most remote areas of the massive U.S.–Mexico land border. In the process, Mexican citizens are caught in a deadly war erupting among crime syndicates seeking control of profitable border crime, and ranchers and residents of rural counties in the Southwest United States are caught in a no-man's-land traversed by hoards of border enforcement personnel and ever more armed and dangerous criminals delivering undocumented immigrants and drugs to employers and drug users in the United States.

All the while, people who make the difficult decision to migrate toward the United States find themselves in the throes of a new group of unscrupulous human smugglers who are just as likely to view the hapless and vulnerable migrants not as paying customers with inalienable human rights, but as contraband to be trafficked and exploited for maximum profitability. Although this unfolding tragedy is evident across the migrant transit routes through Mexico and along the nearly 2,000-mile U.S.–Mexico border, this chapter focuses on how these processes have affected migrants from Central America as they attempt to travel through the rugged Hidalgo and Cochise Counties of New Mexico and Arizona and the Mexican States of Chihuahua and Sonora, which abut them to the south.

Sealing the U.S.–Mexican Border

Sealing the 1,951-mile U.S.–Mexican border is daunting because it includes some of the most desolate and rugged terrain in North America. To that end, U.S. Customs and Border Protection Commissioner Alan Bersin estimated that by the close of 2010, some 655 miles of fencing were in place, along with an expanded Border Patrol force of over 20,000 agents, many stationed at key highway checkpoints and observation towers. Fencing and human systems are augmented by manned and drone aircraft and 38 mobile radar and camera surveillance stations (Testimony of Alan Bersin 2010). This led DHS to conclude that it had achieved what it calls "effective control," enabling it to detect and respond to illegal entries over 837 miles of the U.S.–Mexico border and coastal regions, even though more than half the southern border remains unfenced (Mora 2010).

U.S. Customs and Border Patrol relies on a three-pronged approach to prevent unwanted border crossings and achieve "effective control," including use of fencing and other fixed barriers, Border Patrol personnel, and various forms of technology. The above illustration shows that most of the border fencing is located on the western half of the U.S.–Mexico border. The most stringent fencing and barriers are placed in urban areas where it would only take a few seconds for a crosser to become immersed in the urban population. In this instance the fence, which might only take 20–30 seconds to climb with the aid of ropes, buys the Border Patrol a few additional seconds to intercept the intruder.

In rural areas where there is fencing or barriers, the Border Patrol has minutes to hours to intercept the crossers before they arrive on foot to a spot where they could meld into the U.S. population. Finally, in areas designated as "remote," those who climb or traverse barriers need days or weeks to get to a spot with sufficient population or vehicle traffic to enable them to blend into the population (personal communication, Border Patrol wall and facilities tour: El Paso Sector, February 16, 2011).

When this system is functioning, U.S. Customs and Border Protection (CBP), a subdivision within DHS, maintains that it has achieved "effective control" of that portion of the border. CBP defines this goal as the "appropriate balance of personnel, technology, and infrastructure" that consistently enables it to: "1) detect illegal entries in to the U.S. when they occur; 2) identify the entry and classify its threat level; 3) efficiently and effectively respond to these entries; and, bring each event to an appropriate law enforcement resolution." (U.S. Department of Homeland Security 2010)

Yet in testimony before Congress, Richard Stana of DHS acknowledged that by Sept. 30, 2010, the Border Patrol had achieved operational control in preventing unlawful entry into only 873 of the roughly 2,000 miles of the U.S.–Mexico

Figure 11.1 U.S. Customs and Border Protection Map 2009

Source: Carolyn Gonzales and Richard J. Schaefer 2009

border, though the length of the border under control was increasing annually (Testimony by Doris Meissner 2011, Testimony of Richard Stana 2011). Thus, much of the border itself is not "sealed" and many of the most remote western border regions are easily penetrated by determined crossers who can rely on the many gaps in the systems and their almost unbounded ingenuity and desperation to come north. Nevertheless, these remote migration and smuggling routes can be dangerous, since they require special knowledge to navigate the harsh terrain, adequately prepare for what can be a 20- to 60-mile desert or mountain trek, and arrange for a rendezvous to get them through the checkpoints the U.S. Border Patrol has strategically set up on highways leading north from the border areas.

Although urban regions of the border have the most intimidating walls and barriers, they too are hardly impenetrable. Tunnels and sewers may be the most common routes taken in urban regions, but corruption and deception are also used frequently to bring people through closed urban borders. Mexicans who look like other Mexicans can "rent" legitimate documents to cross at busy border checkpoints, and those with sufficient funds can be waived across by U.S. customs and border officials who are on the take. But both methods require specialized knowledge of the border region and few indigent migrants have sufficient funds to buy their way across the border in such style. The poorest migrants, many who come from rural Mexico or Central America, lack sufficient resources to buy off American authorities. They tend to cross in the most desolate and unforgiving desert or mountainous terrain where the Border Patrol rarely ventures because it considers these areas to be natural barriers to human movement. Many walk for days in the Southwest's most remote areas before reaching their rendezvous point.

This is known as the "funnel effect" because the migrants are literally funneled into the harshest, most dangerous terrain. In 2009 alone, even though the number of crossers and apprehensions appeared to be down, the Border Patrol found a record 417 migrant bodies, mostly in remote deserts and mountainous areas (Medrano 2010). Yet CBIG studies suggest that the official migrant death toll underestimates the actual number of deaths by a factor of three, but their remains are never found in the desolate terrain.[1] Indeed, in this rarely patrolled, scorching terrain, crossers tend to strip naked as they begin to succumb to heat prostration, and animals, insects and extreme heat can obliterate a corpse in less than a month, leaving few traces for searchers to discover (Personal Communication, videotaped interview, Dr. Bruce Parks August 21, 2009). And the Border Patrol has its hands full along the New Mexico and Arizona border detaining and rescuing live crossers, leaving few resources to search for migrant remains.

---

1   For more funnel effect background and the story of one young man who died crossing, see CBIG's "Closing of the Border and Funnel Effect" article, 2009, at: http://www.cbig.unm.edu/ClosingBorder&FunnelEffect.php; and the CBIG video, *Funnel Effect in the Arizona Desert* video, 2009, featuring Raquel Rubio-Goldsmith and Robin Rieneke at: http://www.vimeo.com/11635584.

Despite the dangers, the migrants keep coming. Even areas with high fences are penetrable by desperate journeyers and well-connected smugglers and human traffickers who capitalize on their desperation. Alberto Melis, police chief of Douglas, Arizona, said, "No wall has ever worked." Douglas is a border town in Cochise County that abuts Agua Prieta, Douglas's sister city in the Mexican state of Sonora. Melis, a Cuban immigrant, recalls how migrants, smugglers and human traffickers have cut and driven through various types of fences, dug tunnels, flown over the border in ultra-light planes and even scuba-dived through flooded sewers to enter his community, which has become dependent on what he calls a "law enforcement economy" fueled by hoards of DEA, ICE and Border Patrol agents (Cross-Border Issues Group 2010b, 2010f). He also says that most of the 20,000 residents of Douglas, which he describes as a close-knit Hispanic community, still have relatives on the other side, making them ambivalent about completely sealing the border.

Although the entire border has increasingly become more closed since the Clinton administration initiated Operation Gatekeeper in California in 1994, DHS officials recognize that their agency is unlikely ever to receive the massive amount of funding and personnel required to create a near-impenetrable barrier along the full 1,951 miles shared by Mexico and the United States. Even Commissioner Bersin recently acknowledged that the best way to ensure genuine border security would be to develop a viable labor market between the United States and Mexico, as opposed to depending upon the illegal low-wage worker system that now exists (Mora 2010).

Current work visa policies are at the heart of undocumented immigration. In 2009 the United States granted 30,000 H-2A agricultural work visas, and in 2009 and 2010 Congress capped the number of low-skill H-2B work visas at 78,000 a year, authorizing an annual total of 108,000 low-skill work visas for all types of low-skill work applicants from around the globe. Yet even during the 2008–2009 recession, economists placed the U.S. demand for those types of low-wage, low-skill jobs at four to five times the number of available authorized visas, and the imbalance continues today to fuel a huge demand for undocumented workers.[2] Given that such minimum wage jobs might pay six or more times as much as similar work in Mexico, and perhaps as much as 15 times the wages for equivalent work in Honduras, if such work could even be found, there is little doubt that desperate workers from south of the border will continue to risk life and limb to satisfy the needs of U.S. employers for legal or illegal low-wage labor. And jobs are not the main incentive for the Mexicans and Central Americans who are heading north to reunite with family members. It is difficult to imagine what type of border barriers could deter them, particularly Central Americans, whom many U.S.

---

2 For more background on migrants' reasons for migrating north, see: Cross-Border Issues Group video entitled *North American Trade Policies and Migration*, 2009, available at: http://www.vimeo.com/12730849; and Richard J. Schaefer's, "NAFTA and Immigration" audio story from the radio documentary, *Perspectives on Mexican Immigration*, CBIG, 2008, accessible at: http://www.cbig.unm.edu/PerspectivesMexImmDoc.php.

citizens mistake for Mexicans. Indeed, formal complaints filed by undocumented Central American migrants traveling through Mexico suggest that the journey to the U.S.–Mexican border is generally more perilous than the dangers they face when trying to cross into the United States.[3]

Residents of Hidalgo County in southwest New Mexico typically say that their border with Mexico could be sealed through a combination of visible Border Patrol personnel and technology. They assert that the United States can accomplish nearly anything it decides to do, and that sealing the border is within its grasp, if the nation makes it a priority (Cross Border Issues Group 2010d). Rather than attempting to seal off the entire southern boundary of the United States, the Border Patrol relies on a strategy that conserves its personnel and infrastructure resources. It places most of its personnel at highway bottlenecks that migrants and smugglers need to pass through after they have crossed via the more remote areas along the border. The Border Patrol recognizes that it need not use great haste to intercept those migrants who must walk for days to reach a rendezvous point in the United States. Utilizing this "checkpoint strategy" also enables DHS to reserve costly fencing and other infrastructure for areas where crossers can blend into crowds or easily be picked up and taken to major highways and transportation arteries. "So in an area where it could take hours or days to make it to a pick-up spot, you don't necessarily need pedestrian fencing in that area," says Steven Cribby, public affairs officer for DHS. "You can utilize personnel—agents—and you can utilize technology to detect the entry, and you have more time in those open areas to make an apprehension." (Cribby 2010)

Based on this strategy, much of rural Hidalgo, Grant and Luna Counties in southwestern New Mexico and Cochise, Santa Cruz and Pima Counties in southern Arizona, may have Border Patrol stations located 20, or even 80, miles from the U.S.–Mexican border. With the U.S. Border Patrol focusing on highway choke points that are often scores of miles from the border line, ranchers and farmers whose land lies between the border and those law enforcement chokepoints may see themselves as collateral damage in border politics, living in a no-man's-land awash with migrants, smugglers who guide them, and drug and human traffickers affiliated with violent gangs and transnational crime syndicates.

That degree of illicit traffic was not as evident decades earlier when labor visas were plentiful and more urban transit routes were relatively open. Then there was no "funnel effect" driving migrants through uninhabited terrain, and even those migrants without visas could typically cross the U.S.–Mexico border without the aid of informed people smugglers, who have come to be called "coyotes" or "*polleros*."

---

3 For a glimpse into the types of abuses Central American migrants endure when coming north, see Richard J. Schaefer's PowerPoint video entitled *Casa de Migrante: An Albergue System Profile* at: http://www.vimeo.com/11242603. Also see Associated Press, "Honduras: 10,000 Migrants Kidnapped in Mexico," Dec. 30, 2010 in the *Miami Herald's* Americas AP online: http://www.miamiherald.com/2010/12/29/1992669/honduras-10000-migrants-kidnapped.html.

From the Bracero Program to Smuggling to Human Trafficking

During the 1940s and 1950s, contractors with the Bracero Program were encouraged to recruit large numbers of Mexican workers to come north to take seasonal positions on ranches and farms, and fill other needed low-skill jobs. Long-time Grant County resident Cecil Waldrip describes the program as "abusive" because the Mexicans only cleared about $15 a month after paying fees for room and board, and contractors had taken their cut. "When they work a month of hard labor for $15 and a contractor makes the most out of that, to me that's not right," says Waldrip. "It's abusive; it's practically slave labor." (Cross Border Issues Group 2010a)

From the 1960s (when the Bracero Program ended) through the 1980s, individuals and small groups of workers continued to come across the border, with or without documents, to work on ranches and farms in southern Arizona and New Mexico. Typically they were seasonal employees going to specific worksites guided by prior experience or word-of-mouth. At that time, no one seemed too concerned whether these seasonal workers had documents. "That's always been a part of life out here, having illegals," says former Hidalgo County sheriff, Bill Cavaliere. "Back in the old days usually you would have one or two coming across, and they were looking for work." (Cross Border Issues Group 2010e) During those decades, the Mexican and Central American migrants who were coming north could cross at a border town or simply walk a mile or two outside the border checkpoint to enter the United States.

In the 1980s and early 1990s, Latino migrants often hired coyotes to help them get across the border, obtain fake documents and arrange rides or flights to get the undocumented migrants to their ultimate destination in the United States. The flights would depart from southern-tier U.S. cities, such as Phoenix or Dallas, to places north, such as Chicago, San Francisco or New York. When driving their clients northward, the coyotes paid off people who would drive ahead of them and call back to help them avoid immigration and customs checkpoints set up by the Border Patrol. These "mom and pop" coyotes would advertise in small towns in southern Mexico, and often accompanied their clients northward through Mexico and across the border. Although clearly in the people-smuggling business, their fees were not lucrative, perhaps $350 to $1,500 a person, including U.S. airfare and meals while driving, and they often knew the people they were smuggling and vice-versa. It was a small business operation, in which participants often knew each other and typically enjoyed some personal relationship and sense of trust, as coyotes and clients often came from the same small towns and had family ties.[4]

All that gradually became more difficult in the early 1990s, as political pressures to slow undocumented worker migration began to mount, requiring

---

4 Cross-Border Issues Group participants have interviewed dozens of migrants and several coyotes who crossed the border at various times. This information is taken from those interviews.

the Border Patrol to clamp down on traditional urban border crossing sites and increase its visibility at key chokepoints north of the border. Instead of farm hands and agricultural workers looking for work in the U.S. Southwest, crossers were increasingly headed to California or northern states looking for jobs in the service sector. The Southwest U.S. border counties were no longer destinations for migrant workers, but rather transit routes for migrants being funneled through the region to destinations throughout the United States.

> "Since 1986 I think the number of illegals dropped drastically, and it has continued to drop," says Hidalgo County resident Harold Kuenstler. "Illegals are going through here. They're not stopping here. Ranchers don't hire them here. . . . They can't depend on them because [of the increased presence] of the Border Patrol." (Cross Border Issues Group 2010e)

At that same time, stepped up pressure on the Colombian drug cartels enabled transnational organized crime syndicates based in Mexico to dramatically increase their share of the U.S. illicit drug trade by moving larger quantities of drugs across the U.S.–Mexican border. Residents in rural areas as far as 80 or 100 miles north of the border, such as Cecil Waldrip, perceived an increase in the number of migrants transiting through their ranches and farms, with the new breed of migrant appearing more aggressive and less hard working, as well as more likely to be headed for sites north, than those who had come seeking work in prior decades. Waldrip says New Mexico Route 180, which runs from the Mexican border north through Grant County up to Colorado, gradually became a transit route for both larger numbers of migrants and drugs. As the Border Patrol began to focus its resources further south, the agency reduced its visibility in the northern sections of Route 180. "Twenty, 30 years ago, there were always Border Patrol checkpoints along 180, which I haven't run into in years now," Waldrip recently said. "And they [the Border Patrol] were more aggressive at that time than they are now. They've evidently made their presence in other areas, rather than in this area."

But even though the Border Patrol may have moved its stations and key chokepoints closer to the border in recent years, it still has not satisfactorily addressed the security concerns of ranchers and farmers with property near the border. Cavaliere says that currently, undocumented workers are increasingly coming in larger groups led by someone associated with a criminal organization. He added that if the locals spot one or two lone migrants, they usually represent the type of migrant they used to see commonly. He said that they, too, have been victimized (Cross Border Issues Group 2010e).

Rancher and former schoolteacher Ed Kerr says that in recent years ranchers have avoided hiring Mexican migrants, instead preferring to work through contractors to obtain seasonal labor. He said that by the 1990s landowners could be fined $10,000 for hiring "illegal or undocumented aliens, and when that came out, that's when we stopped working them." (Cross Border Issues Group 2010e)

A border that was hardly sealed came to be viewed by many Americans as a national security risk in the wake of the al-Qaeda attacks on Sept. 11, 2001. Less than two years after 9/11, President George W. Bush and the U.S. Congress created the Department of Homeland Security, charging it with coordinating border security, customs and immigration and naturalization efforts under the direction of cabinet-level leadership. In a climate of near-hysteria over international terrorism and speculation about dangerous foreign nationals entering the United States, the border became a prominent wedge-issue for both major U.S. political parties, as Republicans called for sealing the southern border completely while Democrats courted the growing Hispanic vote by proposing ill-timed and tepidly-backed immigration reform legislation that called for tighter border security as part of its reform packages. Despite a lack of evidence that terrorists had ever managed to exploit the relatively porous U.S.–Mexico border, migration from the south and terrorism had become conflated for many Americans, and DHS had to deal with that political reality. What analyst Edward Alden characterized as the nation with the most open immigration and border policies prior to 9/11, would have to spend billions trying seal its borders from unsubstantiated threats (Alden 2008).

The CBP budget more than doubled from 2004 to 2010, and the number of CBP employees also doubled until there were 20,700 of them in 2010. The overall 2011 DHS budget has grown to more than $56 billion, with immigration and border security units, such as CBP ($11.2 billion), ICE ($5.8 billion), U.S. Citizenship and Immigration Services ($2.8 billion) and the Coast Guard ($10.0 billion), accounting for more than half the total DHS funding (Department of Homeland Security 2011). Furthermore, the FBI, DEA, and the Bureau of Alcohol, Tobacco, Firearms and Explosives (ATF), along with various state and local law enforcement agencies, also spend billions more annually trying to interdict illicit shipments of drugs, firearms and various sorts of transnational contraband, including those who smuggle and traffic in people and false documentation. Finally, the Mérida Initiative, which was signed into law in June 2008, provided nearly another half-billion dollars in law enforcement and military aid to Mexico and Central American countries to combat transnational organized crime and money laundering.

In recent years, the Tea Party, anti-immigrant media commentators who have rallied the populist ranks of U.S. workers fearing competition from cheap foreign labor, and anti-immigrant organizations such as Numbers USA, the Federation for American Immigration Reform and the Center for Immigration Studies, have pushed the U.S. Government to dramatically increase deportations and law enforcement efforts along what has become a highly "militarized," if not perfectly sealed, U.S.–Mexican border (DeParle 2011). Their anti-immigration rhetoric supports policies that limit the number of foreign-entry visas and portray undocumented migrants as criminals in the eyes of many American citizens. These anti-immigrant voices present the stream of Spanish-speaking migrants as a threat to U.S. workers, American cultural values and the rule of law. Proponents of this anti-immigrant movement have called for get-tough zero-tolerance policies that would treat all undocumented immigrants as lawbreakers worthy of swift punishment and removal.

Ironically, the many billions of dollars spent annually on stepped-up border law enforcement, migrant deportations and efforts to prohibit drug trafficking and seal the border to illicit migration have created a more lucrative environment for gangs and transnational criminal organizations. This is because the U.S. demand for illicit drugs and unskilled labor appears to be inelastic—they are relatively unaffected by increasing prices. In this sense, it is like the U.S. demand for foreign oil. When one source of foreign oil becomes threatened or gets cut off, the price of oil rises dramatically but the demand declines only slightly. Those oil companies, producers and cartels that can still deliver oil see their profits rise dramatically. Those elements in the oil import chain that are still open for business realize windfall profits, as the oil importers profit even more when one of their competitors has its import pathway shut down.

Similarly, when it becomes more difficult and expensive for a particular TCO to import drugs into the United States, the demand does not go away; the drugs merely become more expensive, which makes the profit margins even greater for those gangs and transnational cartels that still have the ability to deliver the drugs. The winning cartels can afford to pay more for production, transport and distribution of drugs because the relatively inelastic demand increases the price. Therefore when one route for importing drugs is cut off, another, perhaps more dangerous and risky route takes its place, and the financial incentive for developing new routes grows, as the TCO that controls the new route sees its profits multiply. This has been going on since long before President Richard Nixon officially declared a "war on drugs" in 1972.

Similarly, the pull of low-wage work in the United States has been so great for Mexicans and Central Americans who have little chance of ever making even a few dollars an hour in their home country, that as the border has become better sealed, the price for smuggling people across it has simply increased. Even when the financial crisis and recession drove down U.S. demand for construction workers, the demand for other forms of low-skill labor in the United States did not abate. Furthermore, labor conditions in countries like Honduras had deteriorated so badly during the recession of 2008–2010 that it made more sense than ever for Central Americans to seek jobs in the north. In short, the push-pull migratory factors had not changed; only the price of crossing the border had changed, and that cost went up three or four times faster than the burgeoning annual budgets of DHS, ICE and CBP. An illicit border crossing and transit to a U.S. city that might have cost $500 in 1995, could cost between $3,000 and $6,000 in 2010. And because of the funnel effect, the 2010 migrants had to take a more perilous route and deal with a new kind of coyote guide—anonymous people who took greater risks and had to make more money to pay off gangs and larger organized criminal groups for the privilege of working the newly-developed routes through some of the most hazardous terrain on earth.

Migrants had to deal with men they did not know and who had fewer scruples than the old coyotes from their villages. As the border crossing business became more lucrative and rationalized, migrants were handed off from one coyote to another, with each coyote performing a specialized task along the route, and with each coyote expecting to earn greater profits off the migrants. Coyotes, the weakest and least organized and protected links in a series of highly entrepreneurial, and often competitive, criminal smuggling chains, now have to exact a large enough toll from migrants and their families to pay off gangs, corrupt border officials and TCOs who protect and enable the smuggling and who have no qualms about killing to control what has become a multi-billion dollar a year criminal enterprise.[5]

In such an environment, the line between smuggling and trafficking can be very thin. The United Nations High Commissioner for Human Rights recently defined human trafficking as "the recruitment, transportation, transfer, harbouring or receipt of persons, by means of the threat or use of force or other forms of coercion, of abduction, of fraud, of deception, of the abuse of power or of a position of vulnerability or of the giving or receiving of payments or benefits to achieve the consent of a person having control over another person, for the purpose of exploitation." (Recommended Principles and Guidelines 2002) Given this broad definition, many undocumented Mexican migrants and perhaps a majority of all Central American migrants are trafficked as they head north. Even before they approach the U.S. border, undocumented Central American migrants must traverse parts of Guatemala and the length of Mexico, with its armed gangs and corrupt authorities who assist local gangs that rob migrants, take them hostage to extort money from their families, and force them into the sex trade and to assist in trafficking drugs.[6]

Most undocumented Central American migrants jump aboard freight trains to travel from the Guatemala border through Mexico. Many start out with some cash, jewelry, and perhaps even a cell phone. But they soon are relieved of their cash and any valuable items by various corrupt border guards and thieves they encounter on their way north. The cell phone is the most dangerous item in their possession, as it would typically have the numbers of relatives, which would make them prime targets for kidnapping and ransom. Indeed, migrants quickly learn to destroy telephone numbers or other forms of identification that organized gangs can use

---

5   This information was obtained from dozens of anonymous interviews of migrants and coyotes by Cross-Border Issues Group participants near the U.S.–Mexican border and throughout the Central America-to-United States migrant route, as well as information provided by *Colegio de la Frontera Norte* immigration and human mobility researcher, Dr. Rodolfo Rubias Salas, in a videotaped interview with Richard J. Schaefer in Ciudad Juárez, Chihuahua, México, May 2009.

6   For a sense of the trafficking faced by Central American migrants on their way through Mexico, see Richard Schaefer, *Casa de Migrante: An Albergue System Profile*, a recorded presentation to the Crises and Opportunities in Latin America conference at the University of California, Riverside, in April 2010: http://www.vimeo.com/11242603.

to identify and extort money from migrants' loved ones. Getting kidnapped and having their families shaken down for money is even worse than death for most migrants, who often begin their journey northward to get a job and send home money to relieve financial pressures on their families.

Migrants who ride the rails may stay for free for one, two or three nights and receive meals at various church-run shelters, or "*albergues*," that have been established along the most frequented rail yards to provide migrants with a safe place to sleep and eat. Although perhaps as few as one-in-eight migrants who have been beaten, robbed and trafficked will consent to file an official complaint called a "*denuncia*," many *albergues*, such as the large facility in Ixtepec in the southern Mexico state of Oaxaca that is run by Padre Alejandro Solalinde Guerra, now have thousands of highly detailed complaints about migrant trafficking in various regions of Mexico. These *denuncias* could easily be compiled into a detailed record of criminal culpability on the part of gangs and local law enforcement officials who have participated in robbing, kidnapping and exploiting migrants for the drug and sex trades. Nevertheless, no government officials have bothered to end this impunity by using these thousands of *denuncias* to prosecute or harass the criminals. It was not until December 2010 that the governments of Mexico and Honduras officially acknowledged the problem, and that acknowledgment came only after an unusually well-publicized incident in which seven gunmen kidnapped nine Central Americans from a train near Ixtepec, less than a week after 50 other migrants had reportedly been kidnapped in the same region (Associated Press 2009).

Gangs, sometimes with assistance from coyotes, force vulnerable migrants into "stash houses," where migrants are held captive until they consent to further demands by the traffickers. Sometimes adolescent migrants and young women will be required to enter the sex trade, or simply be repeatedly raped on their journey. At other times, a migrant may be forced to deliver other unsuspecting migrants into the hands of the stash house gang. Others will be required to serve as "mules" to carry drugs through the Southwest desert into the United States. Sometimes, stash house criminals simply threaten migrants with reporting them to authorities who would deport them, forcing migrants to start their journeys anew.

Undocumented migrants will not typically go to the authorities after suffering abuse because they fear that the local authorities work closely with the cartels and stash house gangs, or they worry that the authorities will not acknowledge the migrants' inherent human rights, but will instead treat them like criminals for entering Mexico illegally. In fact, just as Mexican and Central American immigrants are vilified and viewed as criminals by many Americans and the sheriffs they elect, so too in Mexico do some local authorities pander to the immigrant-loathing sentiments of their constituents. For many Mexicans, Central American migrants are to be shunned and punished, just as many residents of Arizona and Georgia would prefer to see local law enforcement adopt a get-tough zero-tolerance stance toward undocumented Mexican immigrants. This leaves most migrants unwilling to report abuses against them, making them vulnerable to the most unscrupulous and corrupt elements in Mexico.

This is the primary reason it is so difficult to get the Central American migrants who have been abused in Mexico to file *denuncias*. Despite local authorities' failure to act upon the thousands of *denuncias* that have been filed, the all-too-common crimes against undocumented migrants came to public attention in August 2010 when a group of Los Zetas executed 72 migrants in a stash house in the northern Mexico state of Tamaulipas. The migrants had reportedly refused en masse to contact their relatives for ransom or to carry drugs across the border.

In April 2011, another 177 bodies were discovered in mass graves in Tamaulipas. This time the migrants, who apparently included some Mexican migrants with papers, had presumably been pulled off buses for traveling under the direction of coyotes who had not paid extortion fees to move their migrants through a region claimed by a rival cartel. Thus, just as with the far more lucrative drug trade, under the cold logic of cartel warfare, one cartel presumably robbed another of its profits by destroying its human cargo, rather than see its territory successfully invaded by a rival. "It's just business," Mexico City security analyst Alberto Islas was reported to have said when blaming the Zetas, whom he claimed had been charging smugglers $400 to $500 (USD) per head to transport migrants through their territory, with $100 to $200 required in advance and the balance paid once the human contraband had reached the United States (Bosque 2011). When the smugglers failed to pay the extortion fee, the Zetas destroyed their cargo.

More than 200 additional undocumented migrants, including several children, who were traveling to the U.S.–Mexico border, were kidnapped from a freight train en route from Ixtepec to Veracruz on June 24, 2011, according to an Amnesty International communication based on accounts by migrant eyewitnesses who escaped and returned to Padre Alejandro's *albergue* to report the incident.[7] Like so many incidents of this type, this event received no coverage in the mainstream U.S. media.

On Dec. 18, 1990, the United Nations General Assembly adopted a resolution, the International Convention on the Protection of the Rights of All Migrant Workers and Members of Their Families. The Convention recognizes the need to respect the human rights of all migrants and members of their families, irrespective of their migratory status. For workers with permission to enter a country, those rights specifically include legal due process prior to expulsion, equal employment conditions to those of native citizens for equal work performed, access to the same educational opportunities for their children as native citizens, and the right to transfer earnings home once employment has been severed. The Convention emphasizes the need to reform policies that support the use of undocumented labor by clamping down on smugglers and employers who hire them, and prevent human trafficking by imposing "effective sanctions on persons, groups or entities that use violence, threats or intimidation against migrant workers or members of

---

7 Amnesty International and the Yahoo Groups listserv "borderworkinggroup" reported this incident in an email sent to various border researchers, including Richard Schaefer, on June 27, 2011, and resent on June 28, 2011.

their families.." This would spread the pain of enforcement to larger segments of the society, rather than strictly punishing migrants (Office of the United Nations High Commissioner for Human Rights 2005).

By 2005, 33 nations, including Mexico, Honduras, El Salvador and Guatemala, had endorsed the Convention, but the United States was not a signatory. Despite signing the Convention, Mexican officials were slow to acknowledge the extent of the trafficking abuses that Central American migrants faced when transiting through the country. It was not until February 2011 that Mexico's National Human Rights Commission formally admitted that at least 11,333 mostly Central American migrants had been kidnapped by cartels during a six-month period in 2010. That acknowledgement also indicated that the numbers of abuses were rising, that kidnappers typically demanded from $1,000 to $5,000 (USD) for each migrant's release, and that the Mexican human trafficking gangs typically utilized Central American informants and ties to Central American crime groups (Castillo 2011). Nor is it at all clear that the Department of Homeland Security and U.S. State Department have made significant efforts to put an end to such abuses. Since it has become a political priority of both U.S. parties to slow the flow of foreign workers across the U.S.–Mexico border, the trafficker brutality might serve that end by discouraging Central American migrants from coming north. And neither the United States nor Mexico appears to have taken advantage of the thousands of *denuncias* filed by Central Americans who suffered and witnessed abuses, to identify and prosecute kidnappers, traffickers and murderers who prey on the Central American migrant stream. In Mexico and the United States, foreign migrants lack sufficient political constituencies to pressure elected and appointed officials to curtail the abuses.

Living in No-Man's-Land

Those who have lived for decades along the U.S.–Mexico border claim that they often view themselves as collateral damage caused by smugglers and drug and people traffickers, as well as ineffective U.S. border policies. People living on isolated ranches and farms often feel that they reside in a lawless no-man's-land in which nearly anything can happen.

In a group interview in the fall of 2010, several Hidalgo County New Mexico residents noted that increases in the number of Border Patrol agents had failed to prevent nuisance crimes and occasional violence on their farms and ranches. "Everyone…could sit here for hours and hours and tell you about the stolen cars, the ranch gates left open, and the rustled cattle," Harold Kuenstler said. "There was this huge increase, not only in the illegals themselves, but in the crimes connected to them." That situation led Kuenstler, who had worked for the Border Patrol for 29 years, to question whether a lack of political will was contributing to violence along the border. "If you go back and look through history, the border has always been violent, but not to the degree it is today. And not with politicians that ignore it." (Cross-Border Issues 2010d)

Against this backdrop—and with passage of Arizona's get-tough immigration law, SB 1070—the murder of Cochise County rancher Rob Krentz on March 27, 2010, drew national attention, particularly from anti-immigration media outlets. Reports suggest that Krentz had stopped his four-wheeler when he came across someone on his land, as he was known to do when encountering migrant foot-traffic. Several hours later, he and his dog were found shot, with tracks leading back toward the Mexican border. This was the most high profile murder of a U.S. citizen in the region since Chad and Betty Grabe were shot by Mexicans in the early 1980s (Archibold 2010a, Cross Border Issues Group 2010e).

Krentz's family offered a statement after his death. "We hold no malice towards the Mexican people for this senseless act but do hold the political forces in this country and Mexico accountable for what has happened," it read. "Their disregard of our repeated pleas and warnings of impending violence towards our community fell on deaf ears shrouded in political correctness. As a result, we have paid the ultimate price for their negligence in credibly securing our borderlands." (Archibold 2010)

In the previously cited group interview, former law enforcement agents Kuenstler and Cavaliere criticized CBP's "checkpoint strategy" when they called upon the U.S. government to place agents on the border literally to seal it and deter unauthorized people from getting across. But these politically conservative border residents also cited concerns over human rights issues and the Obama administration's reluctance to alienate Hispanic voters as reasons preventing the DHS from using more effective tactics to close off illicit border traffic.

Rancher and farmer Sheila Massey lives a few miles south of the small town of Animas in Hidalgo County—an area often referred to as New Mexico's Boot-heel. She too would prefer to have the authorities seal the border rather than rely on the checkpoint strategy. "Is it not easier to patrol 81 miles [along the Boot-heel-Mexico border] than not to secure the border and drive all over the ranches, here in the Boot-heel and in Southern Arizona? If you get to the border and stop them there, you don't have to drive all over the ranches and leave gates open where cattle get out." (Office of the United Nations High Commissioner for Human Rights 2005)

Other Boot-heel residents describe incidents involving delayed responses by Border Patrol and apparent apathy by federal law enforcement as putting them in danger. Rancher Kerr recalled how he and his son investigated a nighttime fire and scattered a large group of presumably undocumented transients who had started a campfire near Kerr's mother's house. Kerr called the Border Patrol. "We're 20 minutes from Lordsburg, where their station is. No one ever showed up. My son and I drove down there [toward the fire]... And looking back, I think we took a high risk to be approaching them like that in the dark... But we were very upset that we called the Border Patrol. They did not even respond to our call. They never did show up." (Cross Border Issues Group 2010c)

Although groups of migrants in transit may not pose a significant enough threat to bring out authorities promptly, border residents claim that signs of drug smuggling will. Most rural residents told CBIG interviewers that they had found parcels of marijuana and other drug trafficking evidence on their lands.

"On our ranch...My son called the Border Patrol," said sheep rancher Tricia Elbrook. "They had a bunch of illegals coming through... And they [Border Patrol] came in with a helicopter and picked up the drugs they had dropped. But they left the illegals running through his backyard. And he called and said, 'Hey, I've got all these illegals running through my backyard. And they [Border Patrol] weren't concerned about that; all they wanted was the drugs. They brought the helicopter up, loaded the drugs and left. They didn't care about the illegals." (Cross Border Issues Group 2010c)

In spite of the priority apparently placed on interdicting drug traffickers, Bootheel residents are particularly concerned about smuggling routes along the Peloncillo Mountains and other north-south mountain ranges that run from northern Mexico into the United States. Farmer Sheila Massey recalled how in a regional meeting with Border Patrol officials, the Border Patrol acknowledged that smugglers "own the mountains." She said that law enforcement officials admitted that they could not control the area's mountain ranges because the smugglers had advanced technology and could see the officials approaching and rain firepower down on them (Cross Border Issues Group 2010e).

Massey also claims that when drug and migrant smugglers have had to cross ranches and farms that are far from the Border Patrol stations, these criminals have intimidated some of her borderland neighbors. She said that "good law abiding citizens, farmers, ranchers" see things going on that normally they would report. "[They] won't report it because of fear of retaliation, especially if you live along the border," she said. She added that failure to report is now the norm and part of the problem. "You should have freedom of speech to report something that's going on that you know is wrong, but you've been told, 'you do and you will suffer the consequences.' And these are people from the other side of the border that are dealing in the illegal activity... You're supposed to turn a blind eye to it. And what's sad is it has become a way of life. Instead of it being a rare thing. It's a normal thing," she said (Cross Border Issues Group 2010e).

Organized Crime Permeates the Border

Greater pressure from law enforcement produces bigger profits for international crime operations that are well-enough networked; sufficiently armed, violent and intimidating; and possessing enough resources to buy off corruptible officials and thereby defeat DHS and Mexican efforts to curb smuggling. As the border tightened, the profits from smuggling drugs and workers to meet the demand in the United States went up.

Contemporary border smugglers and traffickers work closely with organized criminals on both sides of the border, including corrupt Mexican and U.S. border control officials who will often redirect migrants back north if they have been apprehended by honest ICE or Border Patrol. This allows crime syndicates with ties to particular gangs and their stables of coyotes to rationalize the increasingly profitable human smuggling business so that they now can guarantee passage across the border. Of course, all this has raised the cost of crossing, which by the fall of 2010 was running between $3,000 and $6,000 per migrant, depending upon the crossing point, with the California border commanding the highest prices. Nevertheless, this is the cheapest tier of the multi-tier pricing system for smuggling undocumented people across the U.S. southern border.[8]

This lower tier of border crossing activity relies on the vulnerability of undocumented migrants and their families to ensure payment once the migrant has been reunited with family or has obtained work in the United States. Hence, it is the typical mode of entry for unskilled, impoverished migrants from Central America and Southern Mexico without gang connections. Often this type of entry requires migrants to walk for days with a coyote guide through harsh terrain or endure other hardships when crossing. They are something like modern-day indentured servants, because they are still indebted to the smugglers or traffickers after they cross the border. Migrants who fail to make good on their debts risk having themselves or their families punished, or simply turned over to ICE for deportation.

In the Mexican states of Chihuahua and Sonora, which are contiguous with New Mexico and Arizona, there are preordained staging areas for lower-tier migrant crossers to rendezvous with guides who will take them to a crossing point and spirit them across the border. Migrants go to dormitory-like houses, called *"casas de huéspedes,"* or "guest houses," to wait for their final-stage coyotes. Migrants may wait for a few hours or a few days, with food and lodging at the *casa de huéspedes* covered within their pre-arranged crossing fee. The migrants have no idea where they will cross, and must be ready to follow their guide at a moment's notice. The Sonoran city of Altar, located approximately 60 miles south of the Arizona border, is the most notorious place for making such a rendezvous and the most likely departure point for migrants crossing through Cochise or Hidalgo Counties (Gonzales 2010).

Douglas Police Chief Alberto Melis reports that migrants crossing in the Southwest desert may have their debt forgiven by acting as "mules" carrying bales of marijuana for miles across the border for pick-up in the United States. Sometimes, when prospective migrants reach a staging area such as Altar, they have not yet made arrangements with someone who can take them across the border. This is a precarious scenario, particularly for Central and South Americans, because Altar has many "stash houses"—places where unsuspecting migrants are kidnapped and terrorized by often brutal criminals until the migrants' families pay additional ransoms, or the

---

8   This section is based on CBIG's dozens of anonymous interviews with undocumented migrants in transit in Mexico, Guatemala, Honduras and the United States. It also draws upon information provided by shelter workers, the families of migrants and knowledgeable NGO and governmental immigration officials, as well as specifically cited information and press accounts.

traumatized captives agree to cooperate in further illicit activities, such as luring in other clueless migrants, transporting drugs or working as prostitutes.

The trick for stash house criminals is to convince both migrants and local authorities that they will do anything to protect their business without creating incidents that could incur the wrath of Mexican Federales or the U.S. Department of Homeland Security, or produce sufficient moral indignation to threaten their presumably lucrative business operations. For example, the March 27, 2010, murder of Arizona rancher Rob Krentz and the Aug. 24, 2010, execution of 72 migrants in Tamaulipas both made international headlines, which at least temporarily brought new scrutiny from law enforcement officials on both sides of the border (Archibold 2010a, 2010b). Ironically, many Central and South Americans go north to escape the type of violent criminals who now dominate border smuggling and trafficking activities.

Because CBIG researchers have had many opportunities to meet impoverished migrants heading north, the group's researchers obtained far more information about the bottom tier of those reaching and crossing the Southwest border without documentation. Most information about the more elite forms of illicit migration comes from hearsay from lower-tier migrants and anonymous migration and law enforcement sources on both sides of the border. A few former law enforcement officials have gone "on the record" and a few press accounts provide confirmatory glimpses into the more costly modes of transiting the border.

Some migrants will pay from $20,000 to $30,000 to cross, and their transit is less physically arduous than the route taken by impoverished workers coming north. These higher-paying migrants, who sometimes come from Asia, Africa, or the Middle East, typically have transport across the border. CBIG has been shown evidence of semi-trailer trucks that each transported more than 80 migrants through Mexico and toward the United States. Obviously, to be waived through the border, this smuggling involves complicity of U.S. border authorities. It is also very lucrative, with each truckload producing approximately $2.5 million in revenue.

Former U.S. Border Patrol Agent Kuenstler describes this high-income smuggling as a relatively new development in the Southwest: "We've been apprehending smugglers for many, many years. And it used to be a couple hundred dollars to get them up from the border… It is very costly today, and you'll have some illegals that are paying $30,000. They are indentured until that is paid, because they don't have a penny. They are indentured in this country, the land of the free, until that is paid, and sometimes that's many years. It's a bad thing, but it's a profitable thing for these rings that are trafficking human beings." (Cross Border Issues 2010e)

Kuenstler also recognizes that "when you start putting that much money into something, it has the tendency to become more violent, which affects everyone's security along the border, because the person that's paying that wants to succeed, and the person that is receiving that wants to succeed. And sometimes that is at all cost." Although he describes "99 percent of the people along the border, as honest and hard-working," his law enforcement experience also tells him that "money makes people weak." (Cross Border Issues Group 2010e)

An anonymous Mexican immigration official described the highest human smuggling tier on the U.S.–Mexican border as involving multinational operations, typically bringing in well-funded individuals from countries that might ordinarily trigger extensive background checks, such as Iraq or China. These migrants will pay between $70,000 and $85,000 for international transport and a complete set of European documents, which allows them to cross with the aid of compromised immigration officials, despite the fact that the incoming migrants do not generally fit the profile of their European country documents.

A *Wall Street Journal* story on April 16, 2010, described a raid on an international human smuggling network centered in Arizona's Maricopa County as the largest human smuggling bust in U.S. history. In the article, journalist Miriam Jordan quoted ICE chief John Morton as saying human smuggling into the United States had become a multi-billion-dollar international business. Morton stated that the Arizona ring had charged Chinese nationals up to $75,000 apiece to enter the United States at the Arizona border (Jordan 2010). In October 2010, Mexican federal police arrested the purported leader of a global human trafficking ring that brought Chinese migrants to New York via Mexico by issuing counterfeit passports and visas. Some of the migrants, reportedly contracted to pay $80,000 for entry, did not even realize that they were also being brought into Mexico illegally. A CNN report on the arrest noted that approximately 1 percent of undocumented migrants in the United States have come from China, with the U.S. Border Patrol apprehending 6,000 Chinese nationals between 2005 and 2008 (CNN Wire Staff 2010).

Should the human smuggling across the U.S. southern border produce average revenues of between $4,000 and $8,000 per undocumented crosser, it could easily be generating as much as $1-to-3 billion a year in revenues for organized crime. But that figure pales in comparison to frequently cited estimates of the approximately $25 billion annually produced by the illicit cross-border drug trade. $26-to-$28 billion can buy a lot of corrupt law enforcement officials, especially in Mexico where so many honest border citizens fear cartel violence, and high levels of distrust permeate various law enforcement agencies. With such high stakes money involved, it is not too surprising to hear migrants' stories of corruption, theft and abuse at the hands of Mexican criminals as well as immigration and law enforcement officials.

Despite the best efforts of many in law enforcement on the American side of the border, the U.S. Southwest is hardly squeaky-clean or immune to the corrupting influences of big money. Maureen Meyer of the Washington Office for Latin America, an NGO, sees some stylistic similarities between the smuggling and kidnapping of migrants in Tamaulipas and the budding human trafficking business evident in the state of Arizona. Meyer has suggested that such stories highlight the "vulnerability of migrants in both countries." (Frontera NorteSur 2010)

In the small border town of Douglas, Arizona, Mexican Consul Oscar de la Torres Amezua describes such criminal problems as binational. "It's not just the

Mexican cartels that are working here," he said. "It's the Arizona cartels. . . . The most important thing we need to see is that one side does not have responsibility for these things." (personal communication, videotaped interview Consul Oscar de la Torres, October 1, 2010)

Although numerous CBIG interviews suggest that law enforcement corruption is far more prevalent on the Mexican side of the border, clear evidence exists that a number of authorities on the U.S. side have also been recruited by criminal elements. In the fall of 2010, prosecutors convicted six Border Patrol agents of abuse or corruption, including the successful prosecution of agent Martha Garnica, who had been compromising U.S. border security for a dozen years. In a six-year period, 114 U.S. Border Patrol and customs agents had been arrested for corruption (Connolly 2010, Dilanian 2010). "Cartels based in Mexico, where there is a long history of corruption, increasingly rely on well-placed operatives such as Garnica to reach their huge customer base in the United States," *The Washington Post* reported. "It is an argument often made by Mexican officials— that all the attention paid to corruption in their country has obscured a similar, growing problem on the U.S. side of the border." (Connolly 2010) Perhaps even more telling, *The Washington Post* piece also reported that the inspector general of U.S. Customs and Border Protection—the agency that includes the Border Patrol—investigated approximately 775 employees in the 2009–2010 fiscal year, and placed an additional 228 ICE employees under investigation.

According to Mexican Consul de la Torres Amezua, corruption and brutality have also found their way to Cochise County, Arizona. He says that Mexican migrants filed approximately 250 formal complaints against American authorities in Cochise County between 2006 and 2010. Consul de la Torres Amezua blames much of the brutality on a climate in which the migrants are viewed as criminals, rather than as honest people trying to reunite with their families in the north or find work. For Police Chief Melis, the distinction can be tricky. He recounted the story of a rancher who arrived home after a long day riding the range. "[And he finds] four or five undocumented aliens sitting on his front porch waiting to ask for permission to clean up and drink the water out of his horse trough," Melis said. "[They are] waiting to ask for permission to drink from the water that is there for the horses.. And that crystallizes the problem for me. How to tell the people that are such gentlemen and been raised so right that they will not drink water that a horse drinks from, without permission, from the kind that will kill you because you are in their way when they're moving dope." (Cross Border Issues Group 2010b)

For years Mexican government officials have been saying privately that the drug war on both sides of the border has been a failure and a boon for internationally organized criminal syndicates. These Mexicans say they can only hope that the United States will someday come to its senses and emulate what it did 80 years earlier when it repealed the ban on alcohol. That repeal provided the liquor industry with legitimacy at the same time that it deprived Chicago and Detroit mobsters of their greatest source of income and power. That sentiment finally became public in 2011, when the blue ribbon Global Commission on Drug Policy issued a scathing report calling for an end to the failed "War on Drugs" and for the decriminalization of drug use (Global Commission on Drug Policy 2011). Its members not only included former Mexican President Ernesto Zedillo and writer Carlos Fuentes, but former U.N. Secretary General Kofi Annan, former U.S. Federal Reserve Chair Paul Volcker and former U.S. Secretary of State George Schultz.

Drug policy is not the only impediment to border security. As long as U.S. immigration policy fails to address the need for unification on the part of millions of family members now divided by the border, and the very real need for foreign labor on the part of many U.S. employers, it is difficult to imagine a border that will ever be both safe and secure. For her part, rancher Sheila Massey links the overall border policy with U.S. law enforcement's shortcomings in Hidalgo County. "I think there is a lot of stuff that could be stopped, but it's too economically viable to the system," she said. Massey implied that there must have been communication between the U.S. authorities and Mexicans engaged in illicit activities when she recalled how crimes that had been happening on a monthly basis suddenly stopped when some fed-up ranchers told law enforcement officials, "If you don't stop it we will." Massey said, "It stopped. So somebody had to have told somebody, 'Look, they're laying for you.'" (Cross Border Issues Group 2010d)

Furthermore, ramping up various levels of law enforcement to fight smuggling cartels and thwart "undocumented aliens" is not without its unintended consequences. Mexico has learned that its armed forces are blunt instruments that often alienate the local populations they were mobilized to protect. Forced to intercede in the low-intensity wars between competing criminal cartels and to collaborate with local law enforcement, the Mexican Army has revealed its lack of nuance and local knowledge, as well as its inability to preserve human rights as it attempts to take control of the situation. Similarly, the U.S. Department of Homeland Security now has tens of thousands of ICE and Border Patrol agents to deal with smuggling, trafficking and violence along the U.S.–Mexican border. Those agents must implement often-conflicting priorities of local and national interests and be responsive to changing political winds. It is inevitable that friction would exist between them and resident ranchers, farmers and local law enforcement officials who can remember the days when the borders were more open and the few migrants one might encounter were gentlemen looking for work.

Bibliography

Alden, E. 2008. The Closing of the American Border: Terrorism, Immigration and Security since 9/11. Council of Foreign Relations: Harper Collins.

Archibold, R. 2010a. Ranchers alarmed by killing near border. The New York Times [Online, April 4]. Available at: http://www.nytimes.com/2010/04/05/us/05arizona.html [accessed: April 5, 2010].

Archibold, R. 2010b. Massacre in Tamaulipas. The New York Times [Online, August 29]. Available at: http://www.nytimes.com/2010/08/30/opinion/30mon3.html [accessed: August 30, 2010].

Associated Press. 2010. Honduras: 10,000 Migrants kidnapped in Mexico. Associated Press [Online, December 29]. Available at: http://www. miamiherald.com/2010/12/29/1992669/honduras-10000-migrants-kidnapped. html#ixzz19sQmwWOB [accessed: December 30, 2010].

Bosque, M. 2011. Los Zetas' brutal business model. Texas Observer [Online, May 3]. Available at: http://www.texasobserver.org/lalinea/los-zetas-brutal-business-model [accessed: May 5, 2011].

Castillo, E. 2011. More than 11,000 migrants kidnapped in Mexico. The Associated Press [Online, Washington Post Online]. Available at: http://www. washingtonpost.com/wp-dyn/content/article/2011/02/22/AR2011022207120. html [accessed: February 23, 2011].

CNN Wire Staff. 2010. Mexico captures suspected Chinese migrant smuggler. *CNN* [Online, October 23]. Available at: http://www.cnn.com/2010/CRIME/10/23/ mexico.smuggling.arrest/ [accessed: October 24, 2010].

Connolly, C. 2010. Woman's links to Mexican drug cartel a saga of corruption of U.S. side of border. Washington Post [Online, September 12]. Available at: http://www.washingtonpost.com/wp-dyn/content/article/2010/09/11/ AR2010091105687.html [accessed: September 12, 2010].

Cribby, S. 2010. DHS Public Affairs telephone interview with University of New Mexico: Talk radio news service intern Sofia Sanchez [Online, April 19]. Available at: http://www.goear.com/listen/2c5b46b/dhs-steven-cribby-steven-cribby [accessed: October 10, 2010].

Cross-Border Issues Group Video. 2010a. Cecil Waldrip on migration and smuggling in Grant county [Online]. Available at: http://www.youtube.com/ watch?v=-munScXVZo [accessed: December 28, 2010].

Cross- Border Issues Group Video. 2010b. Douglas, Arizona Police Chief Alberto Melis. The Border is not black and white [Online]. Available at: http://www. youtube.com/watch?v=GCqQRLDY [accessed: October 1].

Cross-Border Issues Group Video. 2010c. Rancher and farmer problems on the New Mexico border with Mexico [Online]. Available at: http://www.youtube.com/wa tch?v=pNvgtgx7Imw&feature=related [accessed: December 24, 2010].

Cross-Border Issues Group Video. 2010d. Ranchers & Residents of Hidalgo County, N.M. on Sealing the Border and Intimidation [Online]. Available at: http://www.youtube.com/watch?v=NOb6sZCGxA8 [accessed: July 7, 2010].

Cross-Border Issues Group Video. 2010e. Recent History of Border Crime and Migration in Hidalgo County, New Mexico [Online]. Available at: http://www. youtube.com/watch?v=AAK7rHnILv0&feature=related [accessed: December 24, 2010].

Cross Border Issues Group Video 2010f. Smuggling and the Law Enforcement Economy of Douglas Arizona [Online]. Available at: http://www.youtube. com/watch?v=Kl2_7aEi4D8 [accessed: October 30].

DeParle, J. 2011. The Anti-Immigration Crusader. The New York Times [Online, April 17]. Available at: http://www.nytimes.com/2011/04/17/us/17immig. html?pagewanted=1&_r=1&emc=eta1 [accessed: April 17, 2011].

Department of Homeland Security. 2008. FY 2011 Budget in Brief, Homeland Security [Online]. Available at: http://www.dhs.gov/xabout/budget/ gc_1214235565991.shtm [accessed: February 22, 2011].

Dilanian, K. 2010. Border Patrol is grappling with misconduct cases in its ranks. Tribune Washington Bureau for the Los Angeles Time [Online, September 7]. Available at: http://www.latimes.com/news/nationworld/nation/la-na-border-patrol-20100908,0,5346494.story [accessed: September 7, 2010].

Fronter NorteSur. 2010. FNS Special Report- Mexico's Arizona movement. FSN Online News- email distributed newsletter, fnsnews@nmsu.edu [Online, August 29]. U.S.–Mexico border news, Center for Latin American and Border Studies, New Mexico State University, Las Cruces, New Mexico.

Global Commission on Drug Policy. 2011.War on drugs: Report of the global commission on drug policy [Online, June]. Available at: http://www.glabal commissionondruge.org/Report [accessed: June 30, 2011].

Gonzales, C. 2010. CBIG visits Altar, Sonora, Mexico. UNM Today [Online, October 7]. Available at: http://www.news.unm.edu/2010/10/cbig-visits-altar-sonora-mexico/ [accessed: February 22, 2011].

Jordan, M. 2010. U.S. News: Immigration raid targets vast network—Authorities arrest 47 alleged leaders of human-smuggling chain stretching from Mexico to Phoenix to cities across U.S. Wall Street Journal, 16 April, A-3.

Medrano, L. 2010. Border deaths for illegal immigrants hit record high in Arizona Sector. Christian Science Monitor [Online, December 16]. Available at: http://www. csmonitor.com/layout/set/print/content/view/print/350118 [accessed: December 17, 2010].

Mora, E. 2010. U.S. Government does not have 'Effective Control' of 1,081 miles of the U.S.–Mexico Border, DHS Says. CNSNEWS [Online, October 19]. Available at: http://www.cnsnews.com/mews/article/us-government-does-not-have-effective-co [accessed: October 21, 2010].

Office of the United Nations High Commissioner for Human Rights. 2005. Fact Sheet N.24 (Rev. 1): The International convention on migrant workers and its committee. New York and Geneva: United Nations.

Recommended Principles and Guidelines on Human Rights and Human Trafficking. 2002. Office of the High Commissioner for Human Rights: United Nations. Presented as addendum to Economic and Social Council.

Testimony of Alan Bersin. 2010. Commissioner, U.S. Customs and Border Protection, before the House Appropriations Committee, Subcommittee on Homeland Security. U.S. Department of Homeland Security News Release [Online]. Available at: http://www.dhs.gov/ynews/testimony/ testimony_1274108577939.shtm [accessed: April 15, 2010].

Testimony by Doris Meissner, Former Commission of the U.S. Immigration and Naturalization Service. 2011. Senate Homeland Security and Governmental

Affairs Committee Hearing, March 20. Securing the Border: Building on the progress made: U.S. House of Representatives Documents.

Testimony by Richard Stana.2011. House Homeland Security Subcommittee on Border and Maritime Security Hearing, February 15. Securing our Borders — Operational Control and the Path Forward: U.S. House of Representatives Documents.

U.S. Department of Homeland Security (U.S. Customs and Border Patrol). 2010. Supplemental Environmental Assessment for the SBInet Tucson West Tower Project: Nogales and Sonoita Stations' Area of Responsibility [Online, June]. ES-1. Available at: http://www.cbp.gov/xp/cgov/border_security/ti/ti_mr/ [accessed: June 30, 2010].

Chapter 12

Aftermath of Hurricanes Katrina and Rita: Labor Exploitation and Human Trafficking of Mexican Nationals to the Gulf Coast

Stephanie Hepburn

In the wake of Hurricanes Katrina and Rita, buildings and lives were simultaneously destroyed. There was an immediate need for low-cost labor during a time of lawlessness when worker-protection regulations were suspended and enforcement of existing laws was almost non-existent, creating an ideal scenario for labor exploitation and human trafficking.

To envisage post-Katrina New Orleans and the conditions its workers faced, simply imagine a city of tents erected in what was formerly a popular golf course in New Orleans City Park. Inside those tents were mostly day laborers living in sub-human conditions, without running water or bathroom facilities. Laborers often worked twelve hour days, seven days a week. Most were paid a fraction of what they had been promised or were not paid at all.

In one publicized case, over 500 workers were forced to live in guarded labor camps in Orange, Texas, and Pascagoula, Mississippi. According to the complaint against their employer, Signal International, LLC, the victims were each charged about $20,000 in fees for recruitment, visas, and travel. Upon arrival in the United States, the men were placed in the guarded labor camps, their travel documents were confiscated and their movements were significantly restricted. The workers were housed in groups of two dozen in single modular structures. The aisles between their bunk beds were so narrow that the workers had to turn sideways to walk through them. At one point, five of the workers were illegally detained and locked in a room monitored by armed guards (*David vs. Signal Intern., LLC* 2008).

Another case involves persons brought into the United States ostensibly to engage in agricultural tasks in North Carolina, but who were instead forced to perform demolition work and live in dilapidated New Orleans buildings. Kept in the buildings by an armed guard and with no money for food, the victims at one point had to trap pigeons in order to eat (*Asanok vs. Million Express Manpower, Inc.* 2007).

In both of these cases, the workers appear to have been victims not merely of labor exploitation, but of human trafficking. To date, at least 3,750 persons have been identified as potential victims of human trafficking into the Gulf Coast region in the post-Katrina period. Many of them traveled to the region voluntarily but were forced into debt peonage and indentured servitude after they arrived. As the following discussion will reveal, the rise in labor trafficking in the Gulf Coast region reflects a combination of circumstances, including the weakening of labor protection regulations after Katrina and ambiguities over administration of the H-2B guest worker program.

Latino workers have been particularly vulnerable to labor trafficking into New Orleans and other parts of the Gulf Coast. To date, at least six out of the nine publicized post-hurricane cases of alleged forced labor in the Gulf Coast region have involved Latino victims from the nations of Mexico, Honduras, Peru, Bolivia, the Dominican Republic, Panama, and Brazil. Two of these cases specifically involve Mexican nationals.

A Change in Labor Force Demographics and Resulting Tensions

Prior to Hurricanes Katrina and Rita, the Gulf Coast states already had a growing Latino population. In fact, Mexico has been one of the top-five nations sending migrants to the Gulf Coast states since 2000. According to the 2000 Census, Mexico was the national origin of 8 percent of the foreign born population in Louisiana, 24 percent in Mississippi, and 27 percent in Alabama (Donato and Hakimzadeh 2006). Events in the aftermath of Katrina and Rita have accelerated the growth of the Latino population, particularly in the extensively devastated areas of the Gulf Coast. In November 2005, Andy Guerra, Executive Director of the Gulf Coast Latin American Association, estimated that roughly 30,000 Latino workers had come to the Gulf Coast after Katrina. This includes U.S. citizens and nationals from Mexico, Guatemala, and Honduras, as well as nationals from other Latin American countries (Donato and Hakimzadeh 2006).

Before Katrina, Latinos made up 4.4 percent of the overall population in the New Orleans Metropolitan Statistical Area (MSA). Today, according to 2008 demographic data, the U.S. Census Bureau estimates that Latinos make up 6.3 percent of the New Orleans metro population (Plyer and Ortiz 2009). Whether this percentage is an accurate representation of the Latino population in New Orleans is difficult to say. The Census Bureau readily admits the challenges faced in obtaining accurate data on migrant workers. In fact, in the 2010 Census Tool Kit for Reaching Migrant Workers, the Bureau states, "migrant workers are one of the most difficult-to-count populations in the United States. Many migrant workers frequently move around due to various farming, construction and manufacturing timelines, and lack a permanent address or telephone." (U.S. Census Bureau 2009)

What is known is that immediately after the storm, a steady stream of Latino immigrants came to New Orleans in the hopes of obtaining employment in the rebuilding process (Donato and Hakimzadeh 2006). The most massive response to labor recruitment for the region appears to have been from Mexican nationals. In interviewing the "rapid response" labor force in New Orleans that had arrived in the immediate aftermath of the storm, researcher Elizabeth Fussell (2007) found that 45.5 percent of the Latino interviewees were Mexican nationals. The remaining

54.5 percent of interviewees was made up of nationals from Brazil (20.5 percent), Honduras (13.6 percent), Guatemala (13.3 percent), and El Salvador (6.8 percent) (personal communication, E. Fussell, June 28, 2010).[1]

Similarly, according to the University of California report, "After Katrina, A Population-Based Study of Labor and Human Rights in New Orleans," Latino workers, 54 percent of whom were undocumented, made up nearly half of the post-Katrina reconstruction workforce in New Orleans. The report goes on to say that of the undocumented construction workers, 43 percent were Mexican nationals (Fletcher et al. 2006).

The sudden change in demographics and the dire financial circumstances of local residents led to a rising fear that migrant Latinos would "steal" jobs from resident New Orleanians. These concerns were reflected in an October 2005 town hall meeting with small business owners, when then-mayor Ray Nagin said, "I can plainly see in your eyes that you want to know, 'How do I take advantage of this incredible opportunity?' How do I make sure New Orleans is not overrun with Mexicans?" (Roig-Franzia 2005)

According to alleged trafficking victim Nestor Vallero, misuse of the H-2B visa program by contractors played a significant role in tensions between the local residents and migrant workers as well as the exploitation of migrant workers in post-Katrina New Orleans:

"Here in New Orleans, many contractors are paying $13 or $10 an hour to do cleanup work from the Katrina disaster," Vallero told *Democracy Now*. "However, the contractors have figured out that they can import people from other countries and pay them half that to do the clean-up work. So, this is really a contradiction and this is creating tensions, racial tensions between the African Americans who are local to New Orleans and the Latin Americans who are being imported to work here." (Goodman 2007)

One case that clearly illustrates Vallero's point is that of Decatur Hotels, LLC—a New Orleans based company that allegedly fired local workers and replaced them with undocumented workers and guest-workers.[2] The motivation for the employer was to reduce labor costs:

"...there's a restaurant in New Orleans, and in that single restaurant in New Orleans after Hurricane Katrina, African-American women were working at the kitchen for $10 an hour," Saket Soni, director of the New Orleans Workers'

---

1   In conducting the research, Fussell and her research assistants interviewed every Latino immigrant that they could find – usually in churches, bars, and those living in metro New Orleans neighborhoods (in both Orleans and Jefferson Parish). Fussell states that the reported numbers are illustrative of the interview sample but are not geographically defined.

2   The guest workers in the case against Decatur Hotels are from Peru, Bolivia, and the Dominican Republic.

Center for Racial Justice (NOWCRJ) told *Democracy Now*. "They were all fired and replaced by undocumented workers, who were hired for eight bucks an hour. Those undocumented workers were then fired and replaced by guest workers on H-2B visas, who were given those jobs for $6 [per hour]." (Goodman 2007)

Yet while such practices heightened initial tensions between locals and migrant workers, the two groups ended up collaborating in various efforts to improve the labor situation for migrant workers. As will be described later in further detail, community members such as Curtis Muhammad of the New Orleans Survivors Council (NOSC) helped to pressure the Calcasieu Parish Sheriff's Office to look into and retrieve passports from one withholding employer.

Laws Come Undone

Even though human trafficking is directly prohibited under the federal Victims of Trafficking and Violence Protection Act of 2000 (TVPA), the lack of monitoring of construction sites as well as loosened labor laws in the post-hurricane Gulf Coast resulted in a scenario ripe for forced labor and debt bondage.

On September 5, 2005, the Occupational Safety and Health Administration of the Department of Labor (DOL) temporarily suspended the enforcement of job safety and health standards in hurricane-impacted counties and parishes in Florida, Alabama, Mississippi and Louisiana. On that same day, a memorandum by the Employment Standards Administration of the DOL issued a three-month suspension of Affirmative Action requirements with respect to federal contracts related to Hurricane Katrina relief efforts (COGR 2007, Brown-Dianis et al. 2006).

Presumably to accommodate survivors who had lost documentation and to jump-start the rebuilding process, on September 6, 2005, the Department of Homeland Security (DHS) suspended, for a period of 45 days, the requirement that employers confirm the eligibility and identity of their employees. Two days later, former-President George W. Bush decreed a two-month suspension of the Davis-Bacon Act, which guarantees construction workers the prevailing local wage when paid with federal money (Donato and Hakimzadeh 2006, Fletcher et al. 2006).

These suspensions resulted in a lack of enforcement, not the least of which was a significant decrease in DOL investigations in New Orleans. According to Ohio Representative Dennis Kucinich, the number of DOL investigations in New Orleans dropped from 70 in 2004 to 44 in 2006 (COGR 2007). The result was a 37 percent decrease in investigations at a time when, according to Kucinich and others, the city needed more, not less, labor law enforcement. With the suspensions and lack of enforcement of labor laws throughout the region, it became commonplace for migrant workers in the post-hurricane Gulf Coast to face toxic work conditions with inept or non-existent protective gear, twelve-hour workdays for seven days per week, and non-payment of wages and/or overtime.

Hector, a New Orleans migrant worker, aptly described his post-Katrina experience in the Southern Poverty Law Center report (2006), *Broken Levees, Broken Promises, New Orleans' Migrant Workers in Their Own Words*. He faced non-payment and inhumane working conditions as well as long-term medical side effects:

> "The work we were doing in the schools was horrible," Hector told interviewers. "The hurricanes had left the schools full of mud—three or four feet of mud. All sorts of filth was in the mud. There were horrible smells, and we found snakes, frogs and a lot more."

> "…At five in the morning, we were already standing and waiting for the company bus to pick us up. At seven or eight at night, we would still be at work because the bus hadn't come yet to take us back to the hotel. We would be suffering from the cold and hunger because we only ate once in the evenings. Imagine working a whole day on only water. Since we weren't being paid for our work, we didn't have any money to feed ourselves. We ate only in the evenings when the hotel helped us."

Since working in the schools, Hector hasn't been well. In the mornings when he showers, he finds dried blood in his nose. "I feel like something has damaged me. I had to endure all this just to work in order to earn a living," said Hector.

> "I believe that the contractors don't have a heart to be touched. Poor people come here to work, to better the city, to do the clean-up and to help out. These contractors, all they want is to hoard money. They don't care whether you eat or not. They just want to get the money and run away with it as many companies have done. Many companies have contracted people at a certain wage, but when the time comes to pay them, they just decide they don't want to pay it anymore…" (Southern Poverty Law Center 2006)

Guest Worker Visas

Latinos are the primary population of trafficking victims in the United States. According to the Bureau of Justice Statistics Special Report, *Characteristics of Suspected Human Trafficking Incidents*, 40 percent of victims in alleged human trafficking incidents reported by task forces from 2007–2008 were Latino, compared to those who were White (22.6 percent), Black (20.7 percent), and Asian (13.3 percent). Latinos made up 37.2 percent of alleged victims in sex trafficking cases and 55.8 percent of alleged labor trafficking victims. In confirmed human trafficking cases, the percentage of Latino victims during 2007–2008 was 61.7

percent, making up 66.5 percent of sex trafficking and 31.4 percent of labor trafficking victims (Beck et al. 2009).

It was not only the suspension of worker protection legislation that created the ideal scenario for human trafficking in the Gulf region. The U.S. guest worker program has promoted human trafficking in regions throughout the country. Akin to Japan's government-run Industrial Training Program (ITP) and Technical Internship Program (TIP), the highly unregulated U.S. guest worker program offers the perfect conditions to enable unscrupulous employers to exploit foreign workers. In all nine of the alleged Gulf Coast trafficking cases the victims were visa holders. At least five cases involved victims who held H-2B visas while two other cases involved victims with H-1B or H-2A visas.

The H-1B temporary visa program is designed to attract foreign workers in specialized fields such as technology, engineering and medicine. By contrast, the H-2A visa program allows for the temporary hire of foreign workers to perform agricultural labor, while the H-2B visa allows foreign workers to be hired temporarily to perform non-agricultural labor on a one-time, seasonal, peak load or intermittent basis (U.S. Department of Labor 2010b, 2006).

Both the H-1B and H-2A programs offer visa holders a variety of protections. Under the H-1B program, the worker must be paid a wage that meets or exceeds the prevailing wage in the particular employment sector. The visa holder's family is permitted to live in the United States during the period that the H-1B visa is in effect, although they cannot be employed. H-1B visa holders can also apply for permanent residency during the term the H-1B visa is in effect (USCIS 2010, 2006).

The H-2A program grants workers free housing, access to legal services, the receipt of at least three-fourths of the total hours promised in his/her contract, compensation for medical costs and permanent injury, as well as various other benefits (COGR 2007). By contrast, the H-2B visa program during this time offered few required benefits and minimal regulation, and the regulations that did exist were rarely enforced.

The guest worker program with the least regulation, the H-2B program, has historically been the most commonly utilized. In 2005, for example, employers brought in 121,000 non-agricultural guest workers, 75 percent of whom were from Mexico. The lack of regulation makes the H-2B program particularly prone to abuse, including enabling human trafficking (Testimony of Mary Bauer before the U.S. House of Representatives 2008, Bauer 2007).

The H-2 visa is employer specific and is not valid with any other employer. As a result, the employer who applies for the worker's visa quite literally controls whether the worker's status in the United States is "legal" or "illegal." This places the employer in a position of ultimate control over the visa holder—a power that, historically, has been used to exploit and abuse workers (Testimony of Mary Bauer before the U.S. House of Representatives 2008, Bauer 2007).

One case, not an unfamiliar story in post-Katrina New Orleans, illustrates this point. A group of skilled laborers (welders) were recruited in their home country for jobs in New Orleans. The workers paid their own expenses for training, travel, referral, and visas:

> "The laborers received training in their country of origin by the recruiting company," said Laila Hlass, Staff Attorney at the Loyola Law Clinic in New Orleans. "However, upon arrival in New Orleans, they were told by the recruiter that the work was not there but if they wanted the recruiter could find them work at another place of employment. While the laborers had obtained H-2B visas, the visa is employer specific and is not valid with any other employer. Concerned, the workers went to speak with the assigned employer, who promptly called immigration. ICE arrested the workers and immediately placed them into deportation proceedings. As a result of fraud, the laborers lost thousands of dollars." (personal communication, Laila Hlass, May 18, 2009)

Other kinds of exploitation commonly faced by H-2B visa holders in post-Katrina New Orleans were squalid living conditions, denial of medical benefits for on-the-job injuries, seizure of travel and identification documents by labor brokers and/or employers, and unpaid wages.

As NOWCRJ director Saket Soni reported to *Democracy Now* regarding the Decatur Hotels, LLC, case, "Those H-2B visa holders paid $10,000 to come to New Orleans to chop vegetables, and they were told that if they ever stop chopping, the employer would call Immigration..." (Goodman 2007). "In many cases, they [guest workers] are subjected to horrible living conditions, non-payment for overtime, and non-payment at all," Dennis Kucinich said at the Hearing on Adequacy of Labor Law Enforcement in New Orleans on June 25, 2007. "In the worst case, these guest workers have their passports and visas confiscated by employers rendering them virtual slaves at the hands of someone who used legal means to import them into the U.S." (COGR 2007)

Employers must obtain permission from the DOL to bring in guest workers. For this to occur, the DOL, pursuant to the provisions of Section 101 (a)(15)(h)(ii) of the Immigration and Nationality Act, must ascertain that there are not sufficient U.S. workers available to perform the work. Additionally, the DOL must certify that the terms of employment do not adversely affect the wages and working conditions of workers in the United States who are similarly employed (U.S. Department of Labor 2008b).

Such certifications are not always accurate. In the case of Decatur Hotels, LLC, the assertion was made that there were no available qualified persons in the United States, when in fact local workers who had previously worked in the industry were in New Orleans and desperate to return to work (*Castellanos-Contreras et al. vs. Decatur Hotels, L.L.C.* et al. 2006). As previously described by both Vallero and Soni, this resulted in an unfair pitting of guest workers and undocumented workers against the local low-wage labor force.

While local workers found themselves suddenly unemployed and replaced with persons willing to work for less, many guest workers found themselves in a position of debt bondage. As noted by alleged trafficking victim Vallero, abuses of the H-2B visa became a significant issue after the hurricanes, making guest workers particularly susceptible to human trafficking. Despite U.S. laws which provide some obligation on the part of employers to reimburse guest workers for visa and travel costs, a common way employers abuse the H-2B visa program is to charge recruits exorbitant fees that include visa, travel, and labor broker costs. It is these fees, often with accrued interest, that place guest worker visa holders in indentured servitude and debt bondage (personal communication, Mary Bauer, October 4, 2010).

Yet when Kucinich looked into the lack of labor regulation and enforcement in the post-Katrina period, the DOL claimed to have little or no authority to act on behalf of H-2B visa holders. Technically, under a DOL administrative directive, employers utilizing the H-2B program are obligated to offer full-time employment that pays at the prevailing wage rate. However, because it was an administrative directive[3] instead of a regulation that established the H-2B visa, the DOL claimed that it lacked the legal authority to enforce its wage requirements (Testimony of Mary Bauer before the U.S. House of Representatives 2008, U.S. Department of Labor 1994).

A second reason that the H-2B visa program went unregulated in the post-Katrina period is the jurisdictional confusion between the DOL and the DHS. In 2005, Congress vested DHS with enforcement authority over the H-2B program. As a result, the DOL had no authority to enforce the program's provisions and regulations. "The DOL, which has the authority to grant or deny certification for a foreign labor contract through its Office of Foreign Labor Certification, cannot do so much as deny certification for an employer who has been prosecuted for labor law violations," Kucinich told the Domestic Policy Subcommittee of the Government Reform and Oversight Committee on June 25, 2007. Instead, the DHS is granted complete authority over the enforcement of H-2B contract terms (COGR 2007).

Enforcing the H-2B provisions does not appear to have been the DHS's primary priority. Instead, for nearly four years no governmental agency actually took ownership of the H-2B program. It was not until late 2008 that discussions between DHS and the DOL resulted in an agreement that the DOL should be delegated H-2B enforcement authority (U.S. Department of Labor 2008b).

With its authority over H-2B enforcement clarified, the DOL was in a better position to monitor and protect guest workers. In December 2008, the Employment and Training Administration (ETA) of the DOL amended its regulations to modernize the procedures for issuing labor certifications to employers sponsoring H-2B guest workers, stating that, "… the rule enhances the integrity of the H-2B program through the introduction of post-adjudication audits and procedures for penalizing employers who fail to comply with program requirements." The changes include monetary fines of up to $10,000

---

3   General Administrative Letter 1–95 (U.S. Department of Labor 1994).

per violation, the reinstatement of U.S. workers who were illegally laid off, and potential disbarment of attorneys (agents).

Under the amended ETA regulations that became effective on January 18, 2009, Federal Regulation 20 C.F.R. § 655.22(j) prohibits employers from passing onto foreign workers the cost of attorney or agent fees, the H-2B application, or recruitment associated with obtaining labor certification. As stated by the ETA, these are business expenses associated with aiding the employer to complete the labor certification application and labor market test: "The employer's responsibility to pay these costs exists separate and apart from any benefit that may accrue to the foreign worker." (U.S. Department of Labor 2009, 2008b)

Such regulations, if adequately enforced, could enable the DOL to curb some of the abuses of guest workers under the H-2B program, in New Orleans and elsewhere. As the following section will reveal, one of the conditions that allowed guest worker exploitation and encouraged debt bondage and human trafficking was the lack of regulation of the recruitment system.

Recruitment

In the months and years after Hurricanes Katrina and Rita, the relaxation of labor protection and enforcement fueled the growth of the H-2B labor recruitment industry. Employers seeking inexpensive labor could call upon international recruiters to stock their labor pools with international guest workers under the provisions of H-2B.

Then as now, from the employers' perspective the economic benefits of hiring workers through recruitment companies are compelling. For example, at the MJC Labor Solutions Inc. LatinLabor.com website employers can quickly calculate a rough estimate of what it would cost to hire workers through their recruitment company. A quick snapshot (See Figure 12.1 below) indicates that for 12 workers at 40 hours per week for 5 weeks, after fees as well as the cost of petition and advertising, the net cost per hour per worker would be $3.22 (Costs Petitioned Workers 2010).

In a context such as New Orleans in which minimum wage rates were almost twice this high, using labor recruiters to hire international guest workers made excellent business sense—as long as the employer didn't think too much about why the workers supplied through the labor recruitment firms were so inexpensive. A closer look into the strategies employed by recruitment companies to entice guest workers to the Gulf Coast region reveals that many workers were subjected to manipulation, fraud, and, on occasion, human trafficking.

> "Typically, employers will find a U.S. recruiter and then contract that U.S. recruiter to go in India or Mexico or Peru or Bolivia and find a local recruiter," said Soni. "That local recruiter then places ads aggressively, recruits, at times even knocks on doors in neighborhoods, to get men and women out to meetings

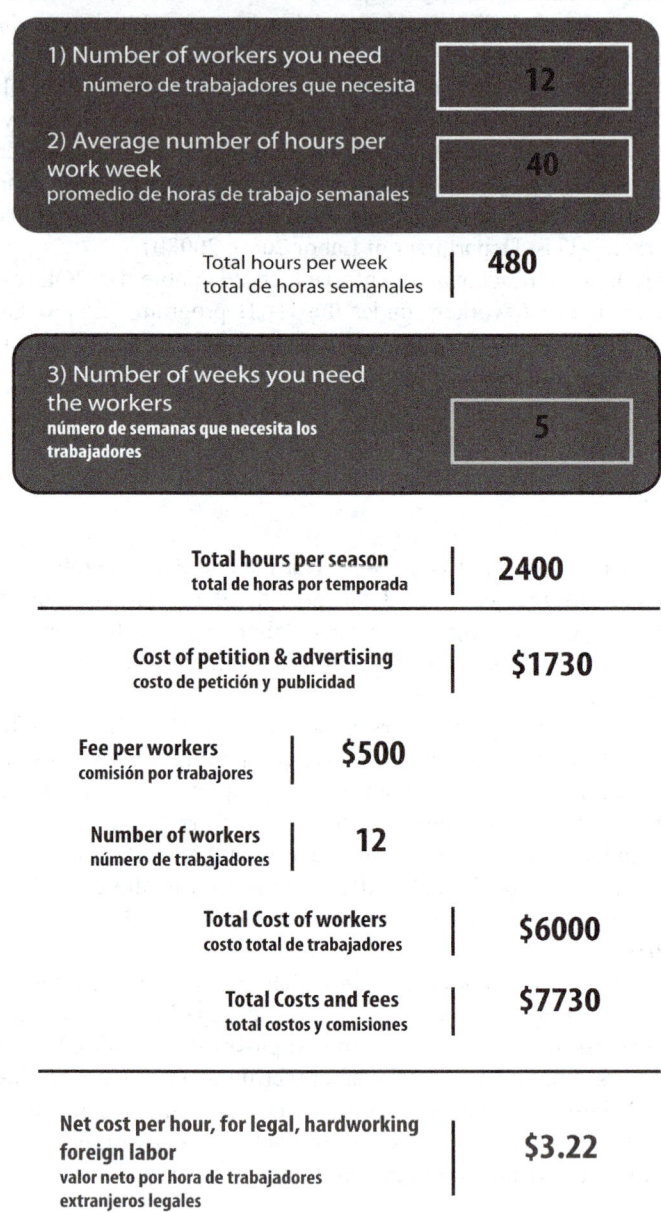

Figure 12.1 Labor Cost Calculator

Source: Data from Latinlabor.com, website no longer accessible

where they are told about the beautiful H-2B program, the nice hotel they will be living in, the great job they will have, the thousands of dollars they'll earn within three months. And then they come." (Goodman 2007)

Consider the case of four Mexican workers recruited to New Orleans in the aftermath of Hurricane Katrina. When Raoul Arcentales, Ricardo Gonzáles, Jesús Blanco, and Eduardo Cruz responded in person to an advertisement printed in their local paper in Mexico, they were promptly shuttled into a small room behind a storefront. There they spoke with an attorney who asked them a variety of questions regarding their personal and work histories. Then each of the four men paid $100 to the United States Consulate for their visa applications (Brown-Dianis et al. 2006).

Several weeks later, the men were informed that a contractor in New Orleans had hired them. They each paid the lawyer $600 and signed a contract and promissory note that committed them to work for a nine month period with a hefty consequence if they failed to satisfy the contract. The men were told by the attorney, "If you don't fulfill the obligation, you pay $3,000 (USD) or go to jail." (Brown-Dianis et al. 2006)

Raoul, Ricardo, Jesús, Eduardo, and 100 other Mexican workers were packed into a bus to begin a three-day journey from Mexico to their new work destinations in the United States. Half were headed to New Orleans and half to Mississippi (Brown-Dianis et al. 2006). Upon arrival in New Orleans, the four men were not given any work except for a single five-hour work day on a construction site. The contractor encouraged them to look elsewhere for work but this violated their contract and the men were fearful of the penalties that could come along with doing so. They were also concerned about accruing living costs such as hotel and food that were to be deducted from their pay. After 18 days in New Orleans, the men had each earned only $70 (Brown-Dianis et al. 2006). Not only had they failed to secure the jobs they had been promised, but each man had lost hundreds of dollars to the recruitment company.

Their experience is not unusual. Recruiters' fees have been reported to be as high as $20,000 (*David vs. Signal Intern., LLC* 2008). Such abuses were able to flourish in the post-Katrina period, when high demand for labor and the relaxation of labor protection regulations created conditions ripe for fraud and other recruitment abuses. As the follow example suggests, in some cases recruiter and/or employer abuses of guest workers subjected them to debt bondage and human trafficking.

The Case of Louisiana Labor, LLC

In the aftermath of Hurricane Katrina, roughly 130 Mexican guest workers were hired by a company called Louisiana Labor, LLC. Matt Redd, owner of the real estate company Redd Properties, LLC, allegedly started Louisiana Labor, LLC, in order to bring in H-2B laborers from Mexico and rent them out to local businesses.

"Matt… went to Mexico," said Soni. "He, himself, became a recruiter. He went to Mexico, recruited workers, promised them that for $400 they would be transported to Louisiana in airplanes—charged them $400 for airfare. When he received the $400, he then packed the Mexican workers into vans like sardines and confiscated their passports and essentially trafficked them across the border to Louisiana." (Goodman, 2007)

According to Soni, once in Louisiana the workers were crammed into apartments in buildings owned by Redd Properties. Redd then leased the workers out to work for various businesses such as restaurants, casinos, car washes, and a fabrication shop. A former employee of Louisiana Labor, LLC, Vallero states that he was promised a stable job, dignified housing, suitable working conditions, and fair wages.

"When we got here, however—well, even before we crossed the border the lies became evident," said Vallero. "They stole our passports. They only gave them to us to present to the immigration officials, but then they took them away again.

Then we got to the apartments and, there, we were crammed into rooms. They had said there would only be four people to an apartment, and they said that we'd have our own bathroom and everything. But the living conditions turned out to be deplorable." (Goodman 2007)

The workers were told that upon arrival they would be working in construction but instead were placed in a variety of menial jobs with wages far below what they had been promised. When workers brought up the issue of wages, Redd and his associates allegedly told them that they could go home if they didn't like the wages. When passports were addressed, the workers were allegedly told that they would only receive their passports if they were going home. The workers were also allegedly charged exorbitant housing costs that placed them further in debt.

"After all of this, we were just forced to take whatever job they were offering us, because we didn't have any money to go home or do anything else," said Vallero. "But that wasn't all. They started to discount the cost of our housing from our wage[s]…we had to pay $1,200 a month for housing. Out of a $300 check that we received for two weeks work, they would take/discount almost $200 off that check. So, they're really, you know, raking in the profits with our work. It's really just a money-making scheme, this whole guest workers program." (Goodman 2007)

This story is echoed by Fernando Rivera, another alleged victim of Redd. According to Rivera, Redd would simply lease out the workers for his own financial gain. When Rivera asked for his passport to be returned to him, Redd refused and threatened to call immigration. "Matt Redd would sell us to the highest bidder," Rivera told *The Nation*. "The money passed through his hands and afterward there was never very much left. It was hell there, but there was nothing else to do but bear it." (Mello 2007)

With pressure from Soni and local community members such as Curtis Muhammad of the New Orleans Survivors Council (NOSC), the Calcasieu Parish Sheriff's Office looked into the matter and retrieved the workers' passports from Redd (Dutton 2007). While Redd admits to taking workers' identification documentation to ensure that they continued to work for him, he claims that he didn't know that confiscation of a passport was illegal. "When we go through this process and pay to get people here, with the attorney's fees and transportation fees, it was some collateral that we had to make sure they stayed and worked for us," Redd told *The Nation* (Mello 2007).

Regardless of whether Matt Redd was actually unaware that confiscation of workers' passports is illegal, it is clear that the lack of labor law enforcement in the post-Katrina period and the confusion between DOL and DHS over H-2B jurisdiction made it possible for labor recruiters to exploit guest workers easily and place them in a position of debt bondage. As the following example demonstrates, the laxity of enforcement also affected guest workers in other parts of Louisiana, who were brought to the United States with H-2A (agricultural work) visas in the post-Katrina period.

The Case against Bimbo's Best Produce

A classic case of trafficking is that of 42 to 118 guest workers from Mexico who were allegedly brought to perform labor in Amite, Louisiana, by Charles Relan, the owner of Bimbo's Best Produce.[4] Relan allegedly confiscated the workers' passports and temporary H-2A visas; threatened them with unlawful eviction, arrest and deportation; and fired a shotgun over their heads in order to prevent the workers from attempting escape (*Antonio-Morales et al. vs. Bimbo's Best Produce, Inc. et al.* 2009).

From an indigenous community in San Luis Potosí, the workers were recruited in Mexico by Relan and allegedly forced to pick strawberries in Amite from 2006 to 2008. Many of the workers spoke Nahuatl as their first language and spoke basic Spanish but little to no English. According to the complaint against Bimbo's Best Produce, Relan "subjected the guest workers to a scheme of psychological coercion, threats of serious harm, and threatened abuse of the legal process to maintain control over them and force them to continue working in his strawberry fields." (*Antonio-Morales et al. vs. Bimbo's Best Produce, Inc. et al.* 2009, Evans 2008)

As stated in the complaint, Relan regularly berated the workers and at times informed them that they were to stay in the bent position of tending to the strawberry

---

4   37 persons were brought from Mexico to work at Bimbo's in 2005/2006; 39 in 2006/2007; and 42 in 2007/2008. It is unknown how many of the workers came back annually.

plants rather than being allowed to stand up. The complaint goes on to state that he physically assaulted at least one worker, plaintiff Reynaldo Reyes-Resendiz. Allegedly, Relan yelled at Reynaldo and accused him of weeding the strawberry plants incorrectly. When Reynaldo tried to continue working, Relan allegedly shoved him (*Antonio-Morales et al. vs. Bimbo's Best Produce, Inc. et al.* 2009).

According to the complaint, Relan frequently carried a gun in the strawberry fields and on occasion would shoot above the workers' heads. One day, the Bimbo's owner allegedly decided to shoot and kill a neighbor's dog—a dog that the workers had befriended. The execution of the dog took place in the same area where the victims were working, which made them more fearful that they could be harmed (*Antonio-Morales et al. vs. Bimbo's Best Produce, Inc. et al.* 2009).

The complaint also states that pesticides were sprayed in the direct vicinity of the laborers while they worked. As a result, the spray and vapor came into immediate contact with the workers' mouths and skin, which in legal terms constitutes a harmful and offensive contact to the victims (*Antonio-Morales et al. vs. Bimbo's Best Produce, Inc. et al.* 2009, Evans 2008).

In 2008, the workers brought suit against Relan for violation of the TVPA, the Fair Labor Standards Act (FLSA), and the guest workers' H-2A employment contracts (*Antonio-Morales et al. vs. Bimbo's Best Produce, Inc. et al.* 2009). On April 20, 2009, the U.S. District Court for the Eastern District of Louisiana granted the federal government an administrative closure in this case. The closure has immobilized the civil suit against Bimbo until the DOJ completes a criminal investigation of Bimbo and any potential prosecution that could result (*Antonio-Morales et al. vs. Bimbo's Best Produce, Inc. et al.* 2009).

An Alliance for Gulf Coast Guest Workers

In response to their own exploitative experiences in the Gulf Coast, a number of guest workers have joined together with the NOWCRJ to create an association called the Alliance of Guest Workers for Dignity. Started in January 2007, the New Orleans based coalition is led by H-2B guest workers whose objective is to advocate for the fair treatment of workers. It also aims to bring attention to guest worker exploitation and the occurrence of debt bondage and indentured servitude that has resulted from lax enforcement of labor law (Olson 2007). Among other nations, members are from Mexico, Peru, Brazil, Bolivia, and India.

The alliance has played a vital role in multiple civil suits against exploitative employers, including Decatur Hotels, LLC. Led by the alliance, workers secretly met for a three-month period before meeting with Mr. F. Patrick Quinn, III, the president of Decatur Hotels, LLC. When the meeting with Quinn was unsuccessful, the workers filed suit against Quinn and Decatur Hotels, LLC, for failure to reimburse the workers for the recruiter-inflated costs of their trip to New Orleans such as airfare, visa processing costs, and other travel expenses (NILC 2007).

Jose Sanchez, a member of the alliance and former employee of Decatur Hotels, LLC, explains that the exploitation that he experienced in their employ motivated him to be active in the alliance in order to protect himself and other guest workers.

> "I worked in Mr. Quinn's hotel for next to nothing because I had to earn enough money to make back what I paid to get here," said Sanchez in a National Immigration Law Center (NILC) press release. "Even though I was so tired at the end of the day, I would go to the [alliance] meetings at night because I knew that this was important not just for our group but for all guest workers in the U.S." (NILC 2007)

While the guest workers won the case against Decatur Hotels, LLC, at the U.S. District Court for the Eastern District of Louisiana, Decatur Hotels filed an appeal and won with the 5th Circuit of Appeals. A panel of judges concluded that employers do not have liability for guest workers under the FLSA, and thereby Decatur Hotels did not have to reimburse the workers for recruitment fees, visa fees, or transportation costs. The guest workers filed a motion for rehearing with the 5th Circuit and the case was reheard before a full court (en banc) in May 2010. On October 1, 2010, the decision came out: the workers lost 8–6 (personal communication, Mary Bauer, October 4, 2010).

In the aforementioned case of Matt Redd, it was the alliance of NOWCRJ, local supporters, and the alleged victims of Matt Redd that pressured the Calcasieu Parish Sheriff's Office to impound and return the victims' Mexican passports (Olson 2007).

Use of FLSA as Opposed to TVPA in Cases against Traffickers

While Kucinich and others describe Redd and similar persons as traffickers, attorneys often turn to the Fair Labor Standards Act (FLSA) instead of the federal Trafficking Victims Protection Act (TVPA) or other state anti-trafficking laws in order to bring suit against them.[5]

According to attorney Lori Johnson of Legal Aid of North Carolina, Farmworker Unit, workers may have legitimate wage claims that precede or are entirely unrelated to the trafficking scenario. For example, one common claim under the FLSA is when guest workers end up paying for costs that are the responsibility of the employer—such as transportation, visa, and/or recruitment fees.

> "Workers pay these costs prior to arrival in the U.S.," said Johnson. "Since these expenses are considered to benefit the employer, the fact that the worker paid the expenses means the worker was essentially paying the employer's expenses out of his own wages. The amount of those expenses is thus treated as a deduction

---

5   It is important to note that as of yet, no suit has been brought against Matt Redd.

from wages. Further, workers may pay recruitment fees. Recruitment fees are illegal and therefore act as a de facto unlawful deduction to wages." (personal communication, Lori Johnson, January 4, 2010)

Dan McNeil, attorney and Associate Director of the Legal Department at the American Federation of Teachers (AFL-CIO), states that in some cases, wage and hour complaints are filed with the DOL, which does not allow for allegations under the TVPA. "But, the DOL can refer such cases to the U.S. Department of Justice (DOJ), which could pursue a TVPA criminal action," said McNeil (personal communication, Dan McNeil, May 2, 2010).

The reality is that the FLSA has been around far longer than the TVPA. As a result, attorneys may feel that using the FLSA in civil suits will be more effective for ensuring a win against the defendants. Yet, utilizing the FLSA does not preclude the use of the TVPA. Furthermore, failing to satisfy one claim would not typically prevent the ability to prevail on another. This means that if attorneys utilize both the FLSA and TVPA but are unable to satisfy the trafficking claim, the suit can still be won in regards to the FLSA claim (personal communication, Lori Johnson, January 4, 2010).

The underuse of the TVPA in civil suits is significant. Contrary to the exclusively financial penalties under the FLSA, when a company loses a civil suit under the TVPA it carries a much stronger social stigma – one that would hopefully deter other companies from engaging in human trafficking practices. Luckily, regardless of the route a victim's attorney takes against his/her trafficker(s), all victims are able to apply for immigration relief through the U or T visa. In fact, there does not have to be a lawsuit associated with the application for either visa. Victims from at least five of the nine alleged Gulf Coast forced labor cases have applied for T or U visas.

Criminal Charges vs. a Civil Suit

Only federal authorities can pursue criminal charges. The DOJ can bring criminal charges against traffickers under a variety of U.S. Codes that target involuntary servitude, involuntary slavery, and forced labor. These anti-trafficking provisions are typically referred to as Chapter 77 offenses, some which were added by the TVPA.

A number of key statutes utilized by the DOJ to bring criminal charges against traffickers are 18 U.S.C. § 1581 (peonage, debt bondage); 18 U.S.C. § 1584 (involuntary servitude); 18 U.S.C. § 1589 (forced labor); 18 U.S.C. § 1590 (Trafficking with Respect to Peonage, Slavery, Involuntary Servitude, or Forced Labor); 18 U.S.C. § 1591 (Sex Trafficking of Children or by Force, Fraud, or Coercion); and 18 U.S.C. § 1592 (Unlawful Conduct with Respect to Documents in Furtherance of Trafficking, Peonage, Slavery, Involuntary Servitude, or Forced Labor). Other provisions of the TVPA give victims an avenue for civil lawsuits (18 U.S.C. § 1595) and provide for mandatory restitution (18 U.S.C. § 1593) (United States Department of Justice, 2008). Under the U.S. Code Title 18,

1595, victims are provided a private right of action, which allows them to file suit against their trafficker(s) in civil court. Additionally, FLSA claims are a civil matter and are consequently filed in civil court. Under the FLSA, there is potential for fines through which victims can obtain back pay of unpaid wages (personal communication, Dan McNeil, May 2, 2010). Under the TVPA, victims can obtain damages and attorneys' fees.

Persons found guilty of trafficking, specifically under 18 U.S.C. § 1590, face fines and up to 20 years imprisonment, which can be increased even up to a life sentence if the offense includes an attempt to kill, aggravated sexual abuse or attempted sexual abuse, kidnapping or the attempt to kidnap (Legal Information Institute).

Thus far, it appears that only two of the publicized Gulf Coast cases may result in a federal prosecution and criminal charges under the TVPA. The first is *Israel Antonio-Morales et al. vs. Bimbo's Best Produce* and the second is that of 361 Filipino teachers brought to Louisiana school districts under the H-2A visa by Universal Placement International (UPI) from June 2007 to August 2009. As noted previously, there was an Administrative Closure of the Bimbo's case until the completion of a federal investigation and proceedings. Currently, the case of the teachers is under federal investigation for violations under the TVPA.

Conclusion

The DOL has taken positive steps to increase their manpower in the Gulf Coast region. The Wage and Hour Division (WHD) of the DOL has added over 35 investigators and mangers to the Gulf Coast offices affected by Hurricanes Katrina and Rita. Four additional investigators and managers and two team leaders were transferred to New Orleans and a satellite office space was opened in Kenner, Louisiana. The WHD has opened at least 1,102 hurricane-related cases, collecting more than $11.3 million in back wages for 17,700 workers in concluded cases and setting the stage for $2 million in back wages to be collected in cases not yet concluded (U.S. Department of Labor 2008).

The new ETA Final Rules on the H-2B guest worker program, if sufficiently enforced, will help to counter employer abuses. But even with these provisions the exploitation of guest workers continues. Unlawful abuses, such as the exorbitant fees charged by recruiters and U.S. employers and the common non-payment or underpayment of workers' wages, are compounded by the fact that H-2B guest workers can only legally work for the petitioning employer. The situation is further exacerbated by demands in the Gulf Coast region for inexpensive labor, creating an atmosphere that continues to be suitable for debt bondage and indentured servitude. As long as employers retain ultimate power over guest workers, with protective regulations weak and the motivation and resources for their enforcement inadequate, the exploitation of guest workers is likely to continue.

Bibliography

Antonio-Morales et al. vs. Bimbo's Best Produce, Inc. et al. [2009] 8:5105 (E.D. La.

Asanok vs. Million Express Manpower, Inc. [2007] No. 07–48 (E.D.N.C.

Bauer, M. 2007. *Close to Slavery, Guestworker Programs in the United States* [Online, The Souther Poverty Law Center]. Available at: http://www.splcenter. org/pdf/static/SPLCguestworker.pdf [accessed: January 3, 2010].

Beck, A.C. 2009. *Characteristics of Suspected Human Trafficking Incidents, 2007–08* [Online, Bureau of Justice Statistics U.S. Department of Justice]. Available at: http://www.bjs.ojp.usdoj.gov/index.cfm?ty=pbdetail&iid=550 [accessed: January 5, 2010].

Brown-Dianis, J.L. 2006. And Injustice For All: Workers' Lives in the Reconstruction of New Orleans [Online, Advancement Project]. Available at: http://www. advancementproject.org/digital-library/publications/hurricane-katrina [accessed: December 22, 2009].

Castellanos-Contreras et al. vs. Decatur Hotels, L.L.C. et al [2006] 2:2006cv04340 (E.D. La. August 16, 2006).

Costs Petitioned Workers [Online, MJC Labor Solutions Inc.]. Available at: http:// www.latinlabor.com/employers/costsPetitioned.htm [accessed: January 10, 2010].

COGR. 2007. *Hearing on Adequacy of Labor Law Enforcement in New Orleans* [Online, Committee on Oversight and Government Reform]. Available at: http://www.oversight.house.gov/index.php?option=com_content&view= article&id=4087:hearing-on-adequacy-of-labor-law-enforcement-in-new-orleans&catid=66:hearings&Itemid=31 [accessed: January 3, 2010].

David vs. Signal Intern., LLC [2008] 588 F. Supp. 2d 718, 727 (E.D. La. 2008).

Donato, K. and Hakimzadeh, S. 2006. *The Changing Face of the Gulf Coast: Immigration to Louisiana, Mississippi, and Alabama* [Online, Migration Information Source]. Available at: http://www.migrationinformation.org/ Feature/display.cfm?ID=368 [accessed: June 28, 2001].

Dutton, M.A. 2007. Guest workers allege slavery locally. *Southwest Daily News* [Online]. Available at: http://www.smfws.com/articles2007/february/ art02162007e.html [accessed: January 4, 2010].

Evans, D. 2008. *Guestworkers sue major Louisiana grower for labor trafficking, slave-like conditions* [Online, Facing South, Institute for Southern Studies (ISS)]. Available at: http://www.southernstudies.org/2008/12/guestworkers-sue-major-louisiana-grower-for-labor-trafficking-slave-like-conditions.html [accessed: December 27, 2009].

Fletcher, L.P. 2006. *Katrina, A Population-Based Study of Labor and Human Rights in New Orleans* [Online, The Human Rights Center at the University of California]. Available at: http://www.hrc.berkeley.edu/pdfs/report_katrina.pdf [accessed: December 22, 2009].

Fussell, E. 2007. *Post-Katrina New Orleans as a new migrant destination* [Online]. Available at: http://www.Princeton.edu:paa2007.princeton.edu/download. aspx?submissionId=70391 [accessed: January 10, 2010].

Goodman, A. 2007. *Indian Guestworker Slits Wrists After Being Fired for Complaining About Squalid Work Conditions* [Online]. Available at: http://www.democracynow.org/2007/3/15/indian_guestworker_slits_wrists_after_being [accessed: June 28, 2010].

Legal Information Institute LII. *U.S. Code: Title 18, 1590, Trafficking with respect to peonage, slavery, involuntary servitude, or forced labor* [Online, Cornell University Law School]. Available at: http://www.law.cornell.edu/uscode/uscode18/usc_sec_18_00001590 [accessed: January 5, 2010].

Louisiana Legislature. 2007. RS 14:46.2, *Human trafficking* [Online]. Available at: http://www.legis.state.la.us/lss/newWin.asp?doc=320889 [accessed: January 10, 2010].

Mello, F. 2007. Coming to America. *The Nation* [Online]. Available at: http://www.thenation.com/article/coming-america-0 [accessed: December 31, 2009].

NILC. 2007. *H-2 Guestworkers Win Landmark Decision in Suit against Luxury Hotel Chain* [Online, National Immigration Law Center]. Available at: http://www.nilc.org/immsemplymnt/LWIW/pressrelease-final.pdf [accessed: January 9, 2010].

Olson, M. 2007. *Two Years after Katrina Workers Center Organizes Day Laborers in New Orleans* [Online, Labor Notes]. Available at: http://www.labornotes.org/node/1329 [accessed: January 9, 2010].

Plyer, A. and Ortiz, E. 2009. *Who lives in New Orleans and the Metro Area now?* [Online, Greater New Orleans Community Data Center]. Available at: http://www.gnocdc.org/2008Demographics/GNOCDC_2008ACSDemographics.pdf [accessed: June 28, 2010].

Plyer, A. 2011. What Census 2010 Reveals about Population and Housing in New Orleans and the Metro Area [Online, Greater New Orleans Community Data Center]. Available at: https://www.gnocdc.s3.amazonaws.com/reports/GNOCDC_Census2010PopulationAndHousing.pdf [accessed: November 17, 2011].

Roig-Franzia, M. 2005. In New Orleans, No Easy Work for Willing Latinos. *Washington Post* [Online]. Available at: http://www.washingtonpost.com/wp-dyn/content/article/2005/12/17/AR2005121700932.html [accessed: May 27, 2009].

Southern Poverty Law Center. 2006. *Broken Levees, Broken Promises, New Orleans' Migrant Workers In Their Own Words* [Online, Immigrant Justice Project]. Available at: http://www.splcenter.org/images/dynamic/legal/IJPorleans.pdf [accessed: January 10, 2010].

Testimony of Mary Bauer before the U.S. House of Representatives. 2008. Testimony of Mary Bauer, Director, Immigrant Justice Project, Southern Poverty Law Center, before the House Subcommittee on Immigration, Citizenship, Refugees, Border Security and International Law, U.S. House of Representatives [Online,

Southern Poverty Law Center]. Available at: http://www.splcenter.org/news/item.jsp?aid=309 [accessed: January 2, 2010].

U.S. Census Bureau. 2009. *Supporting the 2010 Census: Toolkit for Reaching Migrant Workers* [Online, U.S. Census Bureau]. Available at: http://www.2010.census.gov/partners/pdf/toolkit_Migrant_Overview.pdf [accessed: July 1, 2010].

U.S. Department of Justice. 2008. *Involuntary Servitude, Forced Labor, and Sex Trafficking Statutes Enforced* [Online, U.S. Department of Justice, Civil Rights Division]. Available at: http://www.justice.gov/crt/crim/1581fin.php [accessed: Janurary 5, 2009].

U.S. Department of Labor. 1994. *General Administration Letter No. 1–95* [Online, Employment and Training Administration, United States Department of Labor]. Available at: http://www.wdr.doleta.gov/directives/corr_doc.cfm?DOCN=393 [accessed: July 11, 2010].

U.S. Department of Labor. 2006. *Foreign Labor Certification: International Talent Helping Meet Employer Demand* [Online, U.S. Department of Labor, Office of Foreign Labor Certification, Performance Report]. Available at: http://www.foreignlaborcert.doleta.gov/pdf/OFLC_Report_v11_8-23-07.pdf [accessed: September 29, 2010].

U.S. Department of Labor. 2008a. *2008 Statistics Fact Sheet, Wage and Hour collects over $1.4 billion in back wages for over 2 million employees since fiscal year 2001* [Online, U.S. Department of Labor]. Available at: http://www.dol.gov/whd/statistics/2008FiscalYear.htm [accessed: September 30, 2010]

U.S. Department of Labor. 2008b. *ETA Final Rules, Labor Certification Process and Enforcement for Temporary Employment in Occupations Other Than Agriculture or Registered Nursing (H-2B Workers)* [Online, United States Department of Labor]. Available at: http://www.dol.gov/federalregister/PdfDisplay.aspx?DocId=21887 [accessed: June 30, 2010].

U.S. Department of Labor. 2009. Fact Sheet #69: Requirements to Participate in the H-2B Program. [Online, U.S. Department of Labor, Wage, and Hour Division (WHD)]. Available at: http://www.dol.gov/whd/regs/compliance/whdfs69.htm [accessed: June 30, 2010].

U.S. Department of Labor. 2010a. *H-2A Temporary Agricultural Program* [Online, U.S. Department of Labor]. Available at: http://www.foreignlaborcert.doleta.gov/h-2a.cfm [accessed: September 29, 2010].

U.S. Department of Labor. 2010b. *H-2B Certification for Temporary Non-Agricultural Work* [Online, U.S. Department of Labor]. Available at: http://www.foreignlaborcert.doleta.gov/h-2b.cfm [accessed: September 29, 2010].

USCIS. 2010. *H-1B Specialty Occupation Visa Program* [Online, from U.S. Citizenship and Immigration Services]. Available at: http://www.uscis.gov/USCIS/Resources/Resources%20for%20Congress/H1B%20Specialty%20Occupation%20Visa%20Program.pdf [accessed: Septmeber 30, 2010].

USCIS. 2010. *H-1B Specialty Occupations, DOD Cooperative Research and Development Project Workers, and Fashion Models* [Online, U.S. Citizenship & Immigration Services]. Available at: http://www.uscis.gov/portal/site/uscis/

menuitem.b1d4c2a3e5b9ac89243c6a7543f6d1a/?vgnextoid=73566811264a3
210VgnVCM100000b92ca60aRCRD&vgnextchannel=73566811264a3210V
gnVCM100000b92ca60aRCRD [accessed: September 30, 2010].

PART IV
Combating Human Trafficking: Coordinated Responses Across Communities and Borders

Chapter 13

Roadblocks to Legal Help for Trafficking Victims: T-Visas and the Mondragon Raid

Lise Olsen

A big party was in full swing in the seedy bar just off a four-lane road on the northwest fringe of Houston the last night Maximino Mondragon planned to spend in America. After decades as a legal permanent U.S. resident and Houston barman, Mondragon, the owner of the cantina and three other near-by clubs and restaurants, had a one-way ticket back to his home country of El Salvador and was throwing himself a retirement bash.

As usual, the "girls" were there dressed in skimpy skirts and low-cut blouses—clothing he and other cantina operators had bought using the women's own earnings. Mondragon presided over them, displayed along the bar's checkerboard dance floor under the sparkle of a slowly rotating disco ball. The women and teenage girls were compelled to allow anyone who bought the bar's overpriced pony beers to dance with them or to touch them. Virtually all of the money they earned went back to Mondragon and his partners to repay impossibly high fees for the trips the women had made, accompanied by the ring's own smugglers, from their home countries of Honduras and El Salvador.

The midnight raid came as shock. About 100 heavily-armed agents stormed in, bursting into all five bars and restaurants at once. A few girls fled and were never found again. But dozens who happened to be working that night got scooped up and detained along with Mondragon and his accomplices—the very people who had imported them to America and exploited them here.

A marathon set of interrogations was necessary before the victims could be separated from the traffickers, accomplices and cantina operators. Then, even lead investigators from Immigration and Customs Enforcement and the Federal Bureau of Investigation were stunned. They'd rescued almost 120 victims—the biggest human trafficking ring ever identified in the mainland United States.

There were so many that they overflowed the Houston immigration detention center, even though most of the victims were questioned and quickly released. There was not enough space in the local shelters lined up by the International Program of the YMCA to house them all. So some got bussed to Dallas or Austin, where other non-profits offered emergency help. A few got shipped off to jails out-of-town. Some were held for six months.

After the Raid

In the early days, dozens of the victims identified in the round-up got financial assistance—food, clothing and shelter. The federal government sets aside grant money to provide emergency help for trafficking victims through non-profits designated to help in every state.

In theory at least, trafficking victims could qualify for so-called T-visas and be allowed to stay in the United States legally, under a federal program created specifically to help them. As victims waited for the often long, tedious application and review process, they were supposed to be eligible for work permits so they could make money to survive. But most spoke little or no English and had low self-esteem and lacked the skills needed to propel them into good jobs after enduring months or years of physical and emotional abuse.

Three years after the midnight raids and mass rescues, I was assigned, as a reporter from the *Houston Chronicle*, to try to find out what had happened to Mondragon's victims. By November 2008, only about half of the women found back in 2005 had received T-visas—about 67 of the 120. Another 28 were still waiting for decisions or had gotten stuck somewhere in the paperwork process. The rest had drifted away, been rejected or had never applied.

The small percentage of identified victims to receive T-visas is consistent with national trends. Between 2004 and 2007, 1,924 people had received government assistance after being identified as trafficking victims. Yet only 709 of them had received T-visas during the same period.

In the Mondragon case, some victims had never accessed the legal help they needed to apply. Tons of paperwork was required and no victim could do it alone. Some had been discouraged after an initial interview when they learned they would yet again have to tell their stories and provide supporting documents and witness statements. Others had moved and failed to leave forwarding addresses for the volunteer attorneys who tried to help them.

Even in the large and skilled immigration law community in Houston, few knew how to handle T-visas—though a handful of attorneys at Houston non-profits became specialists after helping victims from the Mondragon case and other smaller busts that followed it. It helped that lawyers with one prominent non-profit with offices in Houston's west side, Boat People SOS, had the most experience handling T-visas of anyone in the United States. After the U.S. Department of Justice had exposed a huge trafficking operation at the Daewoosa sweat shop on the island of American Samoa, the non-profit Boat People SOS had raised money to help more than 200 rescued Vietnamese factory workers who had been starved, beaten and forced to work there without pay. Eventually 110 of those victims and their family members got T-visas through the help of attorneys at Boat People SOS offices across the United States. An-Phong Vo, an attorney in the Houston office, had helped some 20 people who had resettled in Texas to get their T-visas and later to apply for a green card. She and other Houston non-profit attorneys had done their best to help the clients they had managed to find from the Mondragon case.

In 2008, Andre Rodriguez, a young attorney who had been hired to work at the YMCA's International Programs a few weeks after the Mondragon raid, worked to assemble an updated list of 99 victims with their phone numbers and current addresses. He contacted them all and tried to find volunteer attorneys to help those who had never applied for visas or who had become discouraged. But more than 20 other Mondragon victims had simply gotten lost. And a few women who had been exploited by the ring but happened to be off work the night of the raid had never been designated as victims at all.

For many of the Mondragon victims' visa applications, attorneys could simply use mass letters of certification that investigators had prepared that listed many victims by name. But some names had been left off those lists. Victims who lacked letters from prosecutors or investigators documenting their hardships could still apply for T visas, but they had less chance of success. Wafa Abdin, an attorney with Catholic Charities in Houston, managed to get T-visas for some trafficking victims without letters but those applicants faced "a higher burden of proof."

T-VISA Troubles

The mission of "saving"—or at least assisting—human trafficking victims is a noble one. Each year many women, men and children are legally or illegally imported into the United States and then exploited here by human traffickers—held prisoner, made to work without pay, and forced to suffer beatings, abuse or even to sell their bodies. They are the victims of what has been called "modern slavery."

But finding trafficking victims can be very difficult. Many criminal trafficking cases involve the rescue of only a handful of victims—or just one person. And a single successful trafficking prosecution can take years to develop and might involve dozens of agents working together on one of the country's elite federal task forces, known as Human Trafficking Rescue Alliances. By 2008, the nation's 40 task forces had arrested 449 traffickers and convicted around 75 percent. Eight of the Mondragon ring members were prosecuted and six were sentenced to prison.

Rescuing victims is a difficult and slow process. The T-visa program was created by the U.S. Trafficking Victims Protection Act of 2000, primarily to help victims who have assisted government anti-trafficking prosecutions as witnesses. In 2001, Congress approved granting as many as 5,000 T-visas a year to victims and to family members whose lives could be endangered because of their relationship with cooperating victims. But according to government statistics, by 2008 only 1,094 T-visas had been granted. In an official response to *Houston Chronicle* questions about why so few visas had been granted compared to the annual quotas, the United States Citizenship and Immigration Services stated, "For the entire US government, identification of trafficking victims is challenging due to the circumstances victims find themselves in, the power and influence of the traffickers, essentially the nature of human trafficking itself."

Still, lawyers and prosecutors in Houston who have been involved in helping victims consider the T-visa program to be of great value. Such visas give women, men and children who have been physically or emotionally abused a chance to recover in a safer environment than the one they would face if deported. Some get jobs and counseling. A few build brand new lives in the United States. Now, under rules passed in December 2008, they can even apply for "green cards" to become legal permanent residents.

But in 2011, questions are still being asked about why some people don't qualify and whether the definition of trafficking victim is too narrow and too tied to cooperation in criminal cases. Many Mondragon victims with T-visas had needed to keep in touch with their attorneys for years to be successful. A few of the luckiest ones had been able to be reunited in America with their children, whom they had left behind in Central America with other relatives after believing traffickers' lies about "legitimate" jobs in Houston, Texas. Some victims with the T-visas lived in tiny crowded apartments shared with other family members or with children—but at least they were working, less fearful and seemed to be enjoying stable lives.

Obstacles to Obtaining T-Visas

But why had only half of the Mondragon victims received T-visas within three years after their rescue? No one was more troubled by that mixed success than the activists and Houston immigration lawyers who had spent countless hours trying to help the victims obtain legal relief.

The explanations were as complex and diverse as the lives of the women exploited by Mondragon and his henchmen. Volunteer advocates, lawyers and victims themselves identified many different obstacles to obtaining T-visas even though the Mondragon case has continued to be trumpeted by the Department of Justice as one of the most successful human trafficking busts in U.S. history. The obstacles fell into several categories:

Victims were never used as witnesses: It is easiest for a victim to get a T-visa when she (or he) has been part of a criminal prosecution and has agreed to act as a witness. But few criminal traffickers are apprehended in the United States, so prosecutions are scarce. Among the many victims trafficked into the country each year, few are rescued; and of those, many are afraid to agree to testify. The reasons are varied: shame about the abuse they suffered; distrust of police because of corruption in their home countries; fear of arrest or deportation; and fear of retribution from the traffickers and their unindicted accomplices either in the United States or abroad.

Technicalities: Sometimes even when arrests get made, victims don't qualify for T-visas or fail to get them for some other technical reason. Some Mondragon victims didn't happen to be at work the day of the arrests. Others escaped prior to the raid. A few of those who were rescued had been too terrified to talk to the law enforcement agents and thus were not included on the initial lists as "victims," so they were unqualified to apply for a T-Visa.

Unstable lives: The instability of victims' lives works against success in drawn-out legal cases. Psychological or economic problems or lingering fears may prompt victims to change addresses and telephone numbers often, making it hard for even the most dedicated volunteer attorneys to keep in touch with clients while T-visas are processed over months or even years. Even those who do get help initially sometimes disappear later on and some even end up being exploited again. According to Diana Velardo, a Houston lawyer who has helped many victims, some are unable to fend for themselves after being rescued and end up being exploited again by other employers or by abusive boyfriends or spouses.

Lack of consistent documentation: Often to succeed, victims' lawyers need to try to get "certification" letters from federal agents, many of whom are too skeptical or too busy to provide them. In other cases, the victims' traffickers are never arrested so their claims of abuse lack legal foundation. Some victims are unable to get the T-visa because they made inconsistent statements to authorities in the confusion after arrests. Others were named—rightly or wrongly—by other victims as "girlfriends" or accomplices of the traffickers so they failed to qualify as legitimate victims.

Daunting hurtles: Victims may just give up. Some qualified victims never get the legal help they need to complete complex T-visa paperwork. Others get discouraged before the process reaches its conclusion as it can take years to proceed through the legal bureaucracy. Other victims who initially receive legal help get discouraged and move away or lose touch with their volunteer lawyers from non-profits—who often receive no pay for helping them and must do their pro bono work on top of regular jobs that can interfere with and slow their progress in assisting the trafficking victims.

Fees: There is no fee to apply for a T-visa. But there is a catch: a $585 fee is required for the waiver that enables them to apply. So-called waivers of "inadmissibility" are required for anyone who entered the United States without being inspected by immigration authorities or who had immigration problems after arrival, such as overstaying a tourist or temporary worker visa. Since many human traffickers bring their victims here illegally, steal their documents and ignore immigration laws, many victims need waivers. Most trafficking victims' lawyers have to find ways to raise money to help their clients pay for the waiver. In hardship cases the $585 fee could be waived, but more paperwork would be required.

Fear: Traffickers often retain power and influence in the community where they are apprehended (and in their home country where victims' families often live) through unindicted co-conspirators, other family members or business associates. So some victims choose to leave the traffickers' turf out of fear, rather than contributing information to authorities that could help get their traffickers arrested. In such cases, not only do they fail to qualify for T-visas, but they provide no information that could help prosecute the traffickers. Thus, another Houston cantina trafficking ring whose members were also indicted in 2005 was able to keep successfully reusing the very same bars and shacks near the Port of Houston to exploit other victims for years after those initial arrests, in part because victims were too afraid to testify against them.

Immigration obstacles: Some victims are quickly deported before being properly interviewed. This happened to at least one juvenile trafficking victim in a Houston case, according to an interview with Wafa Abdin, a prominent immigration lawyer who often works with juveniles at Catholic Charities in Houston. "We worry most about the youngest victims. Some never knew anything but abuse and had no one to take care of them or teach them to protect themselves… some are going to be lost."

Four Women's Stories

To understand more about the experience of the 120 women rescued at Mondragon's cantinas, I spoke at length with four women identified as victims by both lawyers and activists in 2008. I also visited the women's homes and talked to family members, attorneys and activists who knew them. Two had received T-visas after a long struggle. Two had never even applied.

Victims 1 and 2 had recently completed their T-visa process and had parallel success stories. Both had immediately given statements and had cooperated in other ways with government investigators, though neither had ever been required to testify in federal court since Mondragon and his accomplices had all pled guilty to their crimes. Both victims who had been successful in their applications had been paired up early with volunteer lawyers from two different Houston-based non-profits and had earned letters of certification as trafficking victims from government investigators. Though not required in every case, a letter of support from an investigator is of tremendous value to a T-visa seeker. But often getting such letters requires victims' lawyers to lobby busy federal and local agents who are simultaneously trying to investigate new trafficking cases.

Even with the help of lawyers and letters of support, it took more than two years for the two women to obtain T-visas for themselves and their children. They each had to provide detailed accounts in sworn statements of how they had been duped into coming to the United States by traffickers who had promised them legitimate restaurant jobs, and had then brought them to Houston where they were ordered to stay together in guarded apartments, were physically abused, and were forced to work in cantinas for the cash they had been forced to give their captors to repay endless smuggling debts. The accounts had to include details and dates of abuse that required victims to endure long interviews and relate traumatic events that they would have preferred to forget.

Many of the Mondragon victims' documents had been confiscated or stolen by ring members. Both women who had eventually obtained T-visas had children they had left behind in Central America when they had come to the United States for their "jobs," who they hoped could now join them in America. That meant the victims also had to write back to their hometowns in Central America to try to obtain passports or other documents to establish their own identities as well as their claims of relationship to these children.

The need to bring children to the U.S. made the long process more complicated—the mothers needed copies of their children's birth certificates, if the births had been registered, or to obtain sworn statements from people who had seen them pregnant in their home countries. Then they had to try to find and persuade their children's fathers to formally declare they had no objection to the children being brought to the United States. Obtaining such proof often took months, and authenticating the documents often required hiring lawyers in Latin America or asking relatives to make long bus trips to far-off capital cities to visit American embassy officials with limited appointment schedules and little knowledge of the T-visa process.

Yet these two women were among the Mondragon victims who had persisted in their efforts for years and had finally been successful. I watched at the international arrival area at the Houston International Airport as one woman waited to be reunited with her two young sons after a long separation. The boys burst through the metal doors hand in hand with all of their possessions stored in tiny backpacks. It was a tearful yet joyful reunion. The youngest boy had no real memory of his mother, aside from photographs and a voice on the phone. He had been only a baby when she had left to try to build a better life in America, only to end up being trapped by traffickers. This mother had been lucky to get help from an attorney, An-Phong Vo, who was backed by an organization with more experience with T-visas than any other in the United States: Boat People SOS.

The two women victims who had never applied for T-visas had been less fortunate. They had not found lawyers to help them after their rescue and had sadder stories. Both been detained for months following the raids at Mondragon's cantinas. For their own reasons, each had initially been afraid to talk to U.S. authorities. Both felt that they had been treated like criminals. It wasn't an easy thing to confess to a male American FBI agent about being duped and exploited and intimately touched. Each told me that she had been raped against her will. But the two women had different reasons for not obtaining a T-visa.

Victim 3 was a Salvadoran who was a little older than the others who had worked in the cantinas. She had cooperated after a few days in detention but had little new information to offer investigators, who by then had already interviewed dozens of others. The Salvadoran had arrived in the United States only a few months before the raid. More mature and less easily intimidated than the others, she'd been subjected to less physical abuse and had even dared to defend herself verbally to her captors—though once, she said, a friend of Mondragon's had raped her.

By the time I met her in 2008, she felt abandoned by the system and stranded in the United States but she was afraid to return to her native country because her former captors had accomplices who lived and owned businesses in her home town. She had no idea how to get more help once the short-term assistance offered to trafficking victims ran out. Her work permit had expired and she was living in a cheap apartment in Houston and illegally working at cash-only cleaning jobs. I helped her get an appointment to be interviewed by a volunteer attorney, who told her she likely qualified for a T-visa. But running low on cash, she moved out of state before the application process could be completed.

Victim 4 told me she had arrived in the United States as a teenager and was almost immediately forced to become the "girlfriend" of a trafficker—a big burly man old enough to be her father. She said she was kept apart from the other girls and held as a virtual prisoner in an apartment near the cantinas, her movements constantly monitored by a guard or by a security camera. She had worked—without ever actually receiving any real pay—in cantinas with the other victims until she had been made pregnant by the trafficker, whose attentions she said she dared not refuse. Heavily pregnant by the night of the raid, she was no longer working at the bars and so she had not been rescued with others. Despite her advanced pregnancy, she was arrested and then held for months in a jail in East Texas. Eventually, she was interviewed and moved to a more suitable shelter.

Authorities had initially treated the young woman as if she had been an accomplice of the traffickers. Officials apparently viewed her version of events— that she'd been an unwilling victim and not the trafficker's girlfriend—with skepticism, because she was not working on the night of the raid and because some other victims had assumed that, despite her young age, she had willingly submitted to a boyfriend-girlfriend relationship with the trafficker who had impregnated her. She did not win an official letter of support for a T-visa.

Years after the arrest, she obtained her first formal T-visa interview with a volunteer immigration attorney at the Immigration Clinic at the University of Houston Law Center. But after that interview and a review of the documentation, the young woman was told she likely would never qualify. By now the single mother of a toddler, the woman was working illegally in a restaurant. A volunteer advocate who had tried for years to help her worried that she was at risk. The woman lived in poverty only blocks from the bar where she had been exploited— and seemed likely to drift into drinking and depression.

As these examples show, T-visas can be a route to legal status in the United States for trafficking victims, but the road to obtaining them is long and arduous and success is not guaranteed. For the victims of the Mondragon ring who were rescued in one of the largest human trafficking busts in U.S. history, the T-visa system showed at best, mixed success.

Chapter 14

A Model for Coordination in Anti-Human Trafficking Task Forces: The El Paso, Texas, Site Protocol

Virginia McCrimmon

The El Paso Anti-Human Trafficking Task Force operated between March 2005 and April 2009 to integrate and coordinate local and national resources to combat human trafficking and provide immediate and long-term services to victims. The U.S. Department of State has recognized the El Paso site as an exemplary anti-human trafficking task force and has brought many foreign visitors to the site to observe and learn about its operation. The purpose of this chapter is to describe its experience so that other communities with similar goals can learn from its challenges and achievements.

The first comprehensive federal law in the United States to protect victims of trafficking and to prosecute their traffickers—the Trafficking Victims Protection Act (TVPA)—was enacted in October 2000. The intent of the law is to prevent human trafficking overseas, increase prosecution of human traffickers in the United States, and protect and provide federal and state assistance to victims. The provisions of the law apply to all trafficked victims, both U.S. citizens and non-citizens alike.

To combat human trafficking and provide services to victims, whether U.S. citizens or foreign nationals, the U.S. government has established programs at both the national and local levels. At the national level, a Network for Emergency Trafficking Services (NETS) was initiated in March 2005, by the Office of Victims of Crime of the U.S. Department of Justice (DOJ). El Paso, Texas, was designated a Target Site in the Network for Emergency Trafficking Services (NETS) for the Western Region. El Paso's Anti- Human Trafficking Program ended in April 2009 because funding was predicated upon a social service organization and a local law enforcement agency working in partnership, and no local law enforcement agency opted to seek DOJ funding to continue the program. During the four years of its operation, the program and the task force that resulted from it achieved a number of significant gains, including formulation of a protocol for dealing with trafficking cases.

The Anti-Human Trafficking Task Force in El Paso, Texas

The DOJ's Office of Victims of Crime provided funds for the establishment and implementation of anti-human trafficking task forces in various U.S. states. The funds from the DOJ's Bureau of Justice Assistance were to be used by a local law enforcement agency in partnership with a service organization, to implement a program to combat human trafficking. To ensure oversight and appropriate expenditure of the funds, the DOJ required that the partners operate within specified guidelines and requirements established for both the law enforcement agency and the service organization. There were two different categories of objectives—one for law enforcement and the other for social service support. The El Paso Salvation Army was the service organization that took the lead on the initiative.

The Department of Justice grant funded the Salvation Army to have one employee work part time (20 hours per week) on addressing issues related to human trafficking. Within the city police department, funding was provided for one full-time employee. A requirement of the grant was the formation of a task force encompassing members of local law enforcement and social service organizations. Individuals were identified from various community groups to attend regularly scheduled meetings of the task force and to coordinate responses from their particular organizations.

The DOJ named the El Paso Police Department as the lead agency to direct the task force. An individual from the lead agency had the overall responsibility of ensuring that the task force operated as a single, unified unit. The lead individual was expected to establish and maintain a cooperative network of individuals within the task force.

To constitute the membership of the task force, it was necessary to determine what resources within the local community were available to advance the task force's mission. Agencies, organizations and community groups were identified to provide support in meeting the specific objectives of the task force, and each organization identified a representative to the task force. To formalize the types of support that the task force and its constituent agencies would provide for trafficking victims, a Memorandum of Understanding (MOU) was executed between the Salvation Army, law enforcement, and other task force members.

The result was a multi-agency task force able to respond to the complex aspects of human trafficking cases. The multi-disciplinary group represented local law enforcement (police, sheriffs, and U.S. marshals), the Federal Bureau of Investigation (FBI), the Department of Labor, immigration officials, immigration legal advocates, the Salvation Army, religious organizations, and others. Each agency represented in the task force was expected to operate within its own directives and constraints. Members of the task force brought their own unique set of abilities and expertise to provide synergy for the task force. Law enforcement personnel were focused on prosecution of traffickers whereas service agencies' members focused on meeting the needs of trafficked victims. Each task force member had an understanding of the overall purpose of the task force and his or her role in combating human trafficking and assisting victims.

To comply with the requirements of the DOJ, the task force developed and implemented a detailed and comprehensive protocol. Appropriate sections of the protocol were implemented on a case-by-case basis. The focus of the protocol was on the perspective, functions, and responsibilities of the Salvation Army's Victim Service Coordinator, who was a member of the task force.

Following the discussion of the protocol, two cases are presented to highlight the execution of duties performed by the victim service coordinator during the period of DOJ funding. The chapter closes by discussing issues and problems that decreased the effectiveness of the anti-human trafficking task force.

Anti-human Trafficking Task Force Services Protocol

Federal agencies combating human trafficking (such as the FBI) have the primary responsibility for the victims and are involved in decisions concerning service provision. The certification of an individual as being a victim of human trafficking lies solely within the purview of the law enforcement agencies, which conduct investigations and interviews to determine whether the treatment and conditions to which the individual has been subjected meet the criteria for human trafficking. The major initial decisions, such as the type and location of shelter and the level of security needed, are determined by these federal professionals. The major focus of federal agencies is upon prosecuting the traffickers; therefore, victims' advocates groups such as the Salvation Army must work closely with all involved to ensure that the victims' needs and well-being are considered and the most appropriate care is provided to them at all stages of the process. There is no cut-off date for services to victims, regardless of how long the certification process takes. Even after the certification process is complete, services should continue until the individual is able to live independently.

Victims of human trafficking are unlike any other client population served by the Salvation Army. They face many different kinds of dangers and have various needs that are unique to the trafficking experience. The victim service coordinators must be prepared to serve the particular needs of each victim. Many are female victims of sex trafficking, but male and female labor trafficking victims are not uncommon in El Paso or elsewhere in the United States. The typical victims served by anti-trafficking task forces such as El Paso's are undocumented immigrants, though cases may also involve U.S. citizens or authorized migrants. Many victims are highly traumatized and afraid; they may be distrustful of those attempting to help them, or fear that their traffickers will harm their loved ones. Given their circumstances, victims of human trafficking exhibit a wide range of immediate needs that must be addressed along with considerations regarding their security and confidentiality.

Minors are intended to be served under a different federal program, the Unaccompanied Refugee Minor (URM) program, which typically transfers them to foster care. However, minors may still need immediate medical care, housing, food, and clothing until appropriate foster care placement can be arranged.

To ensure an appropriate response to trafficking cases, the protocol developed by the El Paso task force identified two distinct levels of action. The Level 1 Basic Protocol focuses on the immediate actions to be taken when a case of human trafficking is suspected. The Level 2 Advanced Protocol addresses the local, multi-disciplinary group response to trafficking victims. Together the two levels form a continuum of actions aimed at delivering services to trafficking victims.

Level 1: Basic Protocol

The key prerequisite for implementing a response to human trafficking is to identify trafficking victims. Several tools were implemented to help with victim identification in the El Paso community. The initial step in the basic protocol was the telephone hotline. During the time the program was funded by the DOJ, the El Paso Police Department maintained a trafficking information and referral center that was open 24 hours a day, 7 days a week. The individuals staffing the center had a Trafficking Hotline Questionnaire that was used to obtain pertinent information from anyone who might be a trafficking victim or might report having knowledge of one. Based on the content of the completed questionnaire, specific actions would be taken to initiate an appropriate response. The information in the completed questionnaire and any additional data obtained from or about the victim(s) was discussed only with individuals on a need-to-know basis. Precautions were taken to ensure that the completed questionnaire and any additional information related to the victim were secure at all times.

An informational program was developed that could be disseminated periodically through the local news media (print, TV, and radio) to reach the general population. The Salvation Army Victim Services Coordinator/Point-of-Contact gave presentations about the human trafficking problem to groups, organizations, and individuals. The informational program was tailored to the intended audience and stressed the necessity for anyone with knowledge of actual or possible victims of the crime to report such information directly to a trafficking information and referral center.

In the event of an apparent human trafficking case, hotline staff members were instructed to contact the Salvation Army's Victim Services Coordinator (VSC) for further direction.

Level 2: Advanced Protocol

After having followed up on a suspected human trafficking case, the third step was for the VSC to make an initial assessment to screen out cases that did not meet the criteria for human trafficking as specified by the Trafficking Victims Protection

Act. To prevent divulging too much information or tainting the victim's story, the VSC did not ask any open-ended or leading questions. The VSC and/or the legal services advocate would discuss options available to victims to determine whether to report the case to law enforcement for investigation.

In making an assessment, the VSC would employ a compassionate, understanding, and helpful approach to ferret out victims of human trafficking. Potential questions used to identify human trafficking victims include:

- Are you now being (or have you at one time been) held against your will?
- Have you or your family been threatened or beaten to prevent you from leaving your current situation?
- Does someone else decide where you work and how much you work?
- If you work, are you paid what you were promised?
- Can you leave your job or situation if you want?
- Can you come and go as you please?
- Have you been threatened if you try to leave?
- Have you been physically harmed in any way?
- Have you ever been deprived of food, water, sleep or medical care?
- Do you have to ask permission to eat, sleep or go to the bathroom?
- Are there locks on your doors and windows so you cannot get out?
- Has anyone threatened your family?
- Has your identification documentation been taken from you?
- Is anyone forcing you to do anything that you do not want to do?
- What are your working or living conditions like?
- Where do you eat?
- Do you sleep in a bed, on a cot or on the floor?

While the questions in the assessment protocol would likely be most appropriate for the VSC or law enforcement personnel, they could also raise awareness of the potential for human trafficking among the general public. Once the initial assessment was completed, any questionable situations would be treated as potential trafficking cases and would initiate further investigative measures.

The fourth step required a multi-disciplinary group mobilization. In order for the Salvation Army to use DOJ grant funds to serve or repatriate victims of human trafficking, a law enforcement or prosecution professional needed to concur with the initial assessment of human trafficking victim status. The VSC would contact appropriate members of the task force—local law enforcement (police, sheriffs, or U.S. marshals), FBI, Department of Labor, ICE, immigration legal advocates, religious organizations, and so on—to determine and implement the appropriate course of action. After the consultations with the task force had been completed the fifth step was to conduct a follow-up interview to collect additional vital information from the victim. To help facilitate this process the VSC would use a Trafficking Victim Services Checklist as a guide. Regardless of whether an investigation took place, any information regarding the alleged trafficking offenses would only be collected by law enforcement and/or legal advocates with bona fide legal status, and would not be collected by case managers.

The sixth step involved additional emergency assessments. These assessments looked at shelter type and location and were helpful in identifying areas in which the victim would require additional services. To facilitate these assessments an Individual Demographics/Brief Assessment Form and a Trafficking Risk Assessment Form were designed to collect pertinent information. These forms included elements such as safety, determination of trafficking victim status, flight risk, mental health (especially post-traumatic stress disorder, potential for suicide or attachment to traffickers), medical status (injuries and contagious diseases), legal status, and substance addictions.

Repatriation was included in the protocol as an optional seventh step. The protocol recommends that victims not be repatriated immediately. Experience has shown that victims often change their mind about repatriation with increased levels of trust, security, and understanding of the benefits for which they may be eligible. A period of at least a week is recommended before revisiting the issue of repatriation. If after the assessment period the victim still wished to return home, the VSC would contact the Salvation Army's Anti-Trafficking Program Coordinator, who would help coordinate the repatriation process with the DOJ's Office for Victims of Crime and the International Organization for Migration. (It should be noted that none of the victims served during the period requested repatriation.)

The eighth step in this process was to determine the victim's service location. Based on a number of factors including the victim's wishes, it might be determined to be in the best interest of the victim to relocate him or her to another city. On a number of occasions, the El Paso site was prepared to receive and provide services to relocated victims; however these preparations turned out to be unnecessary because the cases were disposed without the need for relocation. A special protocol was designed for trafficking victims who were adolescents with no family members present to care for them, who would be served by the Unaccompanied Refugee Minor program.

For victims who opted to stay within the city, the ninth step was to begin service planning to meet their short- and long-term needs. Before any other service providers were contacted, the victim would sign a Release of Information Form so that sensitive information concerning the victim could be released to other authorized agencies and personnel. The need for release of information was clearly explained to ensure that the victim understood the purpose of the form. Once this step had been completed the victim would be ready for the tenth step of developing and monitoring an individual Service Plan designed to meet his or her unique needs. The case manager would take the lead, but the VSC and law enforcement victim coordinators would collaborate in developing, implementing, and monitoring the plan. The assistance provided, personal items issued, and referrals made would be noted on an Individual Services Provision Record Sheet. The eleventh step in the protocol was to develop a Safety Plan to provide for the security of the victim and relevant service providers. To assist in this effort, the task force developed the Safety Plan For Trafficked And Enslaved Persons, which addresses security safeguards for victims and service providers.

The final steps in the Advanced Protocol address assessment and monitoring. The twelfth step is to conduct follow-up assessments to maintain an accurate understanding of the victim's changing needs and to determine the effectiveness of the provided services. The victim's readiness would be the primary factor in determining the timing of these assessments, which would include mental health and medical status, safety issues, victim's needs and desires or other aspects of the victim's situation. The victim's case manager would perform the thirteenth step of providing and monitoring services specified in the Service Plan. Because the Salvation Army was ultimately responsible for the care of the victims the VSC would monitor each case and coordinate funding for services. A Weekly Case Summary Sheet was used to facilitate the monitoring process to ensure optimal care for the victims and efficient use of the funds. These summary sheets would be completed by the case managers and discussed with the VSC on a weekly basis. Then the POC would provide reports to local Salvation Army officials, other members of the task force, and Headquarters, which would coordinate and report on the service needs of trafficking victims.

Needs of Trafficking Victims

The needs of trafficking victims are extensive and varied. As agreed to in the MOU between the Salvation Army and the multi-disciplinary group, each task force member had specific roles to play in meeting the needs of the victims. The diverse responsibilities and actions employed by the task force members to meet the full array of victims' needs are addressed in the paragraphs below. Each victim was assigned a case manager and a victim services coordinator to help oversee and facilitate the process of obtaining services. General needs of the victims included interpretation/translation, secure shelter, food, clothing, medical services, legal services, transportation, addiction recovery programs, and in some cases, services for children. In addition to the general needs included in this assessment, specific needs could be identified and addressed on a case-by-case basis.

Case Management

Case management was an integral component of the service-delivery system. The role of the case manager was to ensure that victims received all the services they might need during the pre-certification phase. The case manager's tasks included helping the victim navigate and understand available social services, service system advocacy, basic case coordination, needs assessments, and service plan development. In addition, case managers helped with transportation, translation, emotional support or counseling, depending upon their training and resources.

The case manager would also coordinate the victims' transition to the care of appropriate agencies once they were certified as trafficking victims. The El Paso agencies that agreed to coordinate and provide necessary services are listed below:

- The Salvation Army
- Center Against Family Violence (CAFV)
- Diocesan Migrant and Refugee Service (DMRS)
- Las Américas
- Mental Health and Mental Retardation (MHMR)
- Mission on the Border
- Project Vida
- Sisters of Our Lady of Charity
- Thomason Cares

The primary person responsible for coordinating the task force was the Salvation Army's Anti-Trafficking Point of Contact/Victim Services Coordinator. The POC's principal role was to serve as the Salvation Army's anti-trafficking liaison in El Paso and to ensure that the Salvation Army's program was fulfilling all of its commitments to the El Paso community. In addition to helping plan and implement task force activities, the POC was also responsible for various administrative tasks. These included requesting distribution of funds, managing service provider contracts and other formal agreements, recording and submitting program activities reports to the DOJ, and keeping supervisors appraised.

Implicit in the administrative duties of the POC were a number of specific sub-tasks. The POC developed and implemented a Public Awareness and Outreach Plan and a Service Provider Training Plan. The POC coordinated and developed Memoranda of Understanding between federal agencies and service providers. It provided written and/or verbal reports to local Salvation Army officials and other members of the task force. It coordinated and reported on victims' service needs and plans and reported this information to the appropriate supervisors within the Salvation Army. It was also the POC's responsibility to maintain records of all expenditures and to file documentation for reimbursable expenditures such as bills, credit card transactions, and receipts. The POC executed and filed client telephone logs and travel logs. It kept a record of all resources, including food, clothing, shelter, personal hygiene items, cleaning supplies, cooking utensils, and educational materials, that were provided to each victim by the Salvation Army. In a case where no receipts for expenditures were available the POC was required to complete and transmit a Service Payment Request Form to Salvation Army headquarters. All other expenditures were coordinated with appropriate local Salvation Army personnel and accounting staff and were submitted periodically to Salvation Army Headquarters.

Interpretation and Translation

In an effort to meet the needs of non-English speaking victims the task force offered language services. Individuals within the local area were called upon when needed to serve as interpreters and translators. To ensure the security of trafficked individuals, local interpreters and translators were first cleared by federal agencies such as the FBI and Immigration and Customs Enforcement. If needed, federal agency interpreters or translators located in other parts of the country could be drawn upon in coordination with local Salvation Army Headquarters and the federal agencies.

Secure Shelter, Food, and Clothing

Victims of human trafficking have a pressing need for basic services such as housing and food, so a priority of the task force was to make sure these needs were addressed. Housing was provided by the Salvation Army's shelter facility on a space-available basis. It was the responsibility of the law enforcement personnel and the VSC to determine the type and location of shelter and the level of security required. In cases where the victim's location needed to remain confidential, alternative housing was provided in a secure facility. Victims housed in the secure facility followed standard guidelines to ensure the security of all residents. For example, each resident or staff member had to make an entry in an activity log when she traveled or made a telephone call.

Food and clothing were also made available through the Salvation Army. If the victim resided at the Salvation Army meals were prepared by the kitchen staff. For victims living elsewhere, food from the Salvation Army's pantry was provided if available. Otherwise funds were available to purchase groceries for meal preparation. Prepared meals were provided to residents in the secure facility. When available, clothing was provided by the Salvation Army from its stock of donated items; otherwise funds were available to purchase clothing.

Medical Services

Trafficking, enslavement, and exploitation understandably take a toll on a victim's health. A number of providers offered medical, dental, and mental health services as needed. Medical care was provided to the victims by the El Paso County Hospital or by medical personnel. Routine medical care or care for chronic illnesses was provided by Thomason Cares, an El Paso county medical facility. Routine or preventative dental care was provided by Thomason Cares and emergency dental care was available. Victims who needed mental health services could access the El Paso County Mental Health and Mental Retardation (MHMR) facility.

Legal Services

Legal advocacy services available to victims included explanation of rights, legal protections, procedures and proceedings, and assistance with legal status, such as visas. The legal advocate helped ensure that victims' rights were protected throughout the legal process. Legal assistance for immigration issues was provided by Diocesan Migrant and Refugee Services (DMRS). If the victim had been involved in illegal activities and had been arrested by local law enforcement officials, the FBI would be notified— which turned out to be unnecessary because none of the victims served during the period had engaged in illegal activities. In general there was a constant flow of information among service providers and law enforcement officials concerning the behavior of the victims.

Children

The Salvation Army contracted with various El Paso providers to deliver services for victims' children. The Salvation Army itself would provide day care services, and emergency medical care would be provided by the El Paso County Hospital and its medical personnel. Children of school age were to be enrolled in a public or private school. Essential clothing would either be purchased or provided from the Salvation Army's clothing donations stocks. As it turned out, none of the victims served during the period had children, so the efficacy of this provider network went untested.

Transportation

A variety of transportation options were available to the victims, depending on their intended destination. When federal agencies requested victims' presence, the POC transported them to the appropriate agencies. When it was deemed appropriate and safe for the victims to use public transportation, funds were provided to individuals who were capable of using the bus system. Transportation for non-emergency medical care or to attend religious services was provided by public transportation, the victim services coordinator or the victim's case manager. When appropriate, the victim used public transportation to and from school.

Addiction Recovery Programs

Although the protocol specified that victims requiring addiction recovery services would be provided care by the El Paso County Hospital or by medical personnel, none of the victims required this service.

Case Studies from a Service Provider's Perspective

During the 4-year life of the grant, eight individuals were certified as being victims of human trafficking, and another twenty possible victims were served. Four visas are currently being processed for our clients. The following section summarizes two cases to show how the protocol played out in real life situations and to highlight the duties of the victim service coordinators in this process. Although we expected that the cases served by the anti-trafficking task force would mainly involve sexual exploitation, all eight of the cases encountered at the El Paso site involved some other type of servitude.

Case 1: Ms. G

Ms. G. was a 36-year-old Mexican woman who, at the age of 18, was contracted to work in a home in the United States. She and her family had been convinced that she would be doing domestic work and that she would be paid.

When Ms. G. arrived illegally in the United States, she was given a small cot on which to sleep in the basement of the house. She was forced into involuntary servitude, cleaning, washing, cooking, ironing, and doing whatever other work was demanded of her. This routine continued seven days a week from morning to night without rest or food, except for the scraps that were left from the dinner that she had to prepare for the lady of the house and her two sons. At least once a month, the sons would throw parties at the house and Ms. G. would have to wait on them and their guests. She had to be perpetually ready to serve the family at their command. Whenever Ms. G. would ask for her wages, the lady of the house would threaten to call the police and immigration authorities and accuse Ms. G. of theft and violent behavior. In addition to the verbal and emotional abuse, she was deprived of the basic necessities of life such as a toothbrush, toothpaste and deodorant, and she had to beg for feminine hygiene products. The lady of the house would bring old men to the house to introduce to Ms. G. Her reported intentions were to find a man who would marry Ms. G; the true intentions of the lady of the house are left to speculation.

Ms. G was paralyzed by the threats and told no one about her situation. She lived in this abusive environment for 15 years before she gathered the courage to contact the mother-in-law of the son of the lady of the house and secretly request her help. The mother-in-law had no previous inkling that Ms. G was being held in bondage, but she believed Ms. G's story and gave her refuge in her home. She advised her to contact the Diocesan Migrant and Refugee Service (DMRS) which in turn contacted the proper authorities in the anti-trafficking task force. In November 2006, the Salvation Army was initially contacted to provide case management for Ms. G. She was withdrawn, frightened, insecure, and unable to take the initiative for anything because all aspects of her life had been rigidly controlled for those 15 years. Her case manager moved her into the safe haven five days after her initial intake, where she remained until March 2007.

During this time, in accordance with the TVPA, Ms. G. was provided safe housing, food, clothing, linens, towels and other supplies necessary to set up residency at the safe haven. She was also given emotional and spiritual support by the residents of the safe haven and legal support by the Diocesan Migrant and Refugee Service. The Salvation Army helped her obtain an Employment Authorization card, a Social Security card, a Texas Identification card through the Department of Public Safety, and a Registration card for Project Vida, which provides medical services for women. She was given a complete physical, including gynecological services. After five months at the safe haven she was able to move into an apartment of her choosing, and with the help of the Salvation Army she found a job and became financially independent. The Salvation Army periodically interfaces with Ms. G. to offer continued support. Hearing her laugh and seeing her do things on her own is a great joy to all who were involved in the case.

In legal proceedings, Ms. G. provided testimony against the lady of the house, who was declared to be mentally incompetent and therefore was not prosecuted.

Case 2: CD

CD was an undocumented, unaccompanied male minor who fell victim to labor trafficking. He had completed six years of school in his home country of Honduras but poverty had forced him to drop out of school to help farm his father's plot of land. CD lamented all the hard work his family had to perform just to subsist and saw no chance that his own or his family's life could be improved. He also was fearful for his life because dangerous gangs had threatened to kill him. He decided to go to the United States to make a better life for himself. Although he was only 14 years old, his family did not try to prevent him from leaving.

With only a few dollars in his pocket, CD set out on foot for the United States. During his three-month journey, he encountered many dangerous situations and privations. He arrived in Laredo, Texas, by crossing the Rio Grande River alone. His intentions were to go to Houston, Texas, but instead he ended up in El Paso. When he reached the outskirts of El Paso after walking across the desert, he was shoeless and his feet were covered in sores. He encountered some children who were playing in a yard, who asked CD to come to their house so that he could get some attention for his feet. The parents of the children decided to let CD live with them. He was told that he could stay in a camper near the house.

Although their initial treatment of CD appeared to be motivated by pity and kindness, CD was required to do farm chores and domestic work in the house. He also was forced to work in the business run by the owners of the home. He was made to operate dangerous machinery without any safety protection. He did not have regular meals with the family and his only nutrition came from food he scrounged while working in the house. Although he was promised payment for his work, he never received the money and had an ever-increasing amount of work to do. CD was told that he must avoid immigration officials. He was told many times that he was free to leave, but that he would not be able to walk one block before immigration would pick him up, torture him, and perhaps kill him.

One day, CD was seen by some local girls who stopped to talk with him and became concerned. A call was made to the Diocesan Migrant and Refugee Service, which then contacted the El Paso Police Department. The police department, in turn, informed the FBI, who then informed the Border Patrol. After initial law enforcement interviews, the Salvation Army was contacted and asked to provide a secure location for the young man, who had been severely traumatized by the thought of what the family had said would happen to him if he interacted with law enforcement personnel. Believing that he was going to be killed, he attempted to hang himself. He later said that he thought that he would rather die by his own hand than by the guns of immigration officials. He learned that his fear of U.S. authorities was unfounded as the El Paso Anti-Trafficking Task Force exerted its extensive coordination and collaboration efforts to ensure CD's safety and welfare. In the three weeks after his discovery while CD was in El Paso, many agencies including the Department of Labor, FBI, ICE, Diocesan Migrant and Refugee Service (DMRS) and Catholic Charities met with him to learn more about his case and to provide legal and social services. The Salvation Army assumed custodial care and provided not only the basic necessities such as clothing, shoes, underwear and toiletries, but also medical care, vision care, counseling, and guidance. Law enforcement personnel made a determination that the youth should have legal status. The legal status was granted and additional steps were taken to ensure that he would be provided all legal assistance and opportunities to acquire U.S. citizenship.

CD is no longer in El Paso. He is receiving foster care at another location in the United States. He is attending school and learning English. CD is interested in soccer and has joined a soccer league. He is able to talk with his family in Honduras and stays in touch with many of the people from the El Paso task force whose lives he has touched.

The family that was holding CD was not prosecuted because of insufficient evidence.

Reflections and Recommendations for the Future

It is of utmost importance that members of an anti-trafficking task force be capable of performing their duties with expertise and professionalism. Experiences with the El Paso task force have shown that its members were extremely dedicated and went well beyond what was expected to ensure that victims were well served. The U.S. Department of State has recognized the El Paso Site as an exemplary anti-human trafficking task-force and during the four years it was operating brought many foreign visitors to the site to observe and learn about its operations.

The most significant obstacle to combating human trafficking is lack of awareness and understanding on the part of the general community. An educated public is essential to fight against this crime. People need to be aware of the pervasiveness of human trafficking and be able to notice any signs of it occurring in their communities. They need to be able to recognize and support potential victims to keep them out of harm's way. They need to understand that the inability to provide for one's essential needs due to a lack of financial resources and absence of strong family support can put an individual at risk for becoming a victim of human trafficking. If such evidence goes unnoticed—or if people have no idea about the proper channels for reporting any suspicions they might have—actual and potential victims will have little chance of being protected, discovered, and assisted.

Throughout the four-year period of its operation, the task force conducted an active program of outreach to the community. At every presentation, various members of the audience expressed shocked reactions upon learning that human trafficking was taking place in their communities. This suggests that if any of them had been exposed to evidence of its occurrence, they would have missed or misinterpreted these clues.

Contained in an undated pamphlet published by the U.S. Department of Health and Human Services Administration for Families and Children, titled *Look Beneath the Surface*, are a number of questions to help identify potential victims:

- Is the person accompanied by another person who seems controlling (possibly the trafficker)?
- Is the person rarely allowed in public (except for work)?
- Can you detect any physical or psychological abuse?
- Does the person seem submissive or fearful?
- Does the person have difficulty communicating because of language or cultural barriers?
- Does the person lack identification or documentation?
- Is someone else collecting the person's pay or holding their money for "safe keeping"?

The lack of knowledge in the general population is also, in varying degrees, reflected among law enforcement personnel. Human trafficking does not appear to be a high priority for many law enforcement officials and inadequate resources are dedicated to combat it. Lawmakers should ensure that resources are available to identify and prosecute traffickers. Prosecution should be vigorously pursued and traffickers should be quickly given stiff penalties and long sentences. Although there are many challenges and deficiencies in current efforts to combat human trafficking, the successes in offering some victims the opportunity to live as independent and autonomous individuals are rewarding to those who work hard to assist them. It is encouraging to members of the El Paso Anti-Human Trafficking Task Force that the states of Texas and New Mexico have recently initiated programs that focus on combating human trafficking. In 2010, for the first time, New Mexico used the state's 2008 anti-human trafficking law to charge an individual with this crime. Likewise in 2010, Texas formed the Texas Human Trafficking Protection Task Force to address the causes and consequences of human trafficking in the state. With an increasing effort, both states will be able to free more victims and significantly diminish the scourge of modern-day slavery.

Chapter 15

Combating Human Trafficking in the U.S.–Mexico Borderlands

Moira Murphy-Aguilar and Susan Tiano

Human trafficking presents numerous challenges for policymakers, law enforcement agents, service providers and others trying to formulate effective strategies to combat the practice. With its root causes spread across a myriad of interrelated factors that affect the supply of and demand for enslaved workers and promote the criminal networks that profit from their participation in the trade, human trafficking defies simple policy prescriptions.

Clearly, in the long run the ideal scenario would be to eliminate the human trade by transforming the conditions that allow it to flourish. Such a worthy objective is unlikely to be achieved anytime soon, however, because the dynamics that give rise to forced physical and sexual labor are so deeply embedded in the global economy that uprooting them will require fairly drastic social changes. In the meantime, efforts at structural transformation need to go hand in hand with policies intended to retard the human trade by apprehending, punishing, and deterring perpetrators, and to ameliorate its negative effects by protecting, rescuing, and serving actual and potential victims. Achieving both strategic and practical objectives requires educational campaigns to promote awareness and understanding among the public at large as well as the politicians, journalists, and others who shape public opinion and formulate social policy. The human rights perspective presented in this chapter prioritizes protecting and socially reintegrating trafficking victims over prosecutorial goals.

Working to eradicate human trafficking means affirming that all human beings have the indelible right to live in freedom and that no one has the authority to possess or enslave another person. It means putting these value commitments into practice by being willing to devote resources to combat the trade and serve its victims. Even in recessionary epochs, most nations have reserves that could be dedicated to developing anti-trafficking programs, or funds could be reallocated from other, less essential budget priorities. National efforts need to be supported and encouraged by international policy reflecting the global community's shared moral obligation to eliminate the human trade. The benefits to be achieved by enabling all human beings to enjoy freedom of choice, earn a living wage, and be treated with dignity regardless of gender, age, national origin or immigration status far outweigh the costs.

Helping the Victims

An essential first step toward creating a global environment in which all people can exercise their right to protection is to ensure that human trafficking is clearly defined and codified in the criminal statutes of all the world's countries (Schauer and Wheaton 2006: 13–15). Without definitional and legislative consistency across countries, traffickers can avoid prosecution by winding their way through different jurisdictions and sets of regulations while continuing to exploit unprotected victims. Creating consistent definitions and laws will greatly aid in identifying victims so they can be removed from harm's way and offered the necessary services. Yet while countries such as Mexico—which amended its constitution in 2011 to provide new protections for trafficking victims by allowing them to denounce traffickers anonymously—continue to work on their own anti-trafficking legislation, attempts at international harmonization across countries continue to face a significant challenge.

A first step might be to harmonize legislation across sub-national units such as the 50 U.S. states to ensure policy consistency across jurisdictions in a single country. For example, the U.S. Department of Justice's "Model State Anti-Trafficking Criminal Statute" was developed in 2004 as a tool for state legislators and victims' advocates attempting to develop effective anti-trafficking legislation. Though the federal government provides a model for the various states to follow, each has the leeway to adjust its statutes to respond to local variation. The challenges facing law enforcement officials in the U.S.–Mexico borderlands are obviously different from those in America's heartland, for example. Since experience gained by local officials in the field is essential to developing effective processes for discovering victims and their traffickers, incorporating their insights into local laws and practices can help attune federal guidelines to local conditions (Freedom Network USA 2005). The strategy allows sub-national units to improve upon the federal framework in order to adapt anti-trafficking programs to the local or regional context.

Ideally, Mexico and the United States would rally around the issue of human trafficking by moving toward harmonization of regulations for protecting victims and prosecuting perpetrators. The precedent set by the North American Free Trade Agreement (NAFTA), where the three countries' policies were harmonized for their mutual economic benefit, indicates that such harmonization is possible if all parties are willing to negotiate. NAFTA itself could help protect people from human trafficking if the three countries could renegotiate the agreement to offer stronger protections against worker exploitation.

The precedent of the NAFTA indicates that if the Mexican and U.S. governments were as committed to preventing modern-day slavery as they were to promoting economic integration, they would be better able to develop consistent definitions of human trafficking in their criminal codes and to harmonize regulations across their shared border. The ideal scenario would be to develop a collaborative model based on the commonalities between the Mexican and U.S. legal systems, which could then be implemented by the 50 U.S. and 31 Mexican states in a way that allowed for local variation.

In Mexico and the United States, as elsewhere, strong laws in favor of workers' rights can serve to abate labor trafficking and protect potential victims. The existence and enforcement of laws guaranteeing workers' right to organize and work in a safe environment and to be paid at or above a minimum wage level is vital to protect workers from enslavement and other workplace abuses. The suspension of such laws, even for a short period, can be a boon to traffickers—as Stephanie Hepburn shows in Chapter 12 in this volume. Protective legislation must be in place for all workers, including sex workers, for whom strengthened laws against battery and rape are vital to shield them from violence. Workers' rights legislation must be enforced, safeguarded and considered to be a vital component of any anti-trafficking strategy.

Legislation provides the essential framework, but it must be effectively implemented to bring the desired results. And enforcement requires detection: as long as trafficking goes unnoticed in the shadows of the underground economy, its victims will continue to be abused and exploited. All law enforcement and immigration officials must be trained to recognize human trafficking victims and to distinguish them from other kinds of exploited workers or unauthorized migrants. When trafficking victims are at risk for detention and deportation for violating immigration laws, they are understandably reluctant to come forward to identify themselves. Some may have direct experience with corrupt officials in league with traffickers, which would further contribute to their fear and distrust of law enforcement agents. Victims' advocates in law enforcement, non-governmental organizations, and the general community need to be proactive in locating victims who are unwilling or unable to seek help.

Likewise, coordination among relevant sectors—law enforcement, immigration, health provision, and so on—should be encouraged to meet the initial needs of victims, with special additional services directed to children and youth. Many victims are identified by advocates only after they have been confined to—and further traumatized within—an immigration detention facility, rather than at the point of first contact with authorities when service provision could have been initiated more immediately and more effectively (Free the Slaves and Human Rights Center 2004).

Human trafficking victims need to be distinguished from victims of other kinds of violence and exploitation. The types of violence experienced by the homeless, by domestic violence victims, by street prostitutes with abusive pimps, or by laborers in unregulated employment contexts is not the same as that endured by slaves. The horrors that trafficked victims experience typically require specific kinds of services to enable them to recover and reintegrate socially. For example, support groups are often helpful for domestic violence victims but they may be uncomfortable or deleterious for human trafficking victims who have been isolated for long periods of time (Free the Slaves and Human Rights Center 2004). Training must be geared toward helping law enforcement officials and other specialized experts understand that different types of violence create contrasting victim profiles, and to be able to distinguish among them.

The specific needs of victims often depend on the type of trafficking they have endured. Victims must be able to tell their stories in their native language, through the use of a translator if need be, to reveal their victimization experiences. Labor trafficking victims often have broken bones and other physical injuries, while sex trafficking victims stand a high chance of having contracted an illness such as HIV or having undergone one or more forced abortions. Sex workers may have been addicted to sedating drugs in order to subdue them, while forced laborers may have been given central nervous system stimulants to increase their productivity. Understanding that victimization profiles will shape the kind of rehabilitative services rescued victims will require can led to more successful treatment outcomes.

Stereotypical images that all trafficking victims are women and children can make it difficult to find male victims and can limit the efficacy of treatment programs for those who are discovered. Gender role stereotypes such as the notion that men should be strong enough to escape their captors can prevent authorities from recognizing male victims of labor trafficking, who are as or more common than female victims of forced labor. Such stereotypes can also impair efforts to develop services to help men cope with the trauma of enslavement. Service providers who work with victims need to be educated about contrasting kinds of victimization profiles so that they will be able to recognize and assist the whole range of trafficking victims they are likely to encounter.

Victims also need to be educated about their rights and the legal protections available to them. For example, the U.S. government created T-visas to enable trafficking victims to remain in the United States and apply for citizenship, if they are willing to testify against their traffickers. But at the time of this writing, only 4 percent of available visas had been allocated (U.S. Immigration Support 2011). Many victims do not know about these visas, and those who do are often reluctant to apply for them because they fear that they will risk deportation or other penalties by immigration and law enforcement officials, or that they or their families will face retribution from traffickers should they participate in prosecuting them (U.S. Immigration Support 2011). For T-visas to achieve their intended goals of simultaneously safeguarding victims and providing prosecutorial evidence against traffickers, victims need to be informed about their availability and protected against the possible pitfalls of applying for them. Witness protection programs, relocation services, safe houses and other types of protections may afford victims enough tranquility that they will be willing to face the administrative hurdles necessary to secure a T-visa.

Yet many victims may not want to stay in the United States or any other country in which they have been exploited. A possible strategy for ensuring that victims who wish to leave the country can continue to receive services is to strengthen cross-border relationships among service agencies and non-governmental organizations. This may be feasible in the United States and Mexico, where civil society and victims' advocacy groups already have substantial cross-border ties.

In sum, while effective and harmonized legislation is essential to provide a legal framework for assisting victims, if victims remain hidden in the shadows of the underground economy there is no way to protect and assist them. Agencies working directly with actual or possible trafficking victims—law enforcement, immigration, social service organizations, health departments, schools, housing associations, courts, and so on—need to provide their personnel with the necessary training to search proactively for victims, recognize them, and offer them the appropriate services to promote their recovery. Ideally, victims' services would be coordinated across borders through a network of binational governmental and non-governmental social service organizations so that victims who might choose to return to their country of origin could do so while continuing to receive the necessary services to help them recover from their ordeal.

Apprehending the Perpetrators

Apprehending the perpetrators and assisting the victims of human trafficking go hand in hand in both a practical and strategic sense. Victims are often detected via the same investigations or raids that apprehend their traffickers. When victims escape their captivity or become known to officials some other way, their discovery triggers the parallel processes of directing them toward appropriate treatment services and initiating the investigations that will hopefully lead to their traffickers' prosecution. In the long run, the most effective way to protect and serve victims is to eliminate the practice by apprehending and punishing perpetrators to deter them from future crimes and to dissuade others from following in their footsteps. Thus one of the most important recommendations for achieving both objectives is to encourage everyone, from the average citizen to the specialized expert, to understand the nature of human trafficking so they can remain on the look-out for suspicious activity.

The key to combating human trafficking is to shift the risk-benefit equation by reducing the profits of the human trade while increasing the risk of apprehension and the severity of the resulting penalties. When the business becomes high-risk and low-profit, the incentives to human trafficking will greatly diminish and the practice will erode and eventually come to an end.

As Naím (2005) concludes from his research on the illicit global trade, combating contemporary cartels presents a law enforcement challenge because the loosely structured organizational networks of the drug and human trafficking cartels enable them to substitute new leadership when existing kingpins are caught and imprisoned. Thus, while apprehending perpetrators is an important and necessary deterrent, it needs to be supplemented by strategies intended to attack the practice at its roots. Disrupting the supply of money flowing to the traffickers has shown some success in the fight against drug trafficking, and might be employed to thwart human traffickers as well. Interruptions caused by additional restrictions on deposits and on cross-border cash transactions, harsh penalties for financial institutions caught laundering money, and freezing monetary assets of apprehended criminals are potentially useful approaches. If traffickers are forced to make continual transfers of their funds from bank to bank, this can add to the risks and costs of their business and might deter, or at least decelerate, their participation in the trade. Of course, savvy traffickers can and do avoid this potential trap by conducting their economic transactions outside official financial institutions, whether through black market channels or simply by making their transactions in cash. A possible counteractive is to limit what can be purchased with cash and to implement mobile check points along roads and highways in Mexico and the United States. By disrupting cash flows, lowering profits, and increasing the risks of doing business, such financial strategies could shift the incentive structure of the human trade to make it more costly and less lucrative.

Traffickers profit from the demand for services extracted from trafficked victims—so in this sense, the clients who purchase victims' services are as integral to the practice that entraps and enslaves people as the traffickers themselves. Deterring people from purchasing the services of trafficking victims is thus essential to combating the trade. Those who benefit from the products and services of enslaved laborers and sex workers need to be educated about how their activities are contributing to the global human trade so that as many as possible will desist voluntarily.

Sex workers would generally have a more direct link to their clients than slaves in sweatshops producing manufactures for the global market. For the latter, consumer educational campaigns and reliable systems for certifying goods produced through fair labor practices are essential to help consumers make enlightened choices to protect global workers. For the former, promoting campaigns to educate people about the links between the prostitution and human trafficking industries is likely to deter few of those who have come to depend on the services of sex workers. For the rest, a deterrence strategy that balances punitive and rehabilitative approaches is probably the most likely to yield positive outcomes. Rehabilitative resources for sex addicts and pedophiles may have some effect in curbing their demand for (possibly enslaved) sex workers, though treatment is most apt to be effective if the addiction can be detected and treated at an early stage in its evolution.

Demand for forced labor may also be curbed by formulating and consistently implementing laws and policies that regulate employment practices. Frequent checks of restaurants, factories and construction sites, with severe penalties imposed for infractions of labor laws, would dampen the incentives to employing trafficked labor. Similarly, undercover law enforcement agents posing as workers in establishments suspected of harboring trafficked workers could be an effective way to apprehend illicit employers—and if the sting was highly publicized, to deter others by their example. Identifying and training private household workers who, regardless of their immigration status, would be willing to participate as neighborhood advocates might be an effective way to locate victims of domestic labor trafficking trapped inside residences. Apprehending and prosecuting their employers as publicly as possible might reduce demand for enslaved domestic workers by deterring other potential employers from similar behavior.

Creating a cultural climate that is unfriendly to traffickers and those who demand victims' services can be accomplished through programs such as the AMBER alert system for missing children, which functions in both the United States and Mexico. In July 2011, a major police roundup was coordinated between Mexican federal and Chihuahua state law enforcement agencies following a week-long AMBER alert in Cd. Juárez that set off a search for missing children. Referred to by the code word, "Alba," the operation rescued 20 children and youth who were trapped in forced prostitution in Juárez hotels and bars, and captured over 1,000 people suspected of belonging to trafficking networks (Radio Francia Internacional Español 2011). Equally important, the operation interrupted business as usual and left a lasting impression throughout the city.

If traffickers and the consumers of victims' services know that an alert system is in place for missing persons and that it will lead to raids on bars, brothels, restaurants, and other places where trafficking victims may be harbored, this can destabilize the business environment and add an additional risk factor that increases the costs. Anonymous tip lines to report suspected cases of trafficking; "no tolerance" policies in designated tourist areas; enlistment of sex workers and laborers in identifying victims, perpetrators and clients; harsh penalties for traffickers; up-to-date data bases to track suspects, convicts, and victims; and better control over the sale of sex on the Internet can all serve to add expense to what presently is a relatively low risk and highly profitable business.

Altering Structural Conditions that Encourage Trafficking

Human trafficking flourishes not only because of the people involved in it, but also due to the political, social and legal structures that permit it. A global economic system that generates extremes of poverty and wealth creates a category of people who are vulnerable to exploitation. Divergent levels of wealth and development within and among countries encourage immigration in search of economic advancement at the same time that strict immigration regulations push migrants into illegal channels and increase their risk of exposure to human trafficking. Diminishing the global inequalities that encourage and facilitate human trafficking will take concerted commitment from all the world's nations, and will be impossible without wide-scale economic, political, and social changes that are unlikely in the foreseeable future.

Progress in the struggle against human trafficking may be most feasible at the regional level, in bounded geographical areas such as the Mexico–United States borderlands, where changes in favor of human rights require binational rather than global coordination and legal harmonization. Combating human slavery in the borderlands requires changes to both immigration and labor law. Restrictive immigration policies stimulate trafficking along the border because those attempting to cross into the United States get pushed into illegal channels where they are vulnerable to human traffickers. In outlawing an immigration process that responds as much to economic incentives as to ineffectively enforceable legal barriers, U.S. immigration policies create and maintain a pool of vulnerable undocumented residents who are fearful of being deported if they complain about workplace exploitation. Forced labor flourishes when employers can manipulate workers' unauthorized migration status to keep them as silent slaves.

The United States government confronts a choice: It can expand the legal channels for migration, thus reducing migrants' vulnerability and the incentives for criminal traffickers while maintaining information about and control over who is actually in the country. Or it can continue its restrictive immigration system, which pushes people into dangerous unauthorized immigration channels, increases their odds of becoming trafficking victims, and encourages criminal trafficking elements to flourish inside the country—all the while making it impossible to track the numbers and identities of those inside U.S. borders.

If the public dialogue about immigration policy shifted from one that demonizes undocumented immigrants to one that demonstrated how the current restrictive immigration policies perpetuate criminal activity in the U.S. borderlands and heartland, the national conversation around immigration might be refocused. Possible U.S. policy solutions to ensure an adequate supply of labor include effectively regulated guest worker programs, tracking mechanisms to enable each state to monitor the entrance and exit of foreign workers according to seasonal labor needs, and circular migration and temporary work visas allowing for multiple entrances and exits for migratory workers. What is more than clear is that the current restrictive system promotes the exploitation of workers and the growth of criminality, and as long as it exists unchallenged, human trafficking will continue to flourish in the U.S.–Mexico borderlands.

Deportations of criminals back to Mexico, Central America, or elsewhere also need to be reconsidered, because they can contribute to the expansion of criminal cartels in the regions that receive the deported outlaws. Just as trafficking victims could be identified by advocates in detention centers, a mechanism could be put in place to identify traffickers and other criminals who were scheduled for deportation. Identifying perpetrators and their associates before they were deported would give authorities a chance to extract information about their criminal networks and their operations, which the criminals may be more apt to do if they have lived most of their lives in the United States and feel vulnerable about being sent back to their country of origin. The resulting information could enable officials to provide advanced warning to authorities in the receiving country of the potential for increased criminal activity. Better intelligence across borders could serve to deter the creation of new trafficking networks while providing information that might help to disrupt existing ones.

Yet, it is not only the immigration system that needs adjustments in order to battle against human trafficking. Labor laws need to be implemented and enforced to ensure that workers are protected against dangerous or debilitating working conditions. Laws and regulations that ensure wages above federally mandated minimums and that limit the number of hours per day that workers, including domestic workers and other informal sector employees, can be expected to remain on the job are essential to protect against workplace exploitation. Though difficult to monitor and enforce, such laws can serve a deterrence function for some employers, and can help victims find legal redress when they are discovered and removed from their exploitative circumstances.

Promoting Public Awareness

Effective and enforceable laws, and adequate resources for prosecuting perpetrators and rendering assistance to victims, can give professionals the means to combat human trafficking. Yet often the tip to law enforcement agents that leads to the rescue of victims and the prosecution of perpetrators comes from non-professionals, whether escaped victims or observant community members. In late 2011, law enforcement agents broke up a sex trafficking ring that spanned from Baltimore, Maryland, to El Paso, Texas. The male perpetrators posed as concert promoters to lure unsuspecting women into their group, then confiscated their communication devices and their identification papers, and forced them into stripping and prostitution. The female defendants in the case confiscated the victims' earnings and enforced strict rules that limited their communication with anyone outside of the group. The perpetrators met their downfall when an escaped victim contacted the police, who then collaborated with several agencies to design a sting operation that resulted in the arrests of ten traffickers (Kilar and Hermann 2011).

While it stands to reason that victims who have escaped their traffickers' clutches might be highly motivated—if not too fearful of repercussions—to tip off police, such escapes are typically too difficult, and therefore too rare, to be the main avenue for alerting law enforcement to human traffickers operating in their communities. The public must play its role by being alert to possible evidence of the human trade. It is vital for "average" members of a community who notice suspicious activity to report it to the proper authorities, for their reports can initiate the necessary law enforcement efforts to rescue the victims and apprehend the traffickers.

Thus promoting public awareness of human trafficking must be an integral part of any multipronged approach to combat the practice. Public education campaigns can take various forms, but three messages are central: first, that trafficking differs from smuggling and undocumented immigration; second, that trafficking victims can be found in every community; and third, that eradicating human trafficking requires a network of agencies, advocates, law enforcement officials, regular citizens and others to identify victims proactively. Differentiating human trafficking from other types of immigration and smuggling focuses attention on the force, coercion and deceit involved in the human trade and builds sympathy for victims among law enforcement agents and the general community. Focusing on the existence of trafficking in every community empowers people and motivates them to take an interest in events affecting their own neighborhoods. A more local focus can also make the problem seem more manageable. Finally, by providing a community-building message that encourages proactive advocates from different segments of society to work together for the benefit of the collective good to free the slaves in their midst, fighting trafficking becomes a collective struggle for the betterment of all community members.

These three messages, expressed in the language of every country on earth, promoted using not only traditional posters and speakers but also contemporary technology such as social media, and made even more attractive by the involvement of public figures able to disseminate their messages through mass culture, could have far-reaching positive impacts. Existing organizations such as the Ricky Martin Foundation can add star power and bilingualism to public service campaigns that warn potential victims in their own countries about the dangers of human trafficking (Ricky Martin Foundation 2011).

Messages may need to be tweaked to attune them to specific audiences. For example, elementary school children could be educated about the ways in which human traffickers can trick young victims. Older youth could learn strategies to protect themselves and their younger siblings. Immigrant communities could be educated to detect the victims and perpetrators in their midst, while law enforcement agents could be taught how to differentiate between smuggled and trafficked persons. Ideally, a network of well-informed advocates committed to fighting the human trade would form in every country and would consolidate internationally, just as it has around issues related to domestic violence. A campaign focusing on how human trafficking disorganizes and weakens communities could follow the models provided by the successful anti-smoking campaign in the United States.

Conclusion

As long as the profits to be made from human trafficking continue to exceed the risks associated with involvement in the business, modern slavery will continue. Combating it will require multipronged, multi-layered initiatives to find and protect victims; to uncover and punish perpetrators and the users of services supplied by trafficked persons; to change the political, social and legal structures that perpetuate the trade; and to make the commitment to eradicate the human trade into a unifying, community-based, transnational priority.

So far, developing effective policies and strategies to combat human trafficking has proved to be an elusive goal. Particularly at the implementation phase, the challenges of cross-level coordination, conflicting political interests, limited resource availability, inconsistent definitions, regulations, and laws, and public ignorance and indifference, among other factors, create substantial barriers to formulating and implementing effective law enforcement strategies. But we have to make the effort. As long as the global institutional framework remains incapable of addressing modern-day slavery, the human suffering it causes will continue to multiply. The formulation and implementation of effective multifaceted policies in the U.S.–Mexico borderlands could make the region a model for cross-national cooperation elsewhere in the world. The victims of modern-day slavery in the borderlands and across the globe deserve nothing less.

Bibliography

Free the Slaves and Human Rights Center. 2004. *Hidden Slaves: Forced labor in the United States, Forced Labor Paper 8.* [Online, University of California, Berkeley]. Available at: http://www.digitalcommons.ilr.cornell.edu/forcedlabor/8 [accessed: November 23, 2011].

Freedom Network USA. 2005. *Introduction to an Overview of State Model Law on Protection for Victims of Human Trafficking* [Online]. Available at: http://www.legislationonline.org [accessed: November 23, 2011].

Kilar, S. and Hermann, P. 2011. More charges filed in Baltimore sex trafficking case: Forced prostitution scheme being prosecuted in Texas. *The Baltimore Sun* [Online]. Available at: http://www.articles.baltimoresun [accessed: December 5, 2011].

Naím, M. 2005. *Illicit: how smugglers, traffickers, and copycats are hijacking the global economy.* New York: Anchor Books.

Radio Francia Internacional Español. 2011. Mil detenidos en un operative contra la trata de personas-México [Online, July 25]. Available at: http://www.espanol.rfi.fr [accessed: December 5, 2011].

Ricky Martin Foundation. 2011. [Online]. Available at: http://www.rickymartinfoundation.org [accessed: November 23, 2011].

Schauer, E.J. and Wheaton, E.M. 2006. Sex Trafficking into the United States: A Literature Review. *Criminal Justice Review*, 31(1), 1–24.

U.S. Immigration Support. 2011. Very Few Visas for Victims of Human Trafficking Offered [Online]. Available at: http://www.usimmigrationsupport.org [accessed: December 5, 2011].

Zhang, S.X. 2011. Woman pullers: pimping and sex trafficking in a Mexican border city. Crime, Law and Social Change, 56(5), 509–528.

Index